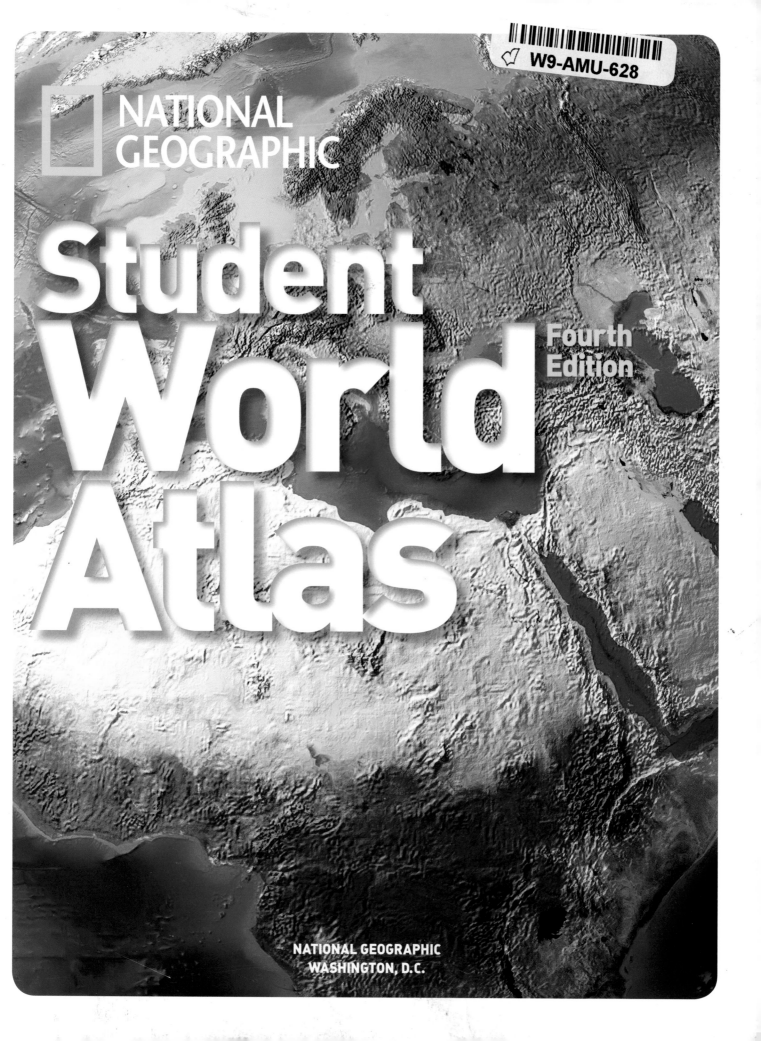

NATIONAL GEOGRAPHIC

Student World Atlas

Fourth Edition

NATIONAL GEOGRAPHIC
WASHINGTON, D.C.

Table of Contents

North America:
Floods, page 68

South America:
Three-toed sloth,
page 78

ASIA 90

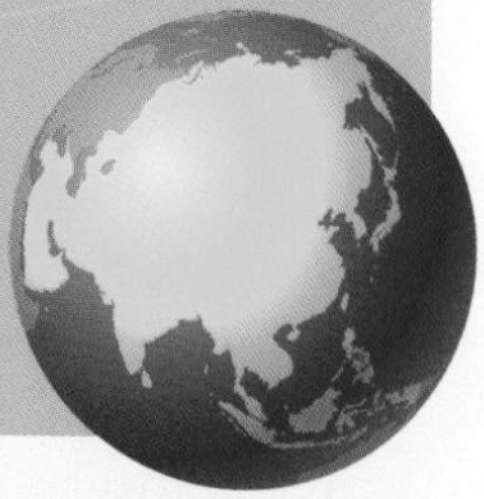

AUSTRALIA & OCEANIA 110

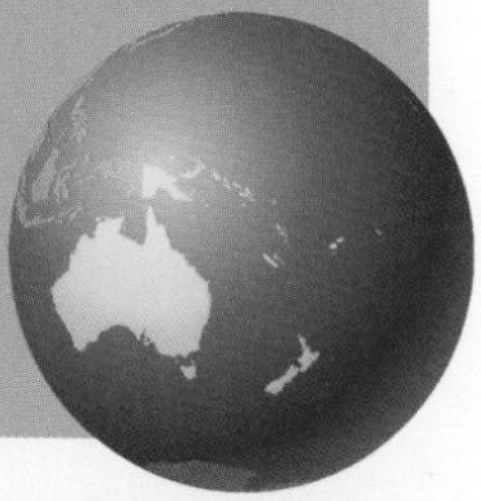

AFRICA 100

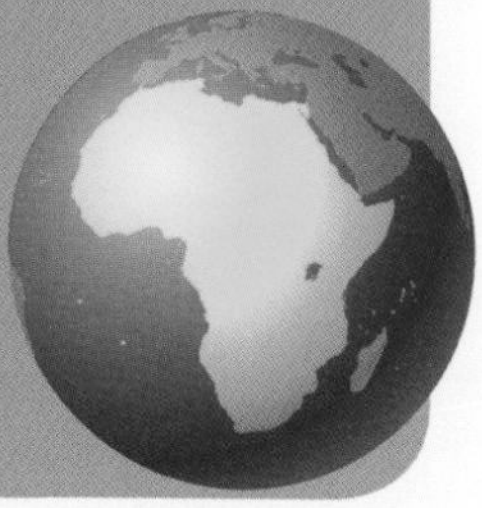

ANTARCTICA 120

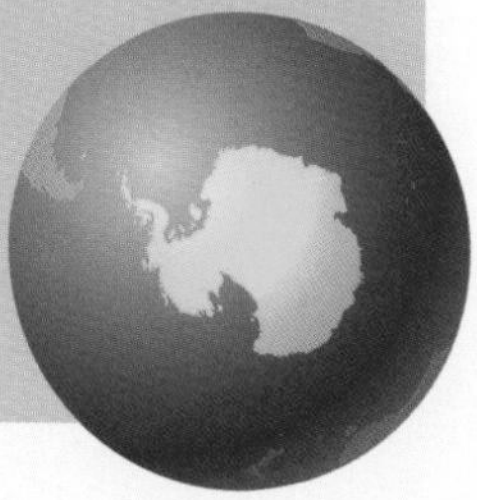

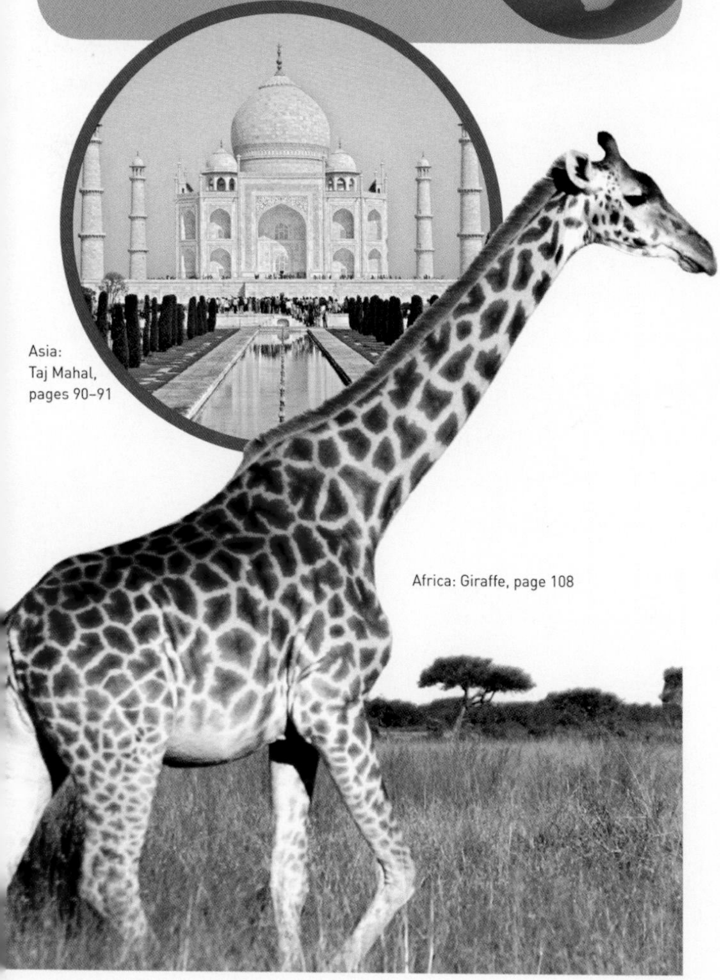

Asia:
Taj Mahal,
pages 90–91

Africa: Giraffe, page 108

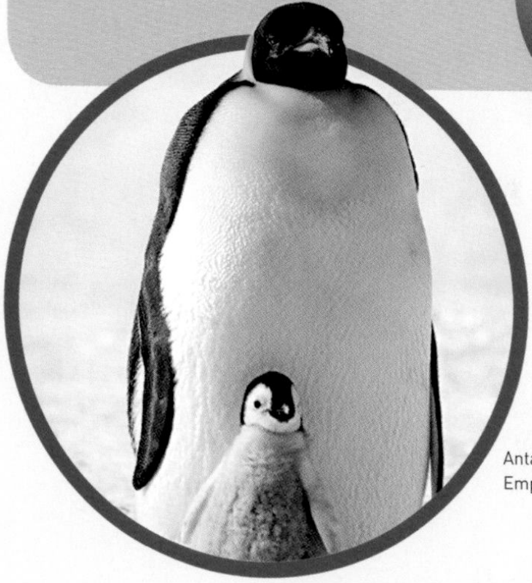

Antarctica:
Emperor penguins, page 125

BACK OF THE BOOK

RESOURCES

ABOUT EARTH

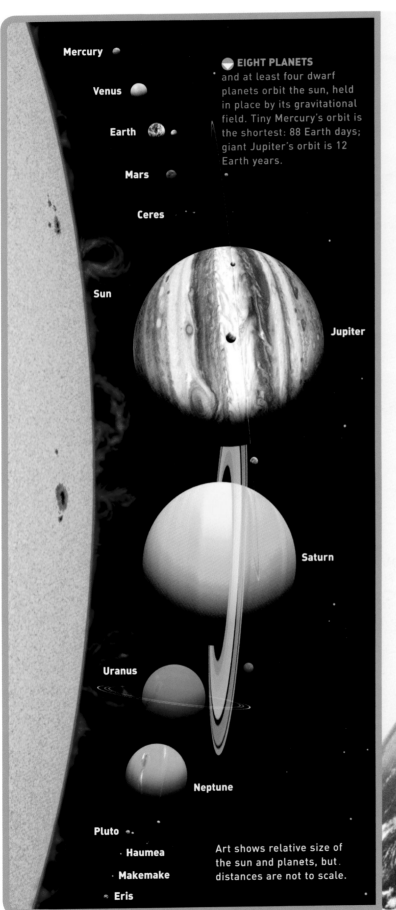

Mercury

Venus

Earth

Mars

Ceres

◐ EIGHT PLANETS
and at least four dwarf planets orbit the sun, held in place by its gravitational field. Tiny Mercury's orbit is the shortest: 88 Earth days; giant Jupiter's orbit is 12 Earth years.

Sun

Jupiter

Saturn

Uranus

Neptune

Pluto

Haumea

Makemake

Eris

Art shows relative size of the sun and planets, but distances are not to scale.

Earth in Space

At the center of our solar system is the sun, a huge mass of hot gas that is the source of both light and warmth for Earth. Third in a group of eight planets that revolve around the sun, Earth is a terrestrial, or mostly rocky, planet. So are Mercury, Venus, and Mars. Earth is about 93 million miles (150 million km) from the sun, and its journey, or revolution, around the sun takes 365¼ days. Farther away from the sun, four more planets—Jupiter, Saturn, Uranus, and Neptune (all made up primarily of gases)— plus at least five dwarf planets (Ceres, Pluto, Haumea, Makemake, and Eris) complete the main bodies of our solar system. The solar system, in turn, is part of the Milky Way galaxy.

◑ **SPRING**
Northern Hemisphere

◐ **WINTER**
Northern Hemisphere

EARTH'S SEASONS change throughout the year because the planet tilts 23.5° on its axis as it revolves around the sun. For example, when the Northern Hemisphere is tilted toward the sun, summer occurs there; when it's tilted away from the sun, it experiences winter.

◐ **SUMMER**
Northern Hemisphere

◑ **FALL**
Northern Hemisphere

North Pole

Tropic of Cancer

Equator

Tropic of Capricorn

South Pole

⬡ **AN ENVELOPE OF AIR SURROUNDS EARTH.** Called the atmosphere, it is made up of a mix of nitrogen, oxygen, and other gases. It is 300 miles (483 km) thick. The troposphere, which extends upward as much as 10 miles (16 km) from Earth's surface, is called the zone of life. The combination of gases, moderate temperatures, and water in this layer supports plants, animals, and other forms of life on Earth.

⬡ **EARTH ROTATES WEST TO EAST** on its axis, an imaginary line that runs through Earth's center from Pole to Pole. Each rotation takes 24 hours, or one full cycle of day and night. One complete rotation equals one Earth day. One complete revolution around the sun equals one Earth year.

Map Projections

Maps tell a story about physical and human systems, places and regions, patterns and relationships. This atlas is a collection of maps that tell a story about Earth.

Understanding that story requires a knowledge of how maps are made and a familiarity with the special language used by cartographers, the people who create maps.

Globes present a model of Earth as it is—a sphere—but they are bulky and can be difficult to use and store. Flat maps are much more convenient, but certain problems result from transferring Earth's curved surface to a flat piece of paper, a process called projection. There are many different types of projections, all of which involve some form of distortion: area, distance, direction, or shape.

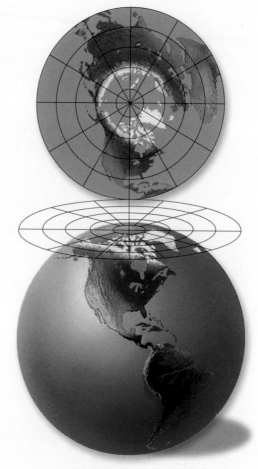

AZIMUTHAL MAP PROJECTION. This kind of map is made by projecting a globe onto a flat surface that touches the globe at a single point, such as the North Pole. These maps accurately represent direction along any straight line extending from the point of contact. Away from the point of contact, shape is increasingly distorted.

MAKING A PROJECTION. Imagine a globe that has been cut in half as this one has. If a light is shined into it, the lines of latitude and longitude and the shapes of the continents will cast shadows that can be "projected" onto a piece of paper, as shown here. Depending on how the paper is positioned, the shadows will be distorted in different ways.

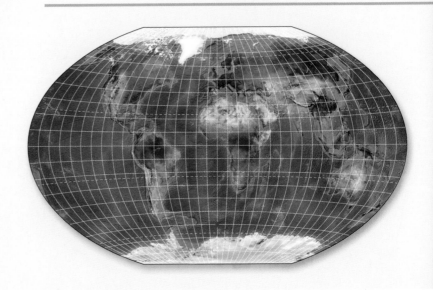

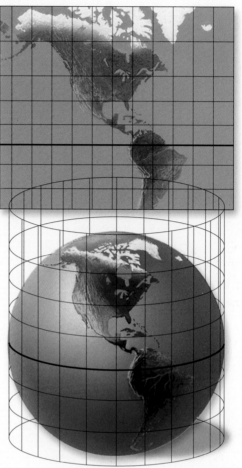

◓ **CONIC MAP PROJECTION.** This kind of map is made by projecting a globe onto a cone. The part of Earth being mapped touches the sides of the cone. Lines of longitude appear as straight lines; lines of latitude appear as parallel arcs. Conic projections are often used to map mid-latitude areas with great east-west extent, such as North America.

◓ **CYLINDRICAL MAP PROJECTION.** A cylindrical projection map is made by projecting a globe onto a cylinder that touches Earth's surface along the Equator. Latitude and longitude lines on this kind of map show true compass directions, which makes it useful for navigation. But there is great distortion in the size of high-latitude landmasses.

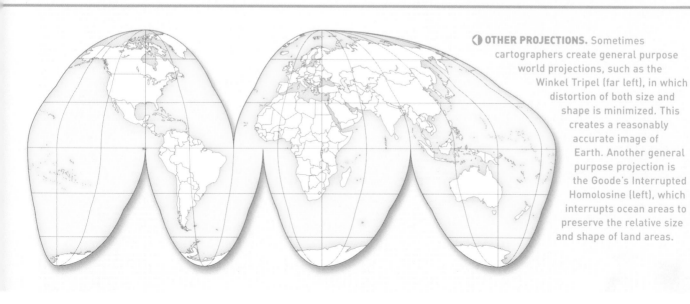

◖ **OTHER PROJECTIONS.** Sometimes cartographers create general purpose world projections, such as the Winkel Tripel (far left), in which distortion of both size and shape is minimized. This creates a reasonably accurate image of Earth. Another general purpose projection is the Goode's Interrupted Homolosine (left), which interrupts ocean areas to preserve the relative size and shape of land areas.

Reading Maps

People can use maps to find locations, to determine direction or distance, and to understand information about places. Cartographers rely on a special graphic language to communicate through maps.

An imaginary system of lines, called the global grid, helps us locate particular points on Earth's surface. The global grid is made up of lines of latitude and longitude that are measured in degrees, minutes, and seconds. The point where these lines intersect identifies the absolute location of a place. No other place has the exact same address.

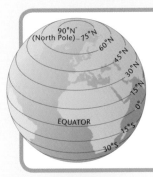

LATITUDE. Lines of latitude—also called parallels because they are parallel to the Equator—run east to west around the globe and measure location north or south of the Equator. The Equator is 0° latitude.

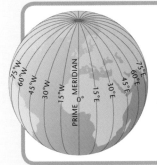

LONGITUDE. Lines of longitude—also called meridians—run from Pole to Pole and measure location east or west of the prime meridian. The prime meridian is 0° longitude, and it runs through Greenwich, near London, England.

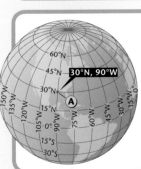

GLOBAL GRID. When used together, latitude and longitude form a grid that provides a system for determining the exact, or absolute, location of every place on Earth. For example, the absolute location of point A is 30°N, 90°W.

DIRECTION. Cartographers put a north arrow or a compass rose, which shows the four cardinal directions—north, south, east, and west—on a map. On this map, point **B** is northwest (NW) of point **A**. Northwest is an example of an intermediate direction, which means it is between two cardinal directions. Grid lines can also be used to indicate north.

SCALE. A map represents a part of Earth's surface, but that part is greatly reduced. Cartographers include a map scale to show what distance on Earth is represented by a given length on the map. Scale can be graphic (a bar), verbal, or a ratio. To determine how many miles point **A** is from point **B**, place a piece of paper on the map above and mark the distance between **A** and **B**. Then compare the marks on the paper with the bar scale on the map.

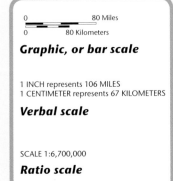

North arrow

Compass rose

```
0          80 Miles
0          80 Kilometers
```

Graphic, or bar scale

1 INCH represents 106 MILES
1 CENTIMETER represents 67 KILOMETERS

Verbal scale

SCALE 1:6,700,000

Ratio scale

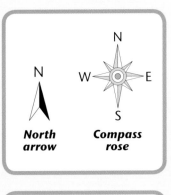

LEARNING ABOUT MAPS

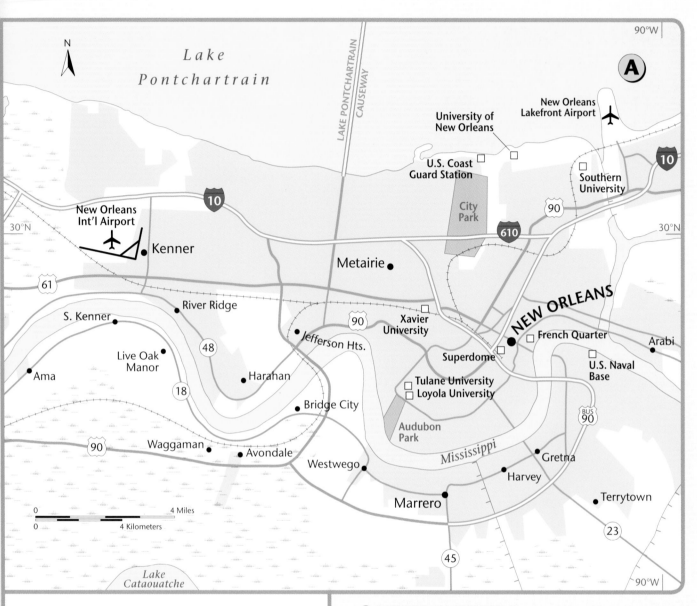

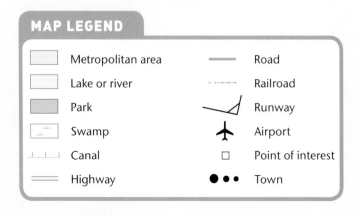

◗ **SYMBOLS.** Finally, cartographers use a variety of symbols, which are identified in a map key or legend, to tell us more about the places represented on the map. There are three general types of symbols:

●● **POINT SYMBOLS** show exact location of places (such as cities) or quantity (a large dot can mean a more populous city).

······ **LINE SYMBOLS** show boundaries or connections (such as roads, canals, and other trade links).

▭ **AREA SYMBOLS** show the form and extent of a feature (such as a lake, park, or swamp).

Additional information may be coded in color, size, and shape.

◖ **PUTTING IT ALL TOGETHER.** We already know from the map on page 8 which states A and B are located in. But to find out more about city A, we need a larger scale map—one that shows a smaller area in more detail (see above).

MAP LEGEND

� Metropolitan area		──	Road
Lake or river		·····+	Railroad
Park		⋀	Runway
Swamp		✈	Airport
Canal		▢	Point of interest
Highway		●●●	Town

Types of Maps

This atlas includes many different types of maps so that a wide variety of information about Earth can be presented. Three of the most commonly used types of maps are physical, political, and thematic.

A **physical map** identifies natural features, such as mountains, deserts, oceans, and lakes. Area symbols of various colors and shadings may indicate height above sea level or, as in the example here, ecosystems. Similar symbols could also show water depth.

A **political map** shows how people have divided the world into countries. Political maps can also show states, counties, or cities within a country. Line symbols indicate boundaries, and point symbols show the locations and sometimes sizes of cities.

Thematic maps use a variety of symbols to show distributions and patterns on Earth. For example, a choropleth map uses shades of color to represent different values. The example here shows the amount of energy consumed each year by various countries. Thematic maps can show many different things, such as patterns of vegetation, land use, and religions.

A **cartogram** is a special kind of thematic map in which the size of a country is based on some statistic other than land area. In the cartogram at far right, population size determines the size of each country. This is why Nigeria—the most populous country in Africa—appears much larger than Algeria, which has more than double the land area of Nigeria (see the political map). Cartograms allow for a quick visual comparison of countries in terms of a selected statistic.

PHYSICAL MAP

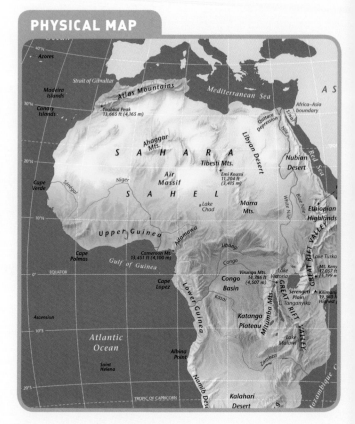

THEMATIC MAP

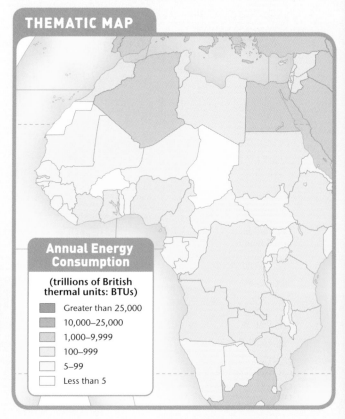

Annual Energy Consumption

(trillions of British thermal units: BTUs)

- Greater than 25,000
- 10,000–25,000
- 1,000–9,999
- 100–999
- 5–99
- Less than 5

◗ **THIS GLOBE** is useful for showing Africa's position and size relative to other landmasses, but very little detail is possible at this scale. By using different kinds of maps, mapmakers can show a variety of information in more detail.

LEARNING ABOUT MAPS

POLITICAL MAP

CARTOGRAM

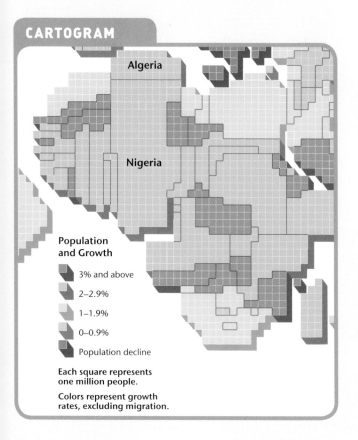

Algeria

Nigeria

Population and Growth

- 3% and above
- 2–2.9%
- 1–1.9%
- 0–0.9%
- Population decline

Each square represents one million people.

Colors represent growth rates, excluding migration.

SATELLITE IMAGE MAPS

Satellites orbiting Earth transmit images of the surface to computers on the ground. These computers translate the information into special maps (below) that use colors to show various characteristics. Such maps are valuable tools for identifying patterns or comparing changes over time.

CLOUD COVERAGE

TOPOGRAPHY/BATHYMETRY

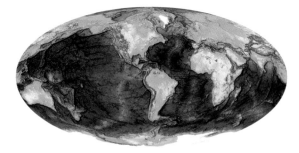

SEA LEVEL VARIABILITY

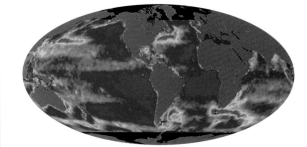

SEA SURFACE TEMPERATURE

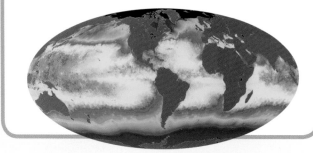

Time Zones

The *Fiji Times*, a newspaper published in Suva, capital of the Fiji Islands, carries the message "The First Newspaper Published in the World Every Day" on the front page of each edition. How can this newspaper from a small island country make such a claim? Fiji lies west of the date line, an invisible boundary designated to mark the beginning of each new day. The date line is just part of the system we have adopted to keep track of the passage of days.

For most of human history, people determined time by observing the position of the sun in the sky. Slight differences in time did not matter until, in the mid-19th century, the spread of railroads and telegraph lines changed forever the importance of time. High-speed transportation and communications required schedules, and schedules required that everyone agree on the time.

In 1884, an international conference, convened in Washington, D.C., established an international system of 24 time zones based on the fact that Earth turns from west to east 15 degrees of longitude every hour. Each time zone has a central meridian and is 15 degrees wide, 7½ degrees to either side of the named central meridian.

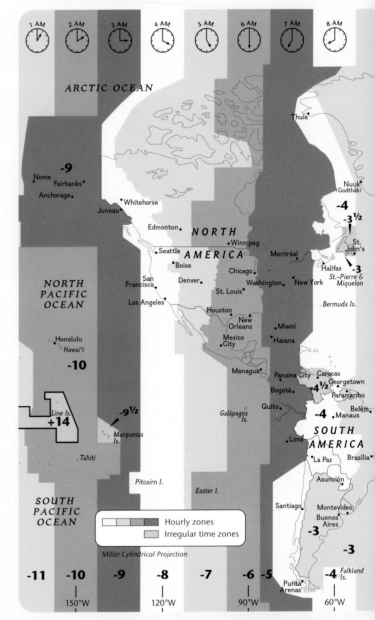

◖ **WORLD TIME CLOCK,** in Alexanderplatz in Berlin, Germany, features a large cylinder that is marked with the world's 24 time zones and major cities found in each zone. The cylinder rises almost 33 feet (10 m) above the square and weighs 16 tons (14.5 MT).

◓ **A SYSTEM OF STANDARD TIME** put trains on schedules which helped reduce the chance of collisions and the loss of lives and property caused by them.

LEARNING ABOUT MAPS

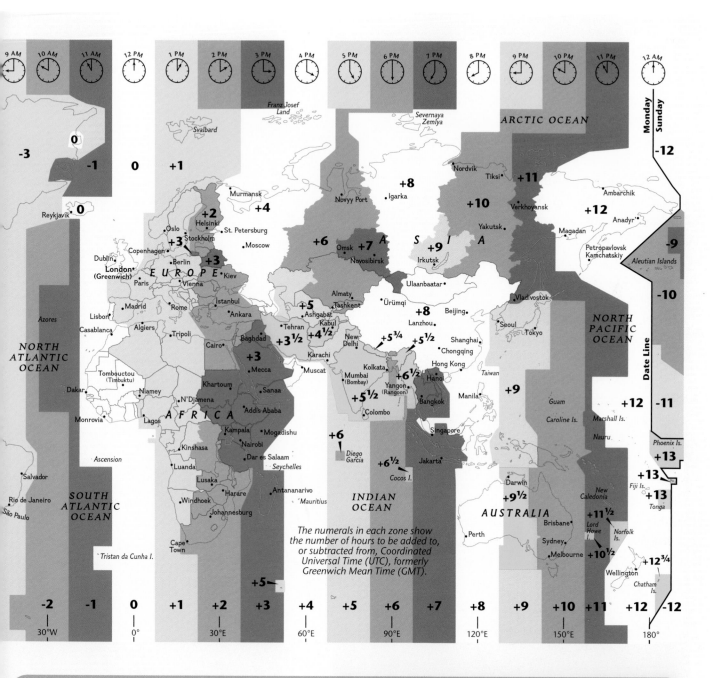

9 AM 10 AM 11 AM 12 PM 1 PM 2 PM 3 PM 4 PM 5 PM 6 PM 7 PM 8 PM 9 PM 10 PM 11 PM 12 AM

The numerals in each zone show the number of hours to be added to, or subtracted from, Coordinated Universal Time (UTC), formerly Greenwich Mean Time (GMT).

THE DATE LINE (180°) is directly opposite the prime meridian (0°). As Earth rotates, each new day officially begins as the 180° line passes midnight. If you travel west across the date line, you advance one day; if you travel east across the date line, you fall back one day. Notice on the map how the line zigs to the east as it passes through the South Pacific so that the islands of Fiji will not be split between two different days. Also notice that India is 5½ hours ahead of Coordinated Universal Time (formerly Greenwich Mean Time), and China has only one time zone, even though the country spans more than 60 degrees of longitude. These differences are the result of decisions made at the country level.

The Physical World

Realms of land and water make up the physical world. More than two-thirds of Earth's surface is covered by water: oceans, lakes, and rivers. The rest is land: continents and islands. People inhabit every continent except Antarctica, which lies frozen beneath a vast ice cap at Earth's South Pole. Each continent is unique, but all show evidence of dynamic forces at work. Some forces build up mountains such as the Rockies, the Andes, and the Himalaya; other forces wear down Earth's surface, creating vast sedimentary plains and lowlands. Powerful rivers such as the Mississippi, the Congo, and the Yangtze (Chang) cut through the land and empty billions of gallons of freshwater into the oceans and seas each day.

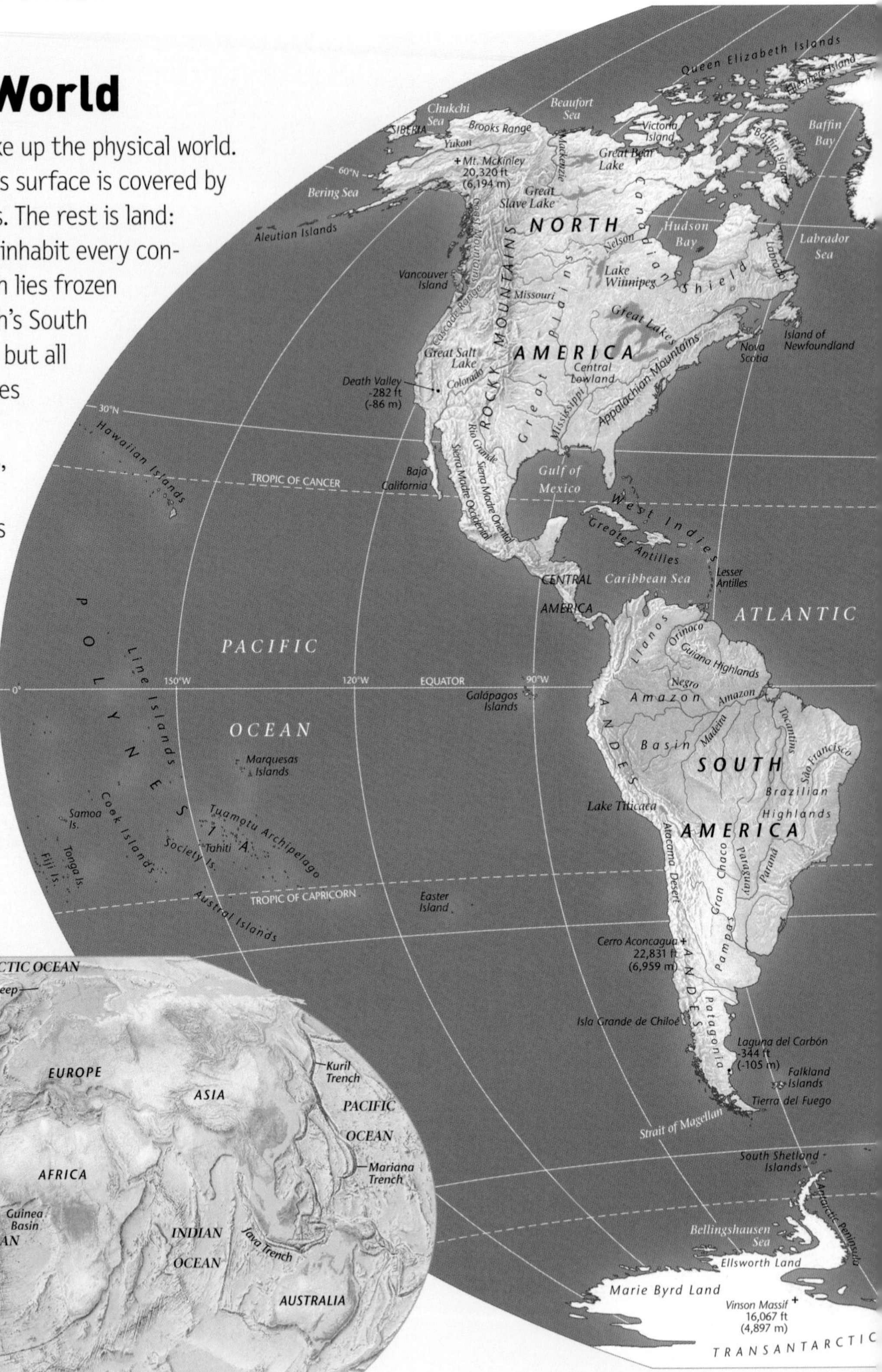

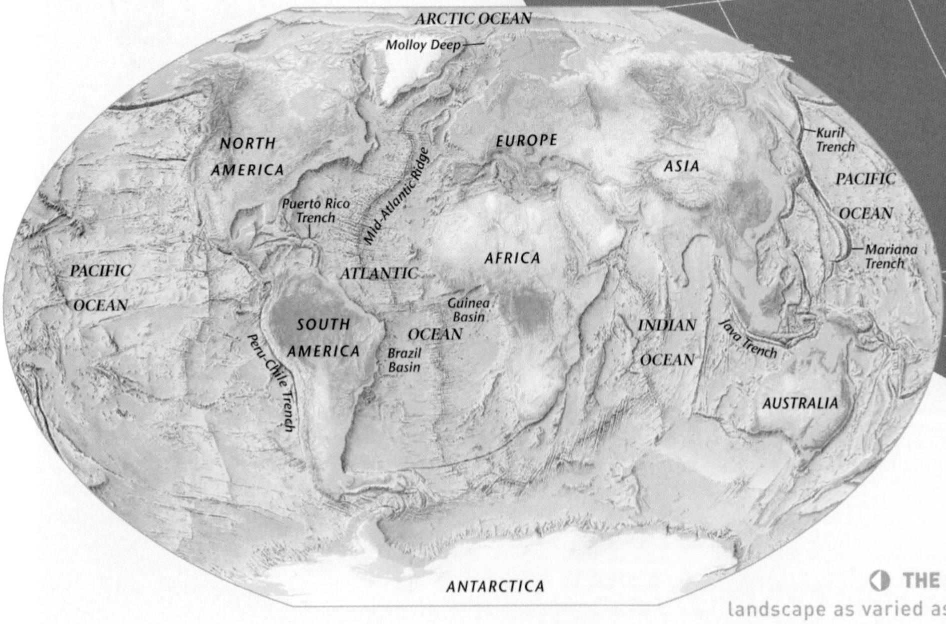

⬤ **THE OCEAN FLOOR.** Beneath Earth's oceans lies a landscape as varied as any on land. The Mid-Atlantic Ridge is part of a global mountain range that winds 40,000 miles (64,000 km) across the ocean floor. Volcanic islands rise up from the seabed, while the Mariana Trench plunges more than 36,070 feet (10,994 m)—deep enough to submerge Mount Everest.

THE PHYSICAL WORLD. Great landmasses called continents break Earth's global ocean into four smaller ones. Each continent is unique in terms of the landforms and rivers that etch its surface and the ecosystems that lend colors ranging from the deep greens of the tropical forests of northern South America and southeastern Asia to the browns and yellows of the arid lands of Africa and Australia. Most of Antarctica's features are hidden beneath its ice cap.

Earth's Geologic History

Earth is a dynamic planet. Its outer shell, or crust, is broken into huge pieces called plates. These plates ride on the slowly moving molten rock, or magma, that lies beneath the crust. Their movement constantly changes Earth's surface. Along one convergent boundary—a place where two plates meet—the Indian Plate moves northward, colliding with the Eurasian Plate and heaving up the still growing Himalaya. Along another convergent boundary, the Nasca Plate dives beneath the South American Plate—a process called subduction that can trigger volcanoes, underwater earthquakes, and giant ocean waves called tsunamis. Along transform faults, such as California's San Andreas Fault, plates grind past each other, resulting in destructive earthquakes. Along divergent boundaries, plates are pushed apart, as in the Mid-Atlantic Ridge where the ocean floor is spreading apart allowing molten rock to rise, and Africa's Great Rift Valley where the continental plate is separating.

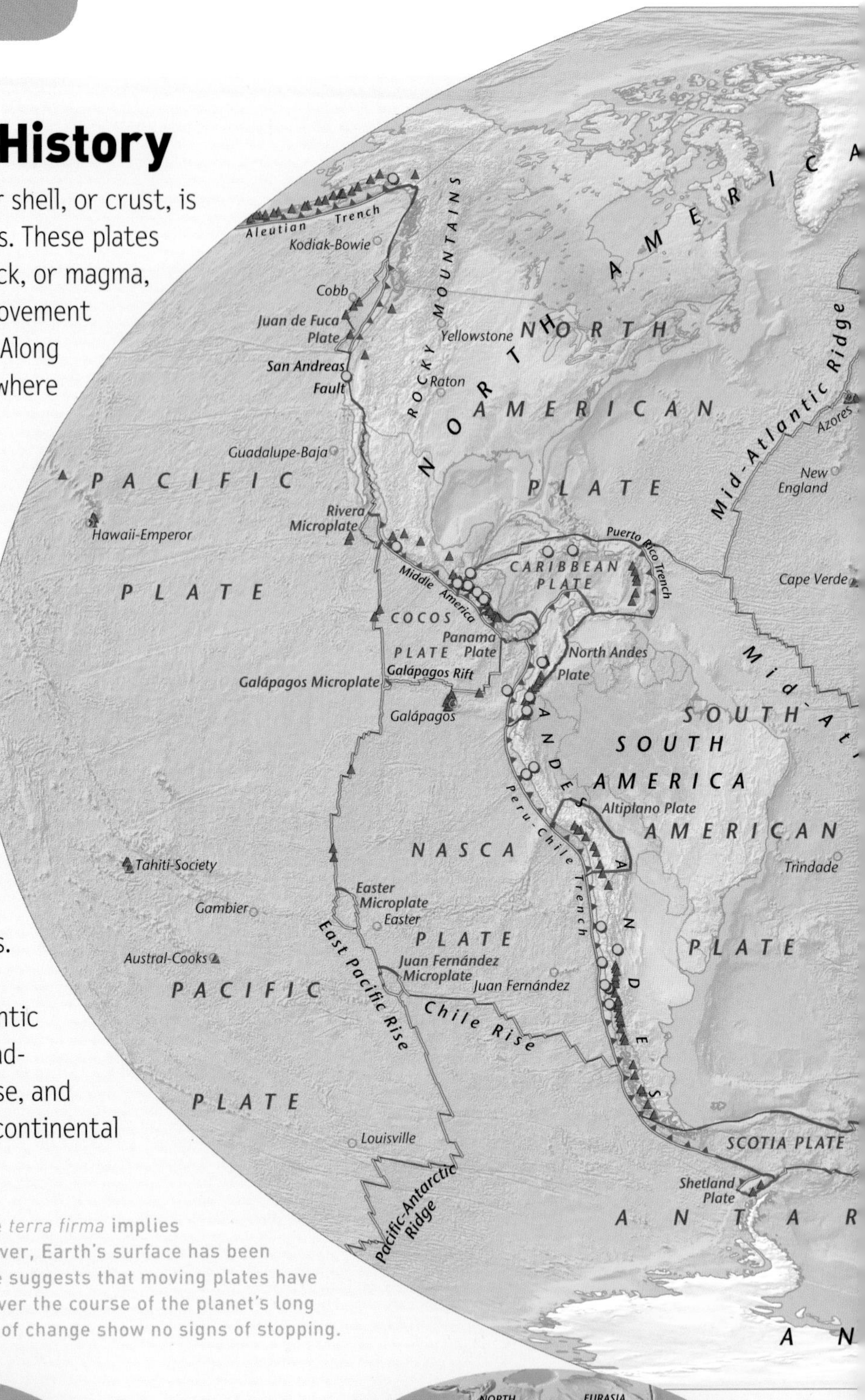

🌀 **OUR CHANGING PLANET.** The Latin phrase *terra firma* implies planet Earth is solid and unchanging. However, Earth's surface has been anything but unchanging. Geologic evidence suggests that moving plates have collided and moved apart more than once over the course of the planet's long history. As the main map shows, the forces of change show no signs of stopping.

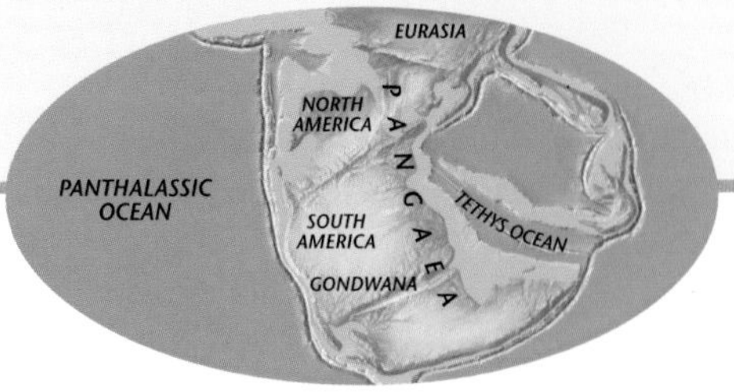

PANGAEA. About 240 million years ago, all of Earth's continents collided to form a vast landmass (now called Pangaea) that stretched from Pole to Pole.

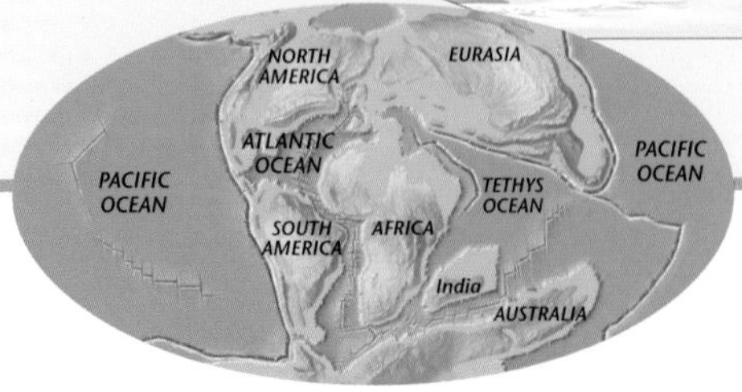

DRIFTING APART. By 94 million years ago, Pangaea had been pulled apart into smaller landmasses. In the warm global climate, dinosaurs evolved into Earth's dominant animal group.

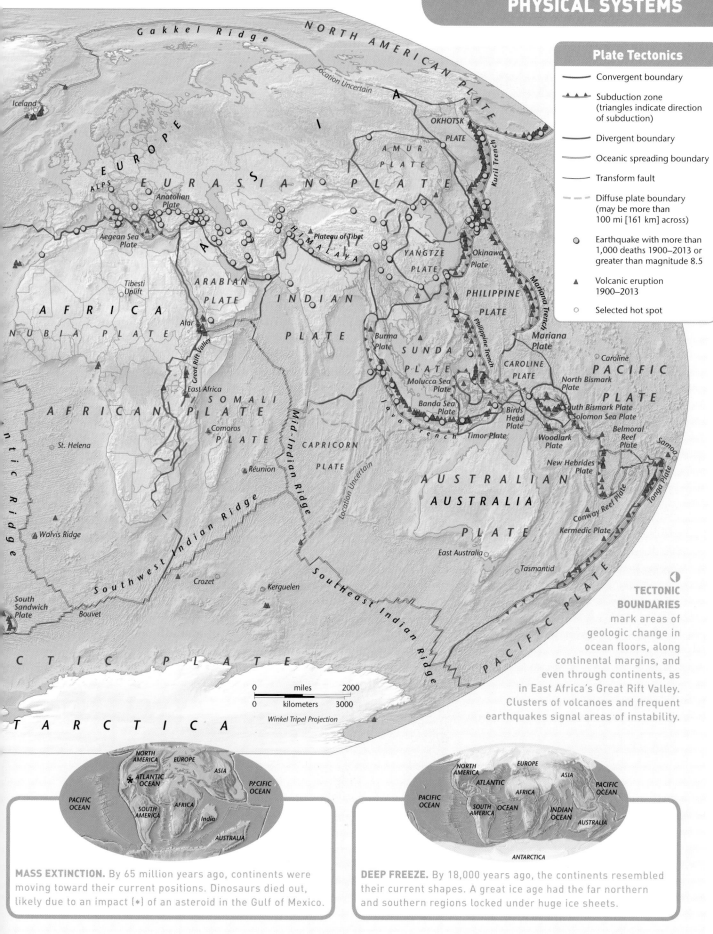

Plate Tectonics

——— Convergent boundary

▲▲▲ Subduction zone (triangles indicate direction of subduction)

——— Divergent boundary

——— Oceanic spreading boundary

——— Transform fault

– – – Diffuse plate boundary (may be more than 100 mi [161 km] across)

○ Earthquake with more than 1,000 deaths 1900–2013 or greater than magnitude 8.5

▲ Volcanic eruption 1900–2013

○ Selected hot spot

Gakkel Ridge

NORTH AMERICAN PLATE

Iceland

EUROPE

EURASIAN PLATE

ALPS

Anatolian Plate

Aegean Sea Plate

OKHOTSK PLATE

AMUR PLATE

Kuril Trench

Location Uncertain

Plateau of Tibet

HIMALAYA

YANGTZE PLATE

Okinawa Plate

Mariana Trench

Tibesti Uplift

AFRICA

ARABIAN PLATE

INDIAN PLATE

PHILIPPINE PLATE

Mariana Plate

NUBIA PLATE

Afar

Great Rift Valley

East Africa

SOMALI PLATE

AFRICAN PLATE

Burma Plate

SUNDA PLATE

Molucca Sea Plate

Banda Sea Plate

Philippine Trench

CAROLINE PLATE

Caroline

PACIFIC PLATE

North Bismark Plate

South Bismark Plate

Solomon Sea Plate

Birds Head Plate

Comoros

CAPRICORN PLATE

Java Trench

Timor Plate

Woodlark Plate

Belmoral Reef Plate

St. Helena

Réunion

Location Uncertain

AUSTRALIAN AUSTRALIA PLATE

New Hebrides Plate

Samoa

Mid-Indian Ridge

Conway Reef Plate

Tonga Plate

Walvis Ridge

Southwest Indian Ridge

Kermedic Plate

East Australia

Tasmantid

Crozet

Kerguelen

Southeast Indian Ridge

PACIFIC PLATE

South Sandwich Plate

Bouvet

TECTONIC BOUNDARIES mark areas of geologic change in ocean floors, along continental margins, and even through continents, as in East Africa's Great Rift Valley. Clusters of volcanoes and frequent earthquakes signal areas of instability.

CTIC PLATE

| 0 | miles | 2000 |
| 0 | kilometers | 3000 |

Winkel Tripel Projection

TARCTICA

NORTH AMERICA · EUROPE · ASIA

ATLANTIC OCEAN

PACIFIC OCEAN

PACIFIC OCEAN

AFRICA

SOUTH AMERICA

India

AUSTRALIA

NORTH AMERICA · EUROPE · ASIA

ATLANTIC

PACIFIC OCEAN

PACIFIC OCEAN

SOUTH AMERICA · OCEAN

AFRICA

INDIAN OCEAN

AUSTRALIA

ANTARCTICA

MASS EXTINCTION. By 65 million years ago, continents were moving toward their current positions. Dinosaurs died out, likely due to an impact (✱) of an asteroid in the Gulf of Mexico.

DEEP FREEZE. By 18,000 years ago, the continents resembled their current shapes. A great ice age had the far northern and southern regions locked under huge ice sheets.

Earth's Land & Water Features

The largest land and water features on Earth are the continents and the oceans, but many other features—large and small—make each place unique. Mountains, plateaus, and plains give texture to the land. The Rockies and the Andes rise high above the lowlands of North and South America. In Asia, the Himalaya and the Plateau of Tibet form the rugged core of Earth's largest continent. These features are the result of powerful forces within Earth pushing up the land. Other landforms, such as canyons and valleys, are created when weathering and erosion wear down parts of Earth's surface.

Dramatic features are not limited to the land. Submarine mountains, appearing like pale blue threads against the deep blue on the satellite map, rise from the seafloor and trace zones of underwater geologic activity. Deep trenches form where plates collide, causing one to dive beneath the other.

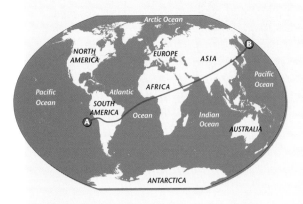

🌐 **A SLICE OF EARTH.** This cross section of Earth's surface extends from Lake Titicaca near South America's Pacific coast to the Kuril Islands in the northwestern Pacific Ocean. It shows towering mountains, eroded highlands, broad coastal plains, and deep ocean basins.

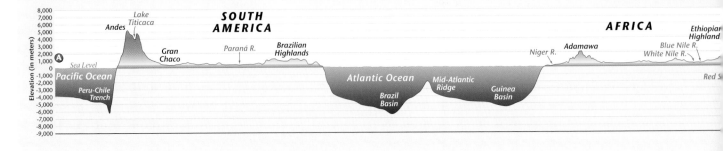

Elevation

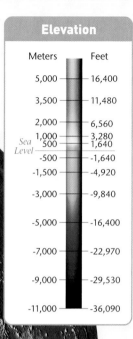

Meters		Feet
5,000		16,400
3,500		11,480
2,000		6,560
1,000		3,280
500		1,640
Sea Level		
-500		-1,640
-1,500		-4,920
-3,000		-9,840
-5,000		-16,400
-7,000		-22,970
-9,000		-29,530
-11,000		-36,090

◖ **EARTH'S HIGHS AND LOWS** above and below sea level are clearly evident in this color-enhanced satellite map. Mountain ranges and ice caps, which rise above the land, stand out in shades of red; broad expanses of lowlands are shown in green. Pale aqua marks shallow seas along continental margins and over peaks and ridges rising from the ocean floor.

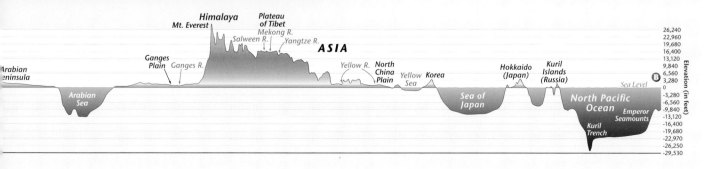

Earth's Climates

Climate is not the same as weather. Climate is the long-term average of conditions in the atmosphere at a particular location on Earth's surface. Weather refers to the momentary conditions of the atmosphere. Climate is important because it influences vegetation and soil development. It also influences people's choices about how and where to live.

There are many different systems for classifying climates. One commonly used system was developed by Russian-born climatologist Wladimir Köppen and later modified by American climatologist Glenn Trewartha. Köppen's system identifies five major climate zones based on average precipitation and temperature, and a sixth zone for highland, or high elevation, areas. Except for continental climate, all climate zones occur in mirror image north and south of the Equator.

CLIMATE GRAPHS. A climate graph is a combination bar and line graph that shows monthly averages of precipitation and temperature for a particular place. The bar graph shows precipitation in inches and centimeters; the line graph shows temperature in degrees Fahrenheit and Celsius. The graphs below are typical for places in the climate zone represented by their background color. The seeming inversion of the temperature lines for Alice Springs, in Australia, and McMurdo, in Antarctica, reflects the reversal of seasons south of the Equator, where January is midsummer. The abbreviations for months are across the bottom of each graph.

Map labels: Resolute, Fairbanks, 60°N, NORTH AMERICA, Subarctic Current, North Pacific Drift, 30°N, Des Moines, Labrador Current, Gulf Stream, North Atlantic Drift, TROPIC OF CANCER, Monterrey, PACIFIC OCEAN, ATLANTIC, Equatorial Countercurrent, 0°, 150°W, 120°W, EQUATOR, 90°W, Belém, South Equatorial Current, SOUTH AMERICA, Peru Current, TROPIC OF CAPRICORN, 30°S, Falkland Current, West Wind Drift, 60°S

0 miles 2000
0 kilometers 3000
Winkel Tripel Projection

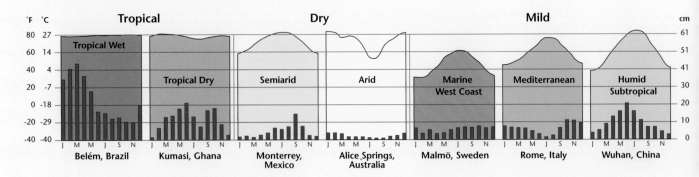

	Tropical		Dry		Mild		
Tropical Wet	Tropical Dry	Semiarid	Arid	Marine West Coast	Mediterranean	Humid Subtropical
Belém, Brazil	Kumasi, Ghana	Monterrey, Mexico	Alice Springs, Australia	Malmö, Sweden	Rome, Italy	Wuhan, China

PHYSICAL SYSTEMS

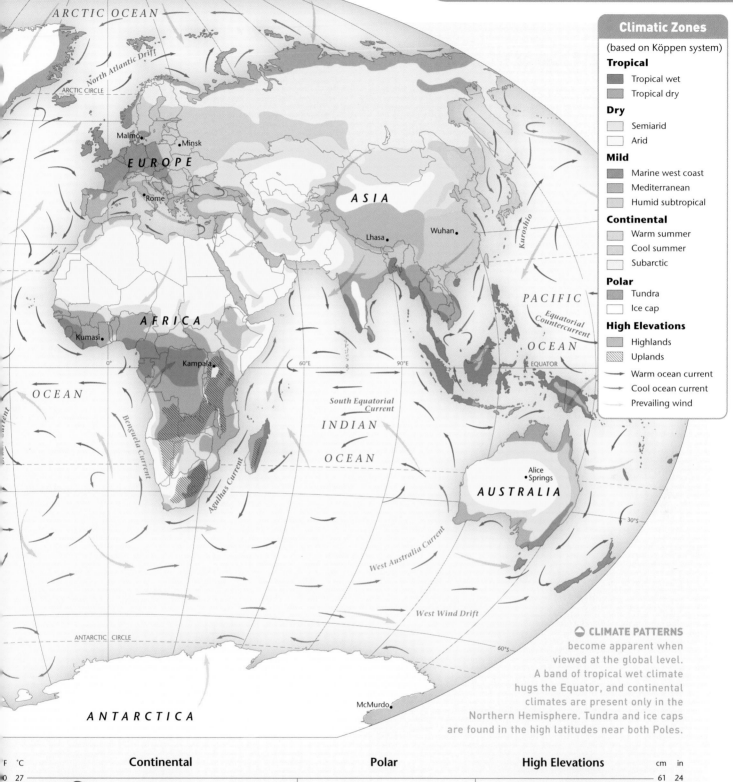

Climatic Zones

(based on Köppen system)

Tropical
- Tropical wet
- Tropical dry

Dry
- Semiarid
- Arid

Mild
- Marine west coast
- Mediterranean
- Humid subtropical

Continental
- Warm summer
- Cool summer
- Subarctic

Polar
- Tundra
- Ice cap

High Elevations
- Highlands
- Uplands

→ Warm ocean current
→ Cool ocean current
→ Prevailing wind

⬤ CLIMATE PATTERNS become apparent when viewed at the global level. A band of tropical wet climate hugs the Equator, and continental climates are present only in the Northern Hemisphere. Tundra and ice caps are found in the high latitudes near both Poles.

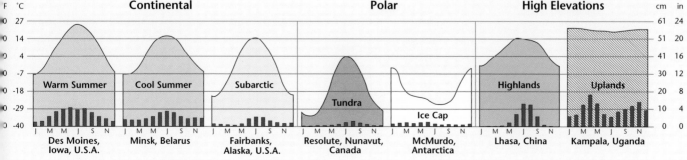

Continental			Polar		High Elevations	
Warm Summer	Cool Summer	Subarctic	Tundra	Ice Cap	Highlands	Uplands
Des Moines, Iowa, U.S.A.	Minsk, Belarus	Fairbanks, Alaska, U.S.A.	Resolute, Nunavut, Canada	McMurdo, Antarctica	Lhasa, China	Kampala, Uganda

Climate Controls

The patterns of climate vary widely. Some climates, such as those near the Equator and the Poles, are nearly constant year-round. Others experience great seasonal variations, such as the wet and dry patterns of the tropical dry zone and the monthly average temperature extremes of the subarctic.

Climate patterns are not random. They are the result of complex interactions of basic climate controls: latitude, elevation, prevailing winds, ocean currents, landforms, and location.

These controls combine in various ways to create the bands of climate that can be seen on the world climate map on pages 20–21 and on the climate maps in the individual continent sections of this atlas. At the local level, however, special conditions may create microclimates that differ from those that are more typical of the region.

ELEVATION

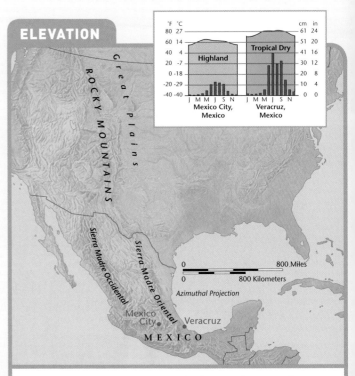

Not all locations at the same latitude experience similar climates. Air at higher elevations is cooler and holds less moisture than air at lower elevations. This explains why the climate at Veracruz, Mexico, which is near sea level, is warm and wet, and the climate at Mexico City, which is more than 7,000 feet (2,100 m) above sea level, is cooler and drier.

LATITUDE

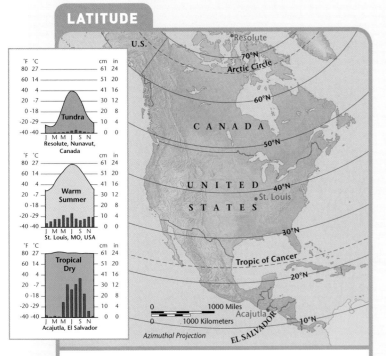

Latitude affects the amount of solar energy received. As latitude (distance north or south of the Equator) increases, the angle of the sun's energy becomes increasingly oblique, or slanted. Less energy is received from the sun, and annual average temperatures fall. Therefore, the annual average temperature decreases as latitude increases from Acajutla, El Salvador, to St. Louis, Missouri, to Resolute, Canada.

LANDFORMS

When air carried by prevailing winds blows across a large body of water, such as the ocean, it picks up moisture. If that air encounters a mountain when it reaches land, it is forced to rise and the air becomes cooler, causing precipitation on the windward side of the mountain (see Portland graph). When air descends on the side away from the wind— the leeward side—the air warms and absorbs available moisture. This creates a dry condition known as rain shadow (see Wallowa graph).

PREVAILING WINDS AND OCEAN CURRENTS

Earth's rotation combined with heat energy from the sun creates patterns of movement in Earth's atmosphere called prevailing winds. In the oceans, similar movements of water are called currents. Prevailing winds and ocean currents bring warm and cold temperatures to land areas. They also bring moisture or take it away. The Gulf Stream and the North Atlantic Drift, for example, are warm-water currents that influence average temperatures in eastern North America and northern Europe. Prevailing winds—trade winds, polar easterlies, and westerlies—also affect temperature and precipitation averages.

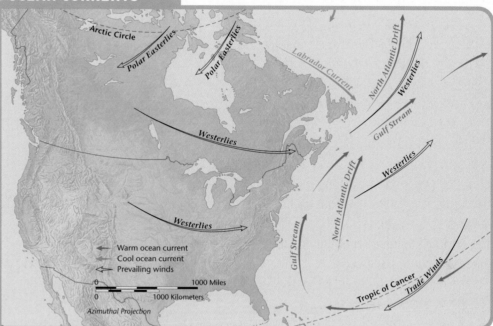

LOCATION

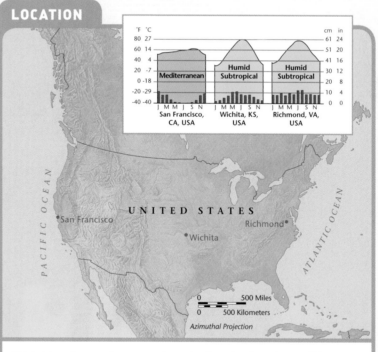

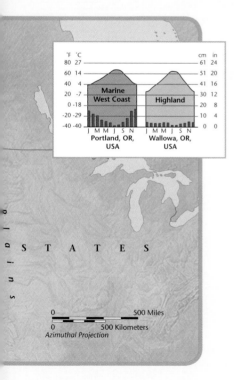

Marine locations—places near large bodies of water—have mild climates with little temperature variation because water gains and loses heat slowly (see San Francisco graph). Interior locations—places far from large water bodies—have much more extreme climates. There are great temperature variations because land gains and loses heat rapidly (see Wichita graph). Richmond, which is relatively near the Atlantic Ocean but which is also influenced by prevailing westerly winds blowing across the land, has moderate characteristics of both conditions.

Earth's Natural Vegetation

Natural vegetation is plant life that would be found in an area if it were undisturbed by human activity. Natural vegetation varies widely depending on climate and soil conditions. In rain forests, trees tower as much as 200 feet (60 m) above the forest floor. In the humid mid-latitudes, deciduous trees shed their leaves during the cold season, while coniferous trees remain green throughout the year. Areas receiving too little rainfall to support trees have grasses. Dry areas have plants such as cacti that tolerate long periods without water. In the tundra, dwarf species of shrubs and flowers are adaptations to harsh conditions at high latitudes and high elevations.

Vegetation is important to human life. It provides oxygen, food, fuel, products with economic value, even lifesaving medicines. Human activities, however, have greatly affected natural vegetation (see pages 28–29). Huge forests have been cut to provide fuel and lumber. Grasslands have yielded to the plow as people extend agricultural lands. As many as one in eight plants may become extinct due to human interference.

⬤ **TYPES OF VEGETATION.** Vegetation creates a mosaic of colors and textures across Earth's surface. Grasslands dominate in places where there is too little precipitation to support trees. In the wet conditions of the tropics, rain forests and mangroves flourish. Desert shrubs are adapted to dry climates, and tundra plants survive a short growing season. These photographs show some of the plants found in various vegetation regions. Each is keyed to the map by color and number.

NORTH AMERICA

ATLANTIC

PACIFIC OCEAN

SOUTH AMERICA

TROPIC OF CANCER

EQUATOR

TROPIC OF CAPRICORN

60°N
30°N
0°
30°S
60°S

150°W   120°W   90°W

| 0 | miles | 2000 |
| 0 | kilometers | 3000 |

Winkel Tripel Projection

TUNDRA

NORTHERN CONIFEROUS FOREST

TEMPERATE BROADLEAF FOREST

TEMPERATE GRASSLAND

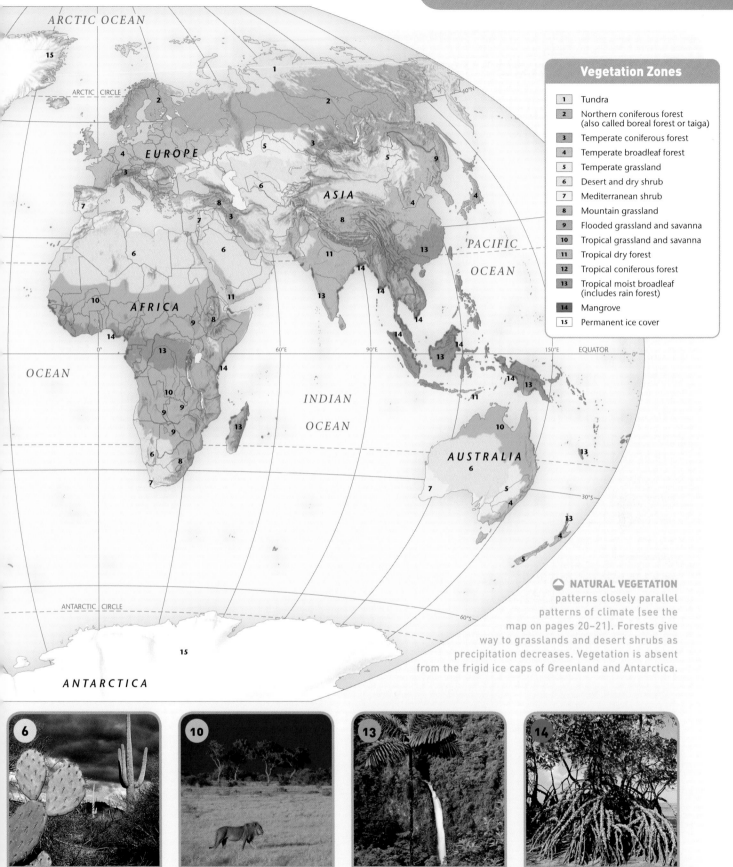

Vegetation Zones

1	Tundra
2	Northern coniferous forest (also called boreal forest or taiga)
3	Temperate coniferous forest
4	Temperate broadleaf forest
5	Temperate grassland
6	Desert and dry shrub
7	Mediterranean shrub
8	Mountain grassland
9	Flooded grassland and savanna
10	Tropical grassland and savanna
11	Tropical dry forest
12	Tropical coniferous forest
13	Tropical moist broadleaf (includes rain forest)
14	Mangrove
15	Permanent ice cover

NATURAL VEGETATION patterns closely parallel patterns of climate (see the map on pages 20–21). Forests give way to grasslands and desert shrubs as precipitation decreases. Vegetation is absent from the frigid ice caps of Greenland and Antarctica.

6 DESERT AND DRY SHRUB

10 TROPICAL GRASSLAND AND SAVANNA

13 TROPICAL MOIST BROADLEAF

14 MANGROVE

Earth's Water

Water is essential for life and is one of Earth's most valuable natural resources. It is even more important than food. More than 70 percent of Earth's surface is covered with water in the form of oceans, lakes, rivers, and streams, but most of this water—about 97 percent—is salty and without treatment is unusable for drinking or growing crops. The remaining 3 percent is fresh, but most of this is either trapped in glaciers or ice caps or lies too deep underground to be tapped economically.

Water is a renewable resource that can be used over and over because the hydrologic, or water, cycle purifies water as it moves through the processes of evaporation, condensation, precipitation, runoff, and infiltration. However, careless use can diminish the supply of usable fresh water when pollution results from industrial dumping, runoff of fertilizers or pesticides from cultivated fields, or discharge of urban sewage. Like other natural resources, water is unevenly distributed on Earth. Some regions, such as the eastern United States, have sufficient water to meet the needs of the people living there. But in other regions, such as large areas of Asia, the demand for water places great stress on available supply (see the map).

NORTH AMERICA

PACIFIC OCEAN

ATLANT

SOUTH AMERICA

TROPIC OF CANCER

EQUATOR

Water Stress

Withdrawls as a Percentage of Available Supply

- Less than 10%
- 10–19.9%
- 20–39.9%
- 40–80%
- Greater than 80%
- Arid with low demand
- No data

WATER USES   Note: Percentages shown are for annual use; 2011 data.

Domestic 12%

DOMESTIC. In many less developed regions, women, such as these in Central America, haul water for daily use.

Agricultural 70%

AGRICULTURAL. Irrigation has made agriculture possible in dry areas such as the San Pedro Valley in Arizona, shown here.

PHYSICAL SYSTEMS

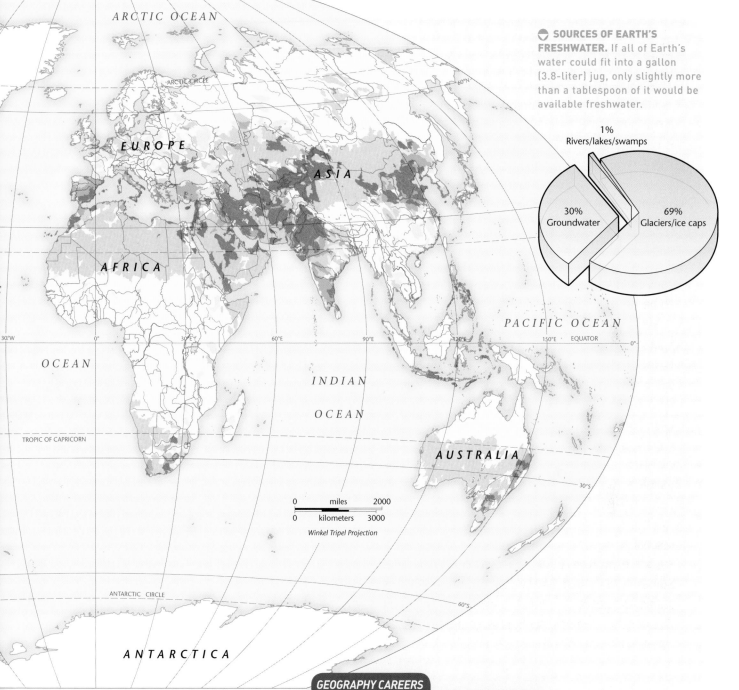

ARCTIC OCEAN

ARCTIC CIRCLE

EUROPE

ASIA

AFRICA

OCEAN

PACIFIC OCEAN

INDIAN

OCEAN

TROPIC OF CAPRICORN

AUSTRALIA

ANTARCTIC CIRCLE

ANTARCTICA

0   miles   2000
0   kilometers   3000

Winkel Tripel Projection

SOURCES OF EARTH'S FRESHWATER. If all of Earth's water could fit into a gallon (3.8-liter) jug, only slightly more than a tablespoon of it would be available freshwater.

1%
Rivers/lakes/swamps

30%
Groundwater

69%
Glaciers/ice caps

Industrial 18%

INDUSTRIAL. Hydroelectric dams, such as this one in Tucuruí, Brazil, generate electricity to power industry.

GEOGRAPHY CAREERS

NG EXPLORER: SANDRA POSTEL

Sandra Postel, a freshwater conservationist, has spent over 25 years promoting water conservation and better water management. She founded the Global Water Policy Project in order to promote the preservation and sustainable uses of Earth's freshwater sources and works to accomplish this goal through research, writing, outreach, public speaking, and teaching. *national geographic.com/explorers/bios/sandra-postel*

Environmental Hot Spots

As Earth's human population increases, pressures on the natural environment also increase. In industrialized countries, landfills overflow with the volume of trash produced. Industries generate waste and pollution that foul the air and water. Farmers use chemical fertilizers and pesticides that run off into streams and groundwater. Cars release exhaust fumes that pollute the air and perhaps also contribute to global climate change.

In less developed countries, forests are cut and not replanted, making the land vulnerable to erosion. Fragile grasslands turn to deserts when farmers and herders move onto marginal land as they try to make a living. And cities struggle with issues such as water safety, sanitation, and basic services that accompany the explosive urban growth that characterizes many less developed countries.

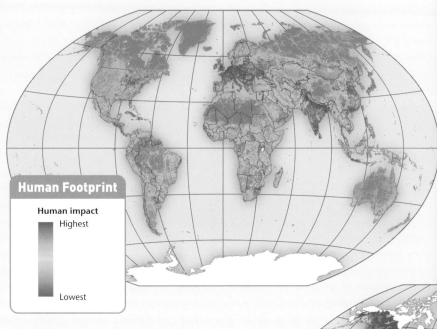

Human Footprint

Human impact

Highest

Lowest

⬒ **HUMAN ACTIVITY** has altered nearly 75 percent of Earth's habitable surface. Referred to as the "human footprint," this disturbance is greatest in areas of high population.

◑ Forests play a critical role in Earth's natural systems. They regulate water flow, release oxygen and retain carbon, cycle nutrients, and build soils. But humans have cut, burned, altered, and replaced half of all forests that stood 8,000 years ago.

Fragile Forests

■ Current frontier forest (large, relatively undisturbed forest)

■ Current non-frontier forest (degraded, regrown, replanted, plantation, or other forest areas)

□ Estimated extent of frontier forest 8,000 years ago

DESERT SANDS, moved by high winds, cover large areas of Mauritania. The shifting sands threaten to cover an important transportation route (upper right), which must be cleared daily. A grid of branches has been laid over the sand to try to slow the advancing desert, which has been expanding since the mid-1960s.

DEFORESTATION in Haiti (left side of photograph above) clearly defines its border with the Dominican Republic. Haiti was once 30 percent forested, but loss of trees for timber and subsistence agriculture has reduced forest cover to less than 2 percent.

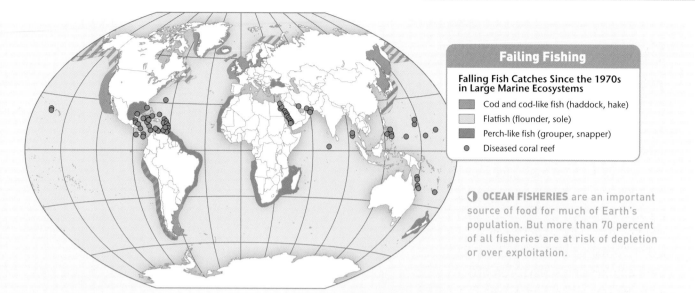

Failing Fishing

Falling Fish Catches Since the 1970s in Large Marine Ecosystems

- Cod and cod-like fish (haddock, hake)
- Flatfish (flounder, sole)
- Perch-like fish (grouper, snapper)
- ● Diseased coral reef

◖ **OCEAN FISHERIES** are an important source of food for much of Earth's population. But more than 70 percent of all fisheries are at risk of depletion or over exploitation.

◕ **CLIMATE CHANGE** may alter Earth's ability to support some forms of life. Rising temperatures may lead to loss of habitat, glacial melting, and flooding of coastal population centers.

Climate Change

Habitat Loss Due to Climate Change
(risk over next 100 years)

- Critical
- High
- Low
- ● City vulnerable to sea-level rise
- △ Melting glaciers

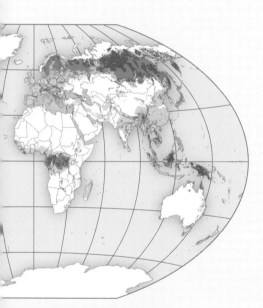

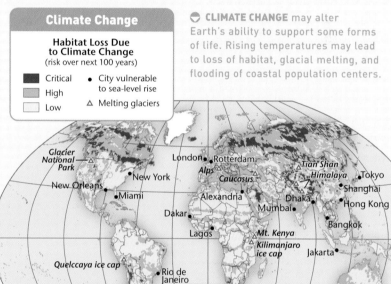

AN OIL SPILL closed this California beach. Clean-up workers are attempting to reduce the amount of damage to the environment.

GEOGRAPHY CAREERS

NG EXPLORER: ERIKA CUÉLLAR

Erika Cuéllar works as a conservation biologist to protect South America's Gran Chaco region, which spans a diverse mix of habitats, climates, topography, and species. Erika trains local people to become environmental protectors by providing courses on conservation, scientific research, and first aid and is working to extend her efforts to South American governments. *nationalgeographic.com/explorers/bios/erika-cuellar*

The Political World

A map with the names and boundaries of countries shows the political world. Boundaries—some arrived at peacefully, others after years of conflict and war—carve up the land into 195 independent units, or countries, early in the 21st century. Boundaries are dynamic, meaning they change over time as political power shifts. For example, in 1990, West and East Germany became one country, removing a boundary that had separated them since 1949. In 2011, a new boundary was established to separate the new country of South Sudan from Sudan.

Countries vary in size. Russia, the largest, stretches across northern Asia into Europe. Other countries are small enough to fit inside another country. For instance, the country of Lesotho lies entirely within the country of South Africa.

◖ THE SCALE OF THIS MAP makes it impossible to name all 195 independent countries and their capital cities. For a complete listing, refer to pages 126–133 or use the place-name index and the political maps in each continent section.

◖ VIEW FROM THE NORTH POLE. Ocean, not land, surrounds the area of the North Pole, so there are no political boundaries there. The Arctic Ocean, icebound much of the year, is part of the coastal waters of Earth's northernmost countries.

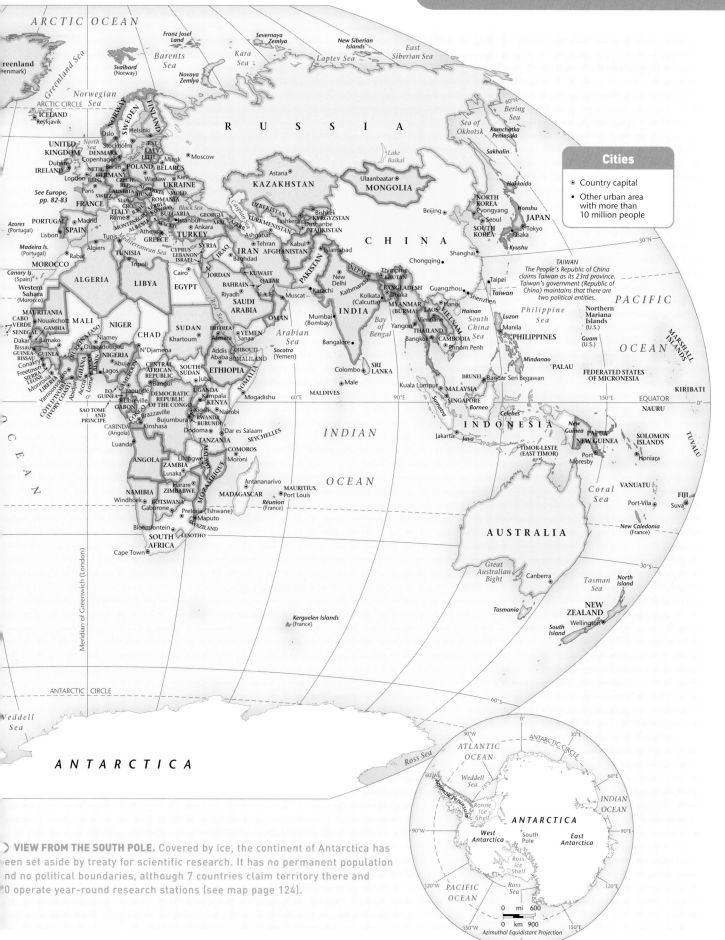

Cities

⊕ Country capital

• Other urban area with more than 10 million people

TAIWAN
The People's Republic of China claims Taiwan as its 23rd province. Taiwan's government (Republic of China) maintains that there are two political entities.

VIEW FROM THE SOUTH POLE. Covered by ice, the continent of Antarctica has been set aside by treaty for scientific research. It has no permanent population and no political boundaries, although 7 countries claim territory there and 30 operate year-round research stations (see map page 124).

World Population

In mid-2013, the United Nations estimated Earth's population to be 7.2 billion. Although more than 86 million people are added each year, the rate, or annual percent, at which the population is growing is gradually decreasing. Earth's population has very uneven distribution, with huge clusters in Asia and in Europe. Population density, the number of people living in each square mile (or square kilometer) on average, is high in these regions. For example, on average there are more than 2,815 people per square mile (1,087 per sq km) in Bangladesh. Other areas, such as deserts and Arctic tundra, have fewer than 2 people per square mile (1 person per sq km).

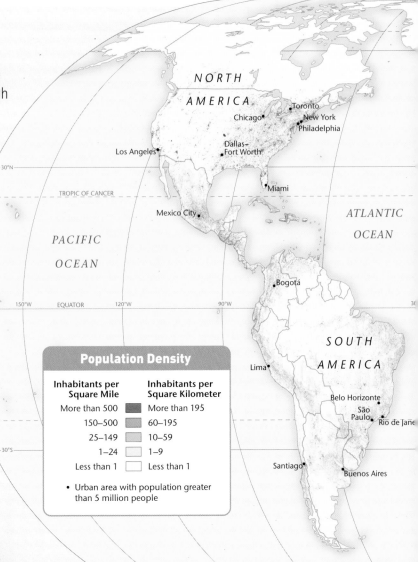

Population Density

Inhabitants per Square Mile	Inhabitants per Square Kilometer
More than 500	More than 195
150–500	60–195
25–149	10–59
1–24	1–9
Less than 1	Less than 1

- Urban area with population greater than 5 million people

CROWDED STREETS, like this one in Shanghai, China, may become commonplace as Earth's population continues to increase and as more people move to urban areas.

POPULATION GROWTH OVER TIME

The population's rate of increase—the percentage by which it changes each year—was slow until industrial and scientific discoveries in the 1800s brought improved health, a more reliable food supply, and other changes that improved the quality of life. Although the rate of increase is slowing, the United Nations projects that Earth's population will reach 9.6 billion by 2050.

9.6 Billion
8.1 Billion
7.2 Billion
6.1 Billion
2.5 Billion
1.6 Billion
900 Million
610 Million
545 Million
425 Million

Billions of people

Year: 1500 | 1600 | 1700 | 1800 | 1900 | 1950 | 2000 | 2025

2013
2050
2012 projections

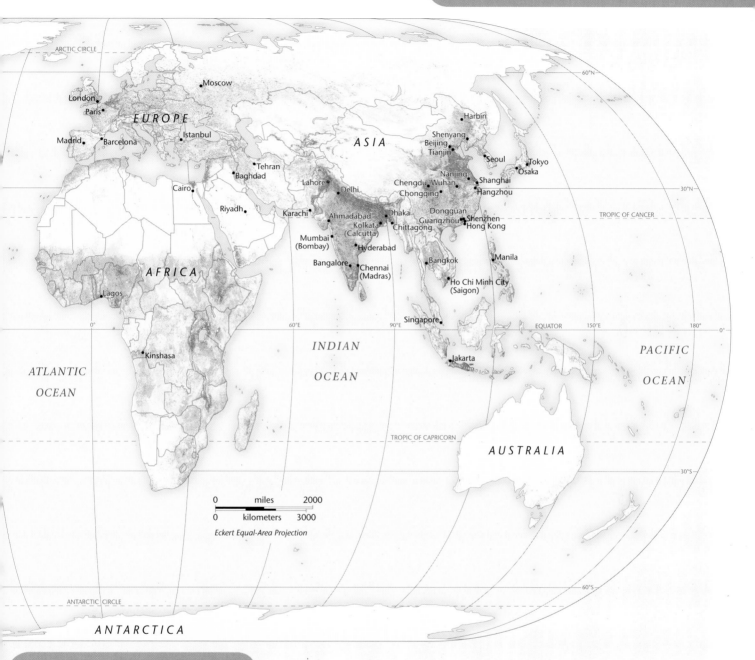

THREE POPULATION PYRAMIDS

A population pyramid is a special type of bar graph that shows the distribution of a country's population by sex and age. Italy has a very narrow pyramid, which shows that most people are in middle age. Its population is said to be aging, meaning the median age is increasing. The United States also has a narrow pyramid, but one that shows some growth due to a median age of about 37 years and a young immigrant population. By contrast, Nigeria's pyramid has a broad base, showing it has a young population. Almost half of its people are younger than 15 years.

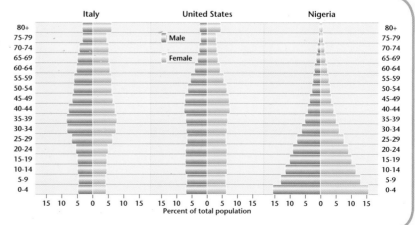

World Refugees

Every day, people relocate to new cities, new states, even new countries. Most move by choice, but some people, called refugees, move to escape war and persecution that make it impossible to remain where they are. Such forced movement creates severe hardship for families who have to leave behind their possessions. They may find themselves in a new place where they do not speak the local language, where customs are unfamiliar, and where basic necessities, such as food, shelter, and medical care, are in short supply.

An agency of the United Nations, the Office of the High Commissioner for Refugees (UNHCR), is responsible for the safety and well-being of refugees worldwide and for protecting their rights. UNHCR works to find solutions to refugee situations through voluntary return to home countries, integration in a host country, or resettlement to another country.

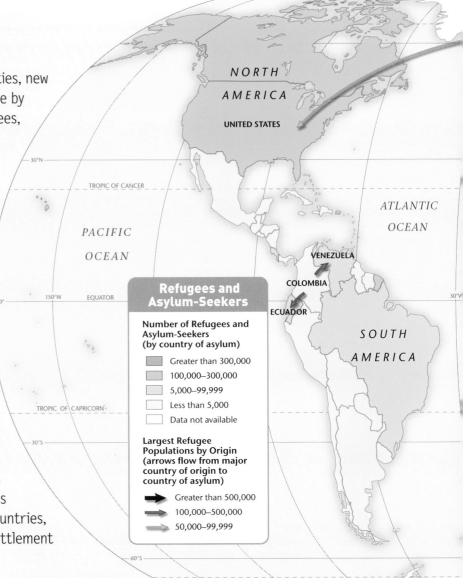

Refugees and Asylum-Seekers

Number of Refugees and Asylum-Seekers (by country of asylum)

- Greater than 300,000
- 100,000–300,000
- 5,000–99,999
- Less than 5,000
- Data not available

Largest Refugee Populations by Origin (arrows flow from major country of origin to country of asylum)

- Greater than 500,000
- 100,000–500,000
- 50,000–99,999

REFUGEE HOST COUNTRIES

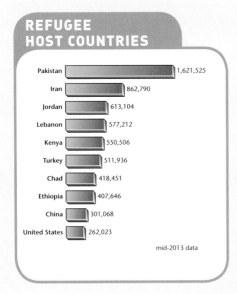

Pakistan	1,621,525
Iran	862,790
Jordan	613,104
Lebanon	577,212
Kenya	550,506
Turkey	511,936
Chad	418,451
Ethiopia	407,646
China	301,068
United States	262,023

mid-2013 data

REFUGEES fleeing hostilities in the Democratic Republic of the Congo (DRC) receive food in a transit camp in Uganda. More than two million people have been displaced—many within the DRC, others crossing into neighboring countries.

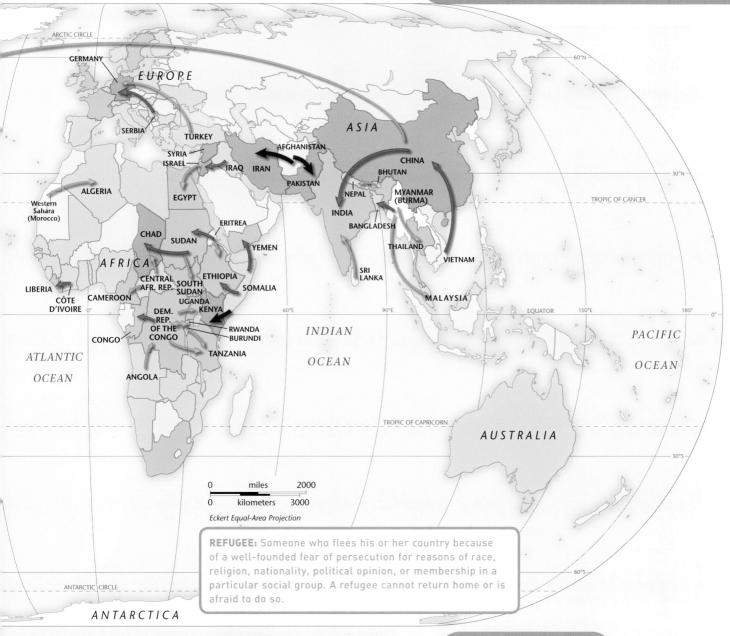

ARCTIC CIRCLE

GERMANY

EUROPE

ASIA

SERBIA

TURKEY

AFGHANISTAN

CHINA

SYRIA
ISRAEL

IRAQ IRAN

BHUTAN

PAKISTAN

NEPAL

MYANMAR
(BURMA)

ALGERIA

EGYPT

INDIA

BANGLADESH

Western
Sahara
(Morocco)

ERITREA

THAILAND

CHAD

SUDAN

YEMEN

VIETNAM

AFRICA

ETHIOPIA

SRI
LANKA

LIBERIA

CENTRAL
AFR. REP.

SOUTH
SUDAN

SOMALIA

CÔTE
D'IVOIRE

CAMEROON

UGANDA

KENYA

MALAYSIA

DEM.
REP.
OF THE
CONGO

RWANDA
BURUNDI

INDIAN

CONGO

TANZANIA

OCEAN

PACIFIC

ANGOLA

OCEAN

ATLANTIC

OCEAN

60°N

30°N

TROPIC OF CANCER

0°

60°E

90°E

EQUATOR

150°E

180°

0°

TROPIC OF CAPRICORN

AUSTRALIA

30°S

60°S

ANTARCTIC CIRCLE

ANTARCTICA

0	miles	2000
0	kilometers	3000

Eckert Equal-Area Projection

REFUGEE: Someone who flees his or her country because of a well-founded fear of persecution for reasons of race, religion, nationality, political opinion, or membership in a particular social group. A refugee cannot return home or is afraid to do so.

⬭ **MANY KURDS,** a people who live mainly in Iraq and Turkey, fled to the remote mountains of northern Iraq to escape spreading hostilities. This region, referred to as Kurdistan, is the traditional homeland of these stateless people.

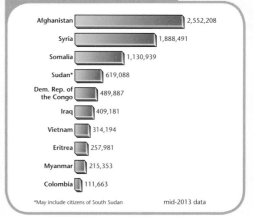

REFUGEES BY ORIGIN

Origin	Refugees
Afghanistan	2,552,208
Syria	1,888,491
Somalia	1,130,939
Sudan*	619,088
Dem. Rep. of the Congo	489,887
Iraq	409,181
Vietnam	314,194
Eritrea	257,981
Myanmar	215,353
Colombia	111,663

*May include citizens of South Sudan   mid-2013 data

Quality of Life

The world's population is unevenly distributed (see map on pages 32–33), and not everyone experiences the same quality of life. The level of development in countries is often measured in economic terms, but beginning in 1990, the United Nations Development Program introduced a different and more complete way to evaluate the condition of life in the world's countries: the Human Development Index (HDI). The HDI combines both social and economic factors to rank the world's countries based on three indicators: health, education, and living standard (see map at right). Health is measured by life expectancy at birth (see map below). Education is measured by average years of schooling. And living standard is measured using gross national income per capita—the total income earned in a country each year divided by the country's population (see graph).

Human Development Index

Level of Human Development

- Very high
- High
- Medium
- Low
- No data

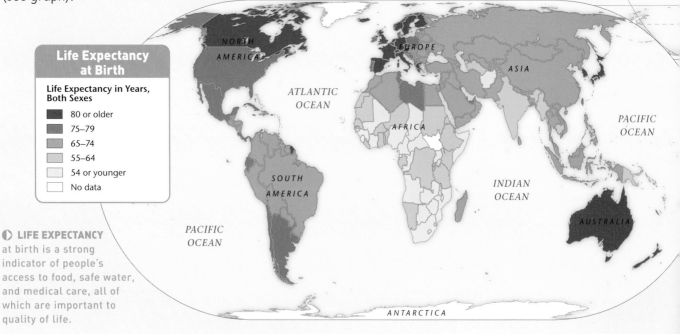

Life Expectancy at Birth

Life Expectancy in Years, Both Sexes

- 80 or older
- 75–79
- 65–74
- 55–64
- 54 or younger
- No data

◗ **LIFE EXPECTANCY** at birth is a strong indicator of people's access to food, safe water, and medical care, all of which are important to quality of life.

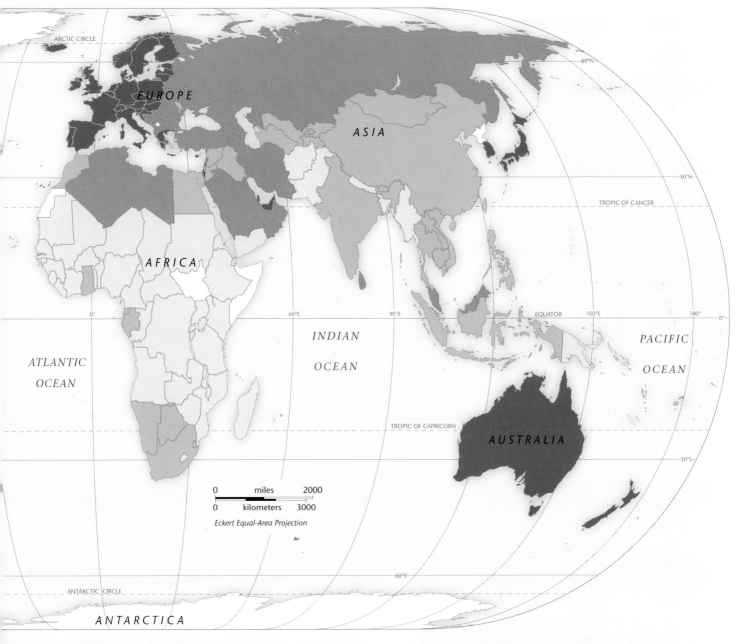

ARCTIC CIRCLE

EUROPE

ASIA

60°N

30°N

TROPIC OF CANCER

AFRICA

0°   60°E   90°E   EQUATOR   150°E   180°   0°

INDIAN

OCEAN

PACIFIC

ATLANTIC

OCEAN

OCEAN

TROPIC OF CAPRICORN

AUSTRALIA

30°S

0   miles   2000
0   kilometers   3000
Eckert Equal-Area Projection

60°S

ANTARCTIC CIRCLE

ANTARCTICA

⬤ **THE HUMAN DEVELOPMENT INDEX** ranks countries of the world in four categories: very high, high, medium, and low human development, based on health, education, and income statistics.

◑ **EDUCATION** opens doors to employment and a better standard of living, but only 59 percent of school-age children in Mozambique are enrolled in school.

◑ **QUALITY OF LIFE,** as measured in terms of income per person, varies greatly among the world's ten most populous countries.

GROSS NATIONAL INCOME

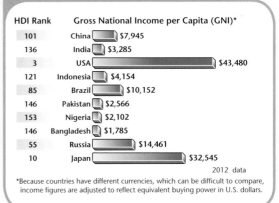

HDI Rank	Gross National Income per Capita (GNI)*
101	China $7,945
136	India $3,285
3	USA $43,480
121	Indonesia $4,154
85	Brazil $10,152
146	Pakistan $2,566
153	Nigeria $2,102
146	Bangladesh $1,785
55	Russia $14,461
10	Japan $32,545

2012 data

*Because countries have different currencies, which can be difficult to compare, income figures are adjusted to reflect equivalent buying power in U.S. dollars.

World Cities

Throughout most of history, people have lived spread across the land, first as hunters and gatherers, later as farmers. But urban geographers—people who study cities—have determined that today more than half of Earth's population lives in urban areas. Urban areas include one or more cities and their surrounding suburbs. People living there are employed primarily in industry or in service-related jobs. Large urban areas are sometimes called metropolitan areas. In some countries, such as Belgium, almost all the population lives in cities. But throughout much of Africa and Asia, only about 40 percent of the people live in urban areas. Even so, some of the world's fastest growing urban areas are towns and small cities in Africa and Asia.

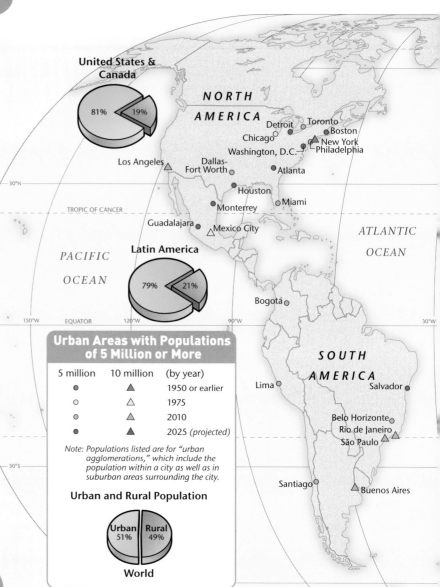

United States & Canada
81% / 19%

Latin America
79% / 21%

Urban Areas with Populations of 5 Million or More

5 million	10 million	(by year)
●	▲	1950 or earlier
○	△	1975
◉	△	2010
●	▲	2025 (projected)

Note: Populations listed are for "urban agglomerations," which include the population within a city as well as in suburban areas surrounding the city.

Urban and Rural Population

Urban 51% / Rural 49%

World

MOST POPULOUS URBAN AREAS

In 1950 New York was the larger of just two urban areas with a population of 10 million or more. By 2011, New York had dropped behind Tokyo, Delhi, and Mexico City in a list of 23 urban areas with populations of at least 10 million. By 2025, the list is projected to include 37 urban areas.

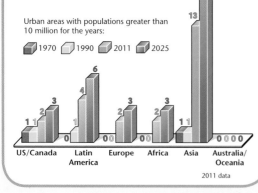

Urban areas with populations greater than 10 million for the years:

◢ 1970 ◢ 1990 ◢ 2011 ◢ 2025

US/Canada | Latin America | Europe | Africa | Asia | Australia/Oceania

2011 data

⬖ **CENTRAL TOKYO,** viewed from high above crowded city streets, contains a mix of modern high-rise and older low-rise buildings. With more than 37 million people, Tokyo is Japan's largest and most densely populated urban area and the world's largest urban agglomeration.

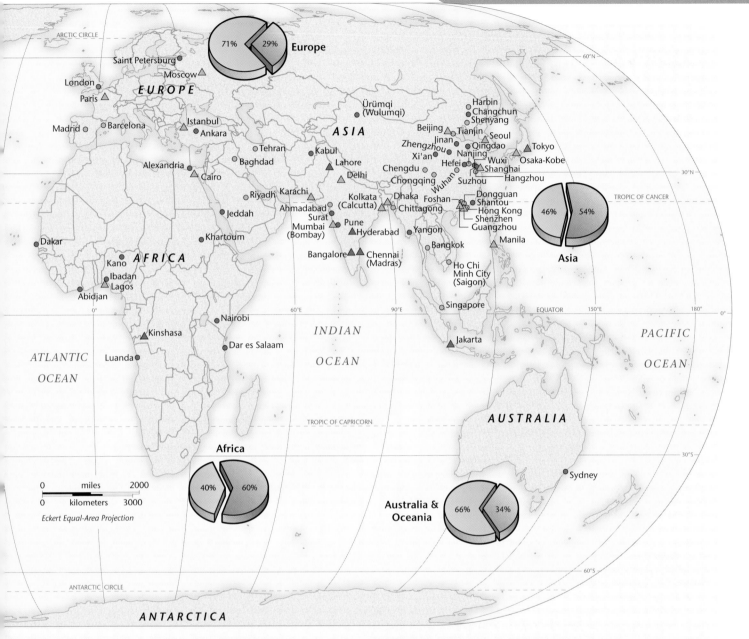

ARCTIC CIRCLE

71% 29% **Europe**

EUROPE

Saint Petersburg
London
Moscow
Paris
Madrid
Barcelona
Istanbul
Ankara

ASIA

Ürümqi
(Wulumqi)

Harbin
Changchun
Shenyang
Beijing Tianjin
Jinan Seoul
Zhengzhou Qingdao Tokyo
Xi'an Nanjing Wuxi Osaka-Kobe
Tehran Kabul
Baghdad Lahore Chengdu Hefei Shanghai
Alexandria Delhi Chongqing Wuhan Suzhou Hangzhou
Cairo

Riyadh Karachi Kolkata Dhaka Foshan Dongguan
Ahmadabad (Calcutta) Chittagong Shantou
Jeddah Surat Hong Kong
Mumbai Pune Shenzhen
(Bombay) Hyderabad Yangon Guangzhou
Khartoum Manila

Dakar
Bangalore Chennai Bangkok
AFRICA (Madras)
Kano Ho Chi
Ibadan Minh City
Lagos (Saigon)
Abidjan Singapore

TROPIC OF CANCER

46% 54%

Asia

EQUATOR

Nairobi

INDIAN

Kinshasa *OCEAN*
Dar es Salaam

ATLANTIC Luanda
OCEAN Jakarta

PACIFIC

OCEAN

AUSTRALIA

TROPIC OF CAPRICORN

Africa

Sydney

0 miles 2000
0 kilometers 3000

40% 60%

Australia &
Oceania

66% 34%

Eckert Equal-Area Projection

ANTARCTIC CIRCLE

ANTARCTICA

URBAN AREAS are home to more than half the world's people. As shown by the symbols on the map, Asia has most of the largest cities, including 13 megacities with at least 10 million people.

RAPID URBAN GROWTH in Africa overwhelms public utilities and contributes to disease, as in this urban slum in Nairobi, Kenya.

NG EXPLORER: THOMAS TAHA RASSAM CULHANE

As part of his work as an urban planner, Thomas Culhane helps developing communities survive and thrive through self-sustainability. His non-governmental organization, Solar C.I.T.I.E.S., assists the residents of Cairo's poorest neighborhoods in installing rooftop solar heaters built from recycled materials. These bring water access to families and help reduce carbon emissions. *nationalgeographic.com/explorers/bios/culhane-thomas*

World Languages

Culture is all the shared traits that make different groups of people around the world unique. For example, customs, food and clothing preferences, housing styles, and music and art forms are all a part of each group's culture. Language is one of the most defining characteristics of culture.

Language reflects what people value and the way they understand the world. It also reveals how certain groups of people may have had common roots at some point in history. For example, English and German are two very different languages, but both are part of the same Indo-European language family. This means that these two languages share certain characteristics that suggest they have evolved from a common ancestor language.

Patterns on the world language families map (right) offer clues to the diffusion, or movement, of groups of people. For example, the widespread use of English, extending from the United States to India, reflects the far-reaching effects of the British colonial empire. Today, English is the main language of the Internet.

About 5,000 languages are spoken in the world today, but experts think many may become extinct as more people become involved in global trade, communications, and travel.

◗ **THE GOLDEN ARCHES** icon helps you identify this restaurant in Moscow even if you don't know how to read the Cyrillic alphabet of the Russian language.

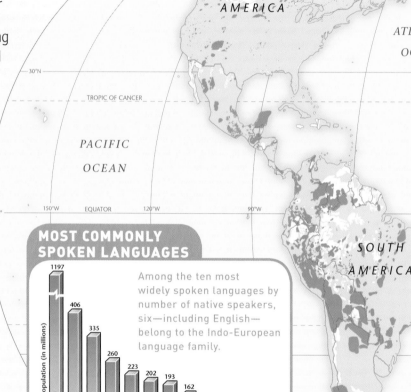

NORTH AMERICA

ATLANTIC OCEAN

30°N

TROPIC OF CANCER

PACIFIC OCEAN

150°W   EQUATOR   120°W   90°W   30°W

0°

SOUTH AMERICA

MOST COMMONLY SPOKEN LANGUAGES

Among the ten most widely spoken languages by number of native speakers, six—including English—belong to the Indo-European language family.

Population (in millions)

Language	Population
Chinese (Mandarin)	1197
Spanish	406
English	335
Hindi-Urdu	260
Arabic	223
Portuguese	202
Bengali	193
Russian	162
Japanese	122
Javanese	84.3

Languages

Макдоналдс

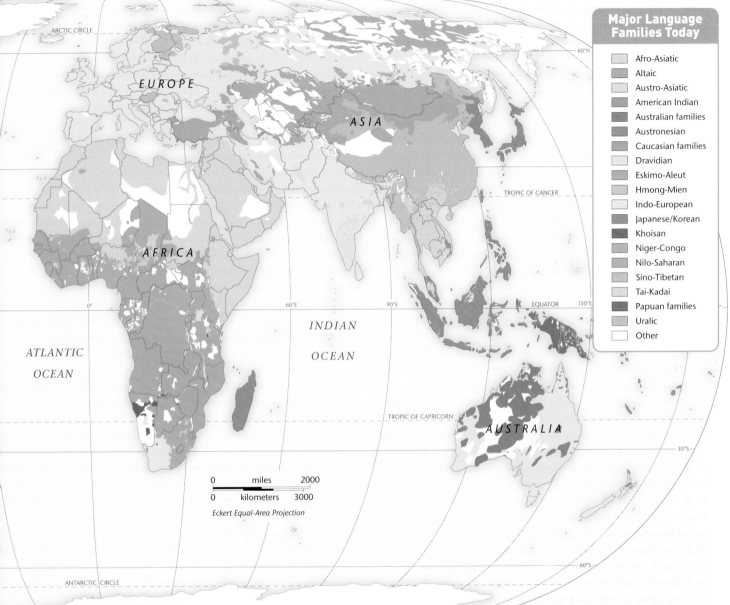

Major Language Families Today

- Afro-Asiatic
- Altaic
- Austro-Asiatic
- American Indian
- Australian families
- Austronesian
- Caucasian families
- Dravidian
- Eskimo-Aleut
- Hmong-Mien
- Indo-European
- Japanese/Korean
- Khoisan
- Niger-Congo
- Nilo-Saharan
- Sino-Tibetan
- Tai-Kadai
- Papuan families
- Uralic
- Other

EUROPE
ASIA
AFRICA
ATLANTIC OCEAN
INDIAN OCEAN
AUSTRALIA
ANTARCTICA

ARCTIC CIRCLE
TROPIC OF CANCER
EQUATOR
TROPIC OF CAPRICORN
ANTARCTIC CIRCLE

60°N
60°E
90°E
150°E
30°S
60°S

0°

```
0        miles       2000
0      kilometers     3000
```
Eckert Equal-Area Projection

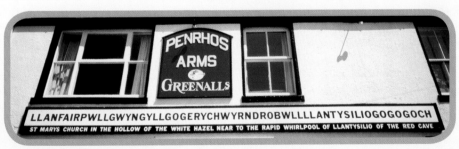

LLANFAIRPWLLGWYNGYLLGOGERYCHWYRNDROBWLLLLANTYSILIOGOGOGOCH
ST MARYS CHURCH IN THE HOLLOW OF THE WHITE HAZEL NEAR TO THE RAPID WHIRLPOOL OF LLANTYSILIO OF THE RED CAVE

SOME WORDS TELL A STORY, like this place-name on the island of Anglesey in Wales. Welsh is an ancient Gaelic language. The alphabet may look familiar, but it has a few more letters than English and different pronunciations.

BENGALI, a language derived from ancient Sanskrit, appears on the walls of a women's health clinic in Kolkata (Calcutta), India. It is just one of the many languages that make up the Indo-European language family.

World Religions

Religious beliefs are a central element of culture. Religious beliefs and practices help people deal with the unknown. But people in different places have developed a variety of belief systems.

Universalizing religions, such as Christianity, Islam, and Buddhism, seek converts. They have spread throughout the world from their origins in Asia. Other religions, including Judaism, Hinduism, and Shinto—called ethnic religions—tend to be associated with particular groups of people and are concentrated in certain places. Some groups, especially indigenous, or native, people living in the tropical forests of Africa and South America, believe that spirits inhabit all things in the natural world. Such belief systems are known as animistic religions.

Places of worship are often a distinctive part of the cultural landscape. A cathedral, mosque, or temple can reveal much about the people who live in a particular place.

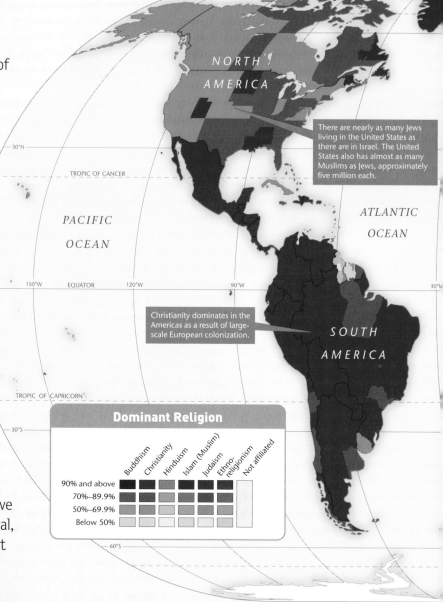

There are nearly as many Jews living in the United States as there are in Israel. The United States also has almost as many Muslims as Jews, approximately five million each.

Christianity dominates in the Americas as a result of large-scale European colonization.

Dominant Religion

	Buddhism	Christianity	Hinduism	Islam (Muslim)	Judaism	Ethno-religionism	Not affiliated
90% and above							
70%–89.9%							
50%–69.9%							
Below 50%							

MOST OF HINDUISM'S 900 million followers live in India and other countries of South Asia. The goddess Durga (above) is regarded as Mother of the Universe and protector of the righteous.

JERUSALEM IS HOLY to Muslims, Christians, and Jews, a fact that has led to tension and conflict. Below, a Russian orthodox church is silhouetted against the Wailing Wall, while sunlight reflects off the Dome of the Rock, a Muslim shrine.

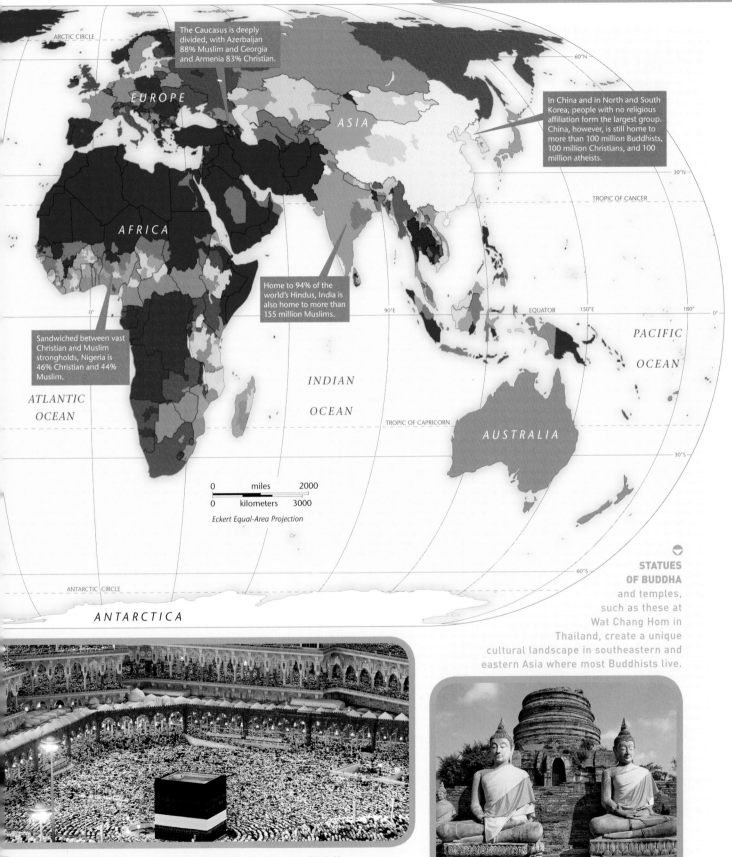

The Caucasus is deeply divided, with Azerbaijan 88% Muslim and Georgia and Armenia 83% Christian.

In China and in North and South Korea, people with no religious affiliation form the largest group. China, however, is still home to more than 100 million Buddhists, 100 million Christians, and 100 million atheists.

Home to 94% of the world's Hindus, India is also home to more than 155 million Muslims.

Sandwiched between vast Christian and Muslim strongholds, Nigeria is 46% Christian and 44% Muslim.

ARCTIC CIRCLE

EUROPE

ASIA

AFRICA

60°N

30°N

TROPIC OF CANCER

0°

90°E

EQUATOR

150°E

180°

0°

PACIFIC
OCEAN

INDIAN
OCEAN

ATLANTIC
OCEAN

TROPIC OF CAPRICORN

AUSTRALIA

30°S

0   miles   2000
0   kilometers   3000

Eckert Equal-Area Projection

60°S

ANTARCTIC CIRCLE

ANTARCTICA

STATUES
OF BUDDHA
and temples,
such as these at
Wat Chang Hom in
Thailand, create a unique
cultural landscape in southeastern and
eastern Asia where most Buddhists live.

MUSLIM WORSHIPPERS surround the sacred Kaaba stone, which lies
shrouded in black cloth at the center of the Grand Mosque in Mecca. Each year
two million Muslims make a hajj, or pilgrimage, here to Islam's holiest shrine.

Predominant World Economies

Economic activities are the many different ways that people generate income to meet their needs and wants. Long ago most people lived by hunting and gathering. Today, most engage in a variety of activities that can be grouped into three categories, or sectors: agriculture, as well as other primary activities such as fishing and forestry; industry, which includes manufacturing and processing activities; and services that range from banking and medicine to information exchange and e-commerce—buying and selling over the Internet. Services and industry, which generate higher incomes, are predominant in more developed countries, while many less developed countries still rely on agriculture.

NORTH AMERICA

PACIFIC OCEAN

ATLANTIC OCEAN

SOUTH AMERICA

30°N

TROPIC OF CANCER

0°   150°W   EQUATOR   120°W   90°W   30°W

TROPIC OF CAPRICORN

30°S

60°S

Predominant Economies

Dominant Economic Sector (as a percentage of GDP)

	Agriculture	Industry*	Services
70%–100%			
50%–69.9%			
0%–49.9%			
No data			

*includes the mining industry

🔵 **SUBSISTENCE AGRICULTURE.** Many people in developing countries, such as these farmers in Bhutan, use traditional methods to grow crops for their daily food requirements rather than for commercial sale.

◗ **FISHING.** Tuna is one of the chief commercial fishes as well as a favorite among big game fishermen. Japan is the world's leading harvester of tuna. Albacore, shown here, is one of the top commercial varieties.

◗ **LOGGING.** Workers ready logs to float down the Columbia River in Washington State. Processing plants will turn the logs into paper products or cut them into lumber for the construction industry.

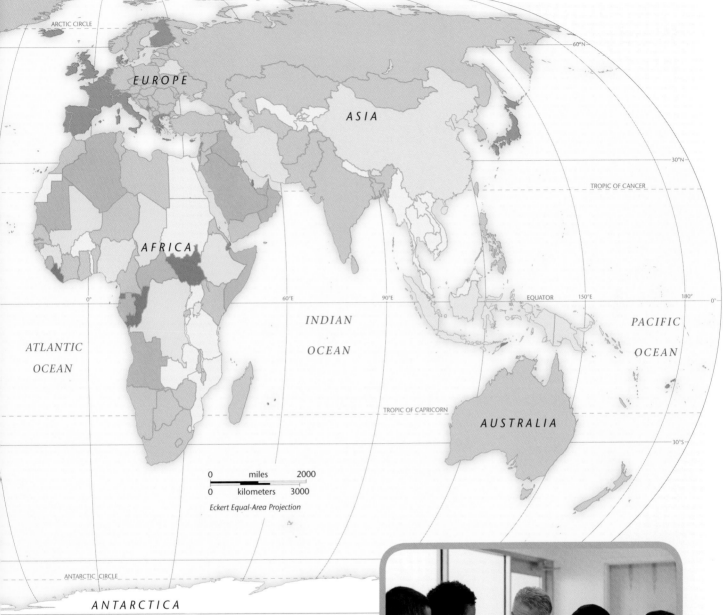

ARCTIC CIRCLE

60°N

EUROPE

ASIA

30°N

TROPIC OF CANCER

AFRICA

0°   60°E   90°E   EQUATOR   150°E   180°   0°

INDIAN

OCEAN   PACIFIC

ATLANTIC   OCEAN

OCEAN

TROPIC OF CAPRICORN

AUSTRALIA

30°S

```
0        miles        2000
0        kilometers      3000
```
Eckert Equal-Area Projection

ANTARCTIC CIRCLE

ANTARCTICA

MANUFACTURING. This mill in Slovakia processes raw materials—coal and iron ore—to make steel, which in turn is used by other industries to produce cars, machinery, and other manufactured goods.

COMMUNICATIONS AND TECHNOLOGY. Medical professionals use computers as they consult about patient treatment. The Internet and advanced technologies have introduced new ways of exchanging information and accessing the latest research in order to solve problems. E-mail connects people in places near and far, while e-commerce makes possible buying and selling from home or office.

World Food

In mid-2013, the world's population reached 7.2 billion people—all needing to be fed. However, the productive potential of Earth's surface varies greatly from place to place. Some areas are good for growing crops; some are better for grazing animals; others have little or no agricultural potential. Grains, such as rice, corn, and wheat, are main sources of food calories, while meat, poultry, and fish are sources of protein.

NORTH AMERICA

ATLANTIC OCEAN

PACIFIC OCEAN

SOUTH AMERICA

30°N

TROPIC OF CANCER

0° 150°W EQUATOR 120°W 90°W 30°

60°S

TOP FISHING COUNTRIES

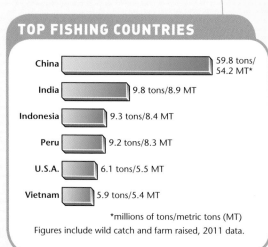

China	59.8 tons/54.2 MT*
India	9.8 tons/8.9 MT
Indonesia	9.3 tons/8.4 MT
Peru	9.2 tons/8.3 MT
U.S.A.	6.1 tons/5.5 MT
Vietnam	5.9 tons/5.4 MT

*millions of tons/metric tons (MT)
Figures include wild catch and farm raised, 2011 data.

FEEDING THE WORLD. Fish and other seafood are important in the diets of much of the world's population. But rising demand has raised concerns that this important food source is at risk due to overharvesting.

GEOGRAPHY CAREERS

NG EXPLORER: BARTON SEAVER

Barton Seaver is a chef who has dedicated his career to restoring the ocean's fragile ecosystems. Barton pursues solutions to overfishing through innovations in sustainability and education, and works to promote the concept of seafood sustainability. He also is involved in promoting healthier eating lifestyles, and works with various organizations in the fight against hunger. *nationalgeographic.com/explorers/bios/barton-seaver*

WHEAT, the world's leading export grain, is a ma ingredient in bread and pasta and is grown on ever inhabited continent. Each year, trade in this grain exceeds 143 million tons (130 million MT).

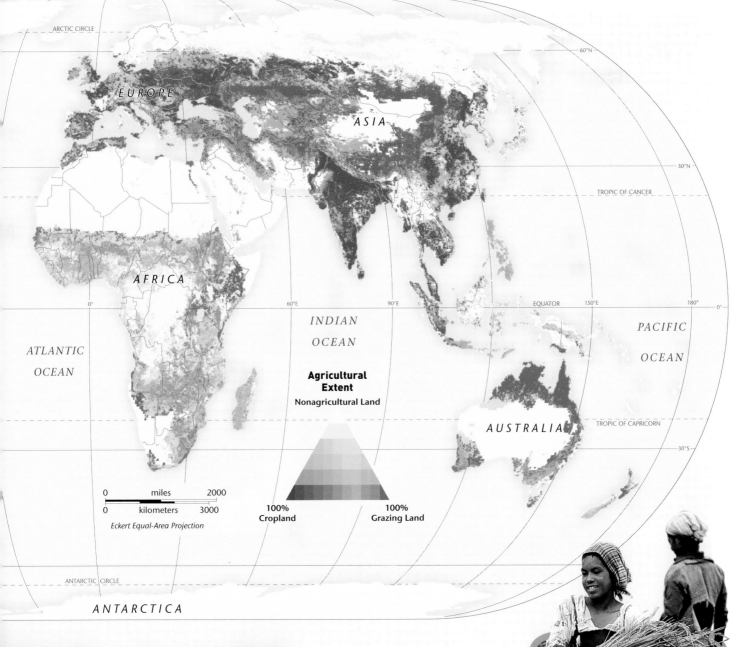

ARCTIC CIRCLE

60°N

EUROPE

ASIA

30°N

TROPIC OF CANCER

AFRICA

0°   60°E   90°E   EQUATOR   150°E   180°   0°

INDIAN
OCEAN

PACIFIC
OCEAN

ATLANTIC
OCEAN

**Agricultural
Extent**
Nonagricultural Land

AUSTRALIA

TROPIC OF CAPRICORN

30°S

| 0   miles   2000 |
| 0   kilometers   3000 |

Eckert Equal-Area Projection

100%
Cropland

100%
Grazing Land

ANTARCTIC CIRCLE

ANTARCTICA

◖ **CORN,** which originated in the Americas, is an important food grain for both people and livestock. Corn is also used to make ethanol, which is added to gasoline to make a cleaner fuel.

◖ **RICE** is an important staple food crop, especially in eastern and southern Asia. Although China produces about one-third of the world's rice, it is also a major importer of rice to feed its population of more than a billion people.

World Energy & Mineral Resources

Beginning in the 19th century, as the Industrial Revolution spread across Europe and around the world, the demand for energy and non-fuel mineral resources skyrocketed. Fossil fuels—first coal, then oil and natural gas—have provided the energy that keeps the wheels of industry turning. Non-fuel minerals such as iron ore (essential for steel production) and copper (for electrical wiring) have become increasingly important.

Energy and non-fuel minerals, like all nonrenewable resources, are in limited supply and are unevenly distributed. Exporting countries with major deposits can influence both supply and prices of these resources, thus playing an important role in the global economy.

🌀 **RENEWABLE ENERGY,** including energy from the sun, wind, running water, and heat from within Earth, is an important alternative to fossil fuels, supplies of which are rapidly being depleted. (Numbers on the map correspond to numbers on the photographs on page 49.)

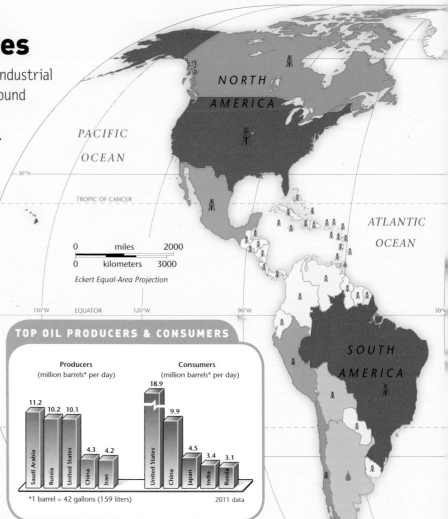

TOP OIL PRODUCERS & CONSUMERS

Producers
(million barrels* per day)

11.2	10.2	10.1	4.3	4.2
Saudi Arabia	Russia	United States	China	Iran

Consumers
(million barrels* per day)

18.9	9.9	4.5	3.4	3.1
United States	China	Japan	India	Russia

*1 barrel = 42 gallons (159 liters)   2011 data

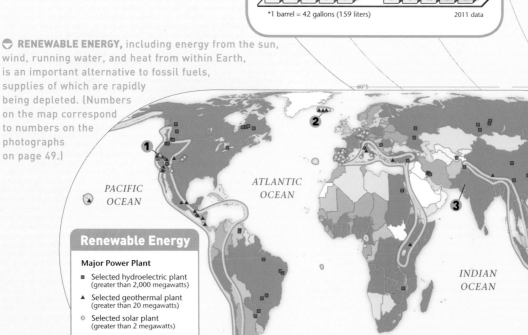

Renewable Energy

Major Power Plant

■ Selected hydroelectric plant (greater than 2,000 megawatts)

▲ Selected geothermal plant (greater than 20 megawatts)

✲ Selected solar plant (greater than 2 megawatts)

Potential Geothermal Resources

◉ High temperature geothermal regions

Annual Fuelwood Production (in thousands of cubic meters)

■ More than 10,000	■ 1,000–3,999	☐ less than 50
■ 4,000–10,000	■ 50–999	☐ no data

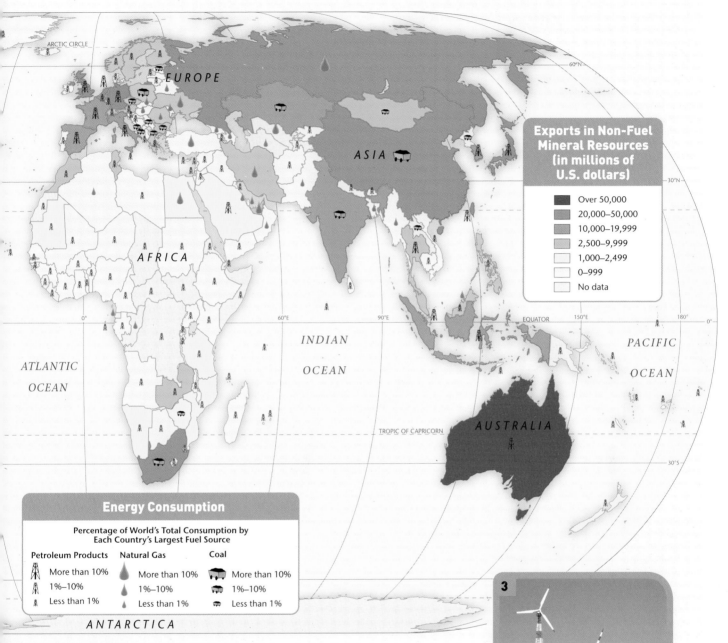

ARCTIC CIRCLE

EUROPE

ASIA

AFRICA

ATLANTIC
OCEAN

INDIAN
OCEAN

PACIFIC
OCEAN

AUSTRALIA

TROPIC OF CAPRICORN

ANTARCTICA

60°N

30°N

0°   60°E   90°E   EQUATOR   150°E   180°   0°

30°S

Exports in Non-Fuel Mineral Resources (in millions of U.S. dollars)

- Over 50,000
- 20,000–50,000
- 10,000–19,999
- 2,500–9,999
- 1,000–2,499
- 0–999
- No data

Energy Consumption

Percentage of World's Total Consumption by Each Country's Largest Fuel Source

Petroleum Products	Natural Gas	Coal
More than 10%	More than 10%	More than 10%
1%–10%	1%–10%	1%–10%
Less than 1%	Less than 1%	Less than 1%

1 **NUCLEAR REACTORS AND SOLAR PANELS** near Sacramento produce renewable energy for California's power-hungry population.

2

WINDMILLS rising above ancient temples near Jaisalmer, India, generate electricity by capturing the energy of winds blowing off the Indian Ocean.

A GEOTHERMAL POWER PLANT, fueled by heat from deep within Earth, produces energy to heat homes in Iceland. Runoff creates a warm pool for bathers.

3

Globalization

The close of the 20th century saw a technology revolution that changed the way people and countries relate to each other. This revolution in technology is part of a process known as globalization.

Globalization refers to the complex network of interconnections linking people, companies, and places together without regard for national boundaries. Although it began when some countries became increasingly active in international trade, the process of globalization has gained momentum in recent years, expanding to include political and social interactions, but not all countries are major players in the global arena.

Improvements in communications and transportation have enabled companies to employ workers in distant countries. Some workers make clothing; some perform accounting tasks; and others work in call centers answering inquiries about products or services. Technology also allows banking transactions to take place faster and over greater distances than ever before. Companies that conduct business in multiple countries around the world are called transnational companies.

An important part of today's global communications system is the Internet, a vast system of computer networks that allows people to access information around the world in seconds. Ideas and images now travel over the Internet, introducing change and making places more and more alike.

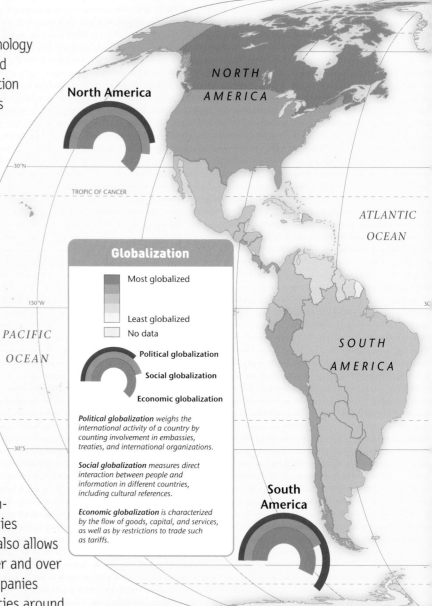

Globalization

Most globalized

Least globalized

No data

Political globalization

Social globalization

Economic globalization

Political globalization weighs the international activity of a country by counting involvement in embassies, treaties, and international organizations.

Social globalization measures direct interaction between people and information in different countries, including cultural references.

Economic globalization is characterized by the flow of goods, capital, and services, as well as by restrictions to trade such as tariffs.

◗ **MAQUILADORAS,** foreign-owned assembly plants located in Mexico, import parts and materials duty-free to produce finished goods for consumers in the U.S. and around the world. Maquiladoras, such as this one in Ciudad Juárez, employ a large workforce.

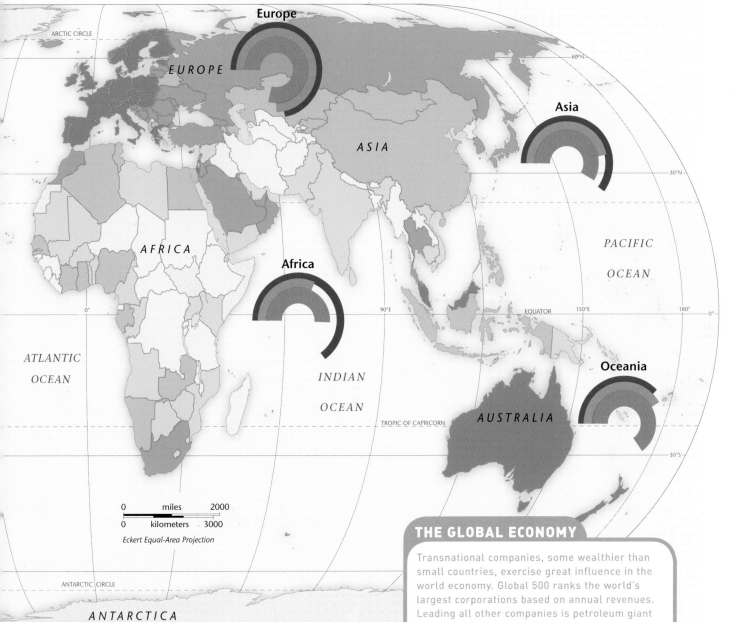

Europe

EUROPE

Asia

ASIA

AFRICA

Africa

PACIFIC OCEAN

INDIAN OCEAN

ATLANTIC OCEAN

Oceania

AUSTRALIA

ANTARCTICA

```
0    miles    2000
0  kilometers  3000
```
Eckert Equal-Area Projection

◖ **OLD MEETS NEW** as a Miao woman, wearing traditional garments, takes a photo of herself using a cell phone camera. The Miao, who live in southwestern China, are one of the country's largest ethnic minorities.

THE GLOBAL ECONOMY

Transnational companies, some wealthier than small countries, exercise great influence in the world economy. Global 500 ranks the world's largest corporations based on annual revenues. Leading all other companies is petroleum giant Royal Dutch Shell, based in the Netherlands.

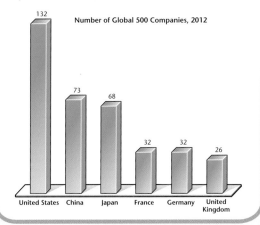

Number of Global 500 Companies, 2012

United States 132 · China 73 · Japan 68 · France 32 · Germany 32 · United Kingdom 26

Cultural Diffusion

In the past, when groups of people lived in relative isolation, cultures varied widely from place to place. Customs, styles, and preferences were handed down from one generation to the next.

Today, as a result of globalization, cultures all around the world are encountering and adopting new ideas. New customs, clothing and music trends, food habits, and lifestyles are being introduced into cultures everywhere at almost the same time. Some people are concerned that this trend in popular culture may result in a loss of cultural distinctiveness that makes places unique. For example, fast food chains once found only in the United States can now be seen in major cities around the world. And denim jeans, once a distinctively American clothing style, are worn by young people everywhere in place of more traditional clothing.

An important key to the spread, or diffusion, of popular culture is the increasing contact between people and places around the world. Cellular telephones, satellite television, and cybercafés have opened the world to styles and trends popular in Western countries. And tourists, traveling to places that were once considered remote and isolated, carry with them new ideas and fashions that become catalysts for bringing about cultural change.

International Tourism

International Tourist Arrivals

- More than 25,000,000
- 5,000,000–25,000,000
- 500,000–4,999,999
- 100,000–499,999
- Less than 100,000
- No data

THE INFLUENCE OF IMMIGRANT CULTURES on the American landscape is evident in ethnic communities such as Chinatown in the heart of New York City.

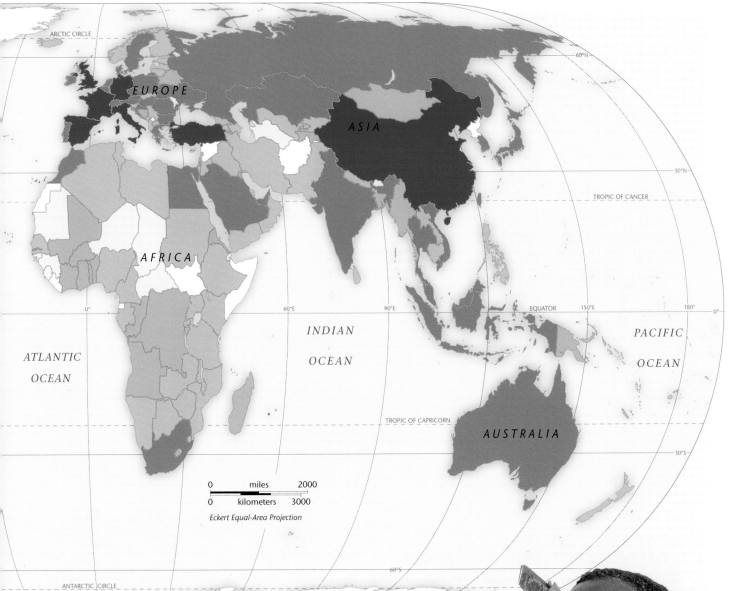

ARCTIC CIRCLE

EUROPE

ASIA

60°N

30°N

TROPIC OF CANCER

AFRICA

INDIAN

OCEAN

PACIFIC

OCEAN

ATLANTIC

OCEAN

0°   60°E   90°E   EQUATOR   150°E   180°   0°

TROPIC OF CAPRICORN

AUSTRALIA

30°S

| 0 | miles | 2000 |
| 0 | kilometers | 3000 |

Eckert Equal-Area Projection

60°S

ANTARCTIC CIRCLE

ANTARCTICA

◖ **A COUPLE IN TRADITIONAL ROBES** strolls through a modern shopping mall in Doha, Qatar. Stores and movie theaters bring Western fashions, technologies, and ideas into contact with long-established Arab culture and values.

◖ **TAKING A BREAK** from a tribal ceremony, a Maasai warrior in Kenya enjoys a soft drink that was once uniquely American.

North America:
A View From Space

Viewed from high above, North America stretches from the frozen expanses of the Arctic Ocean and Greenland to the lush green of Panama's tropical forests. Hudson Bay and the Great Lakes, fingerprints of long-departed glaciers, dominate the continent's east, while the brown landscapes of the west and southwest tell of dry lands where water is scarce.

Rays of the setting sun light up the Golden Gate Bridge in San Francisco, California

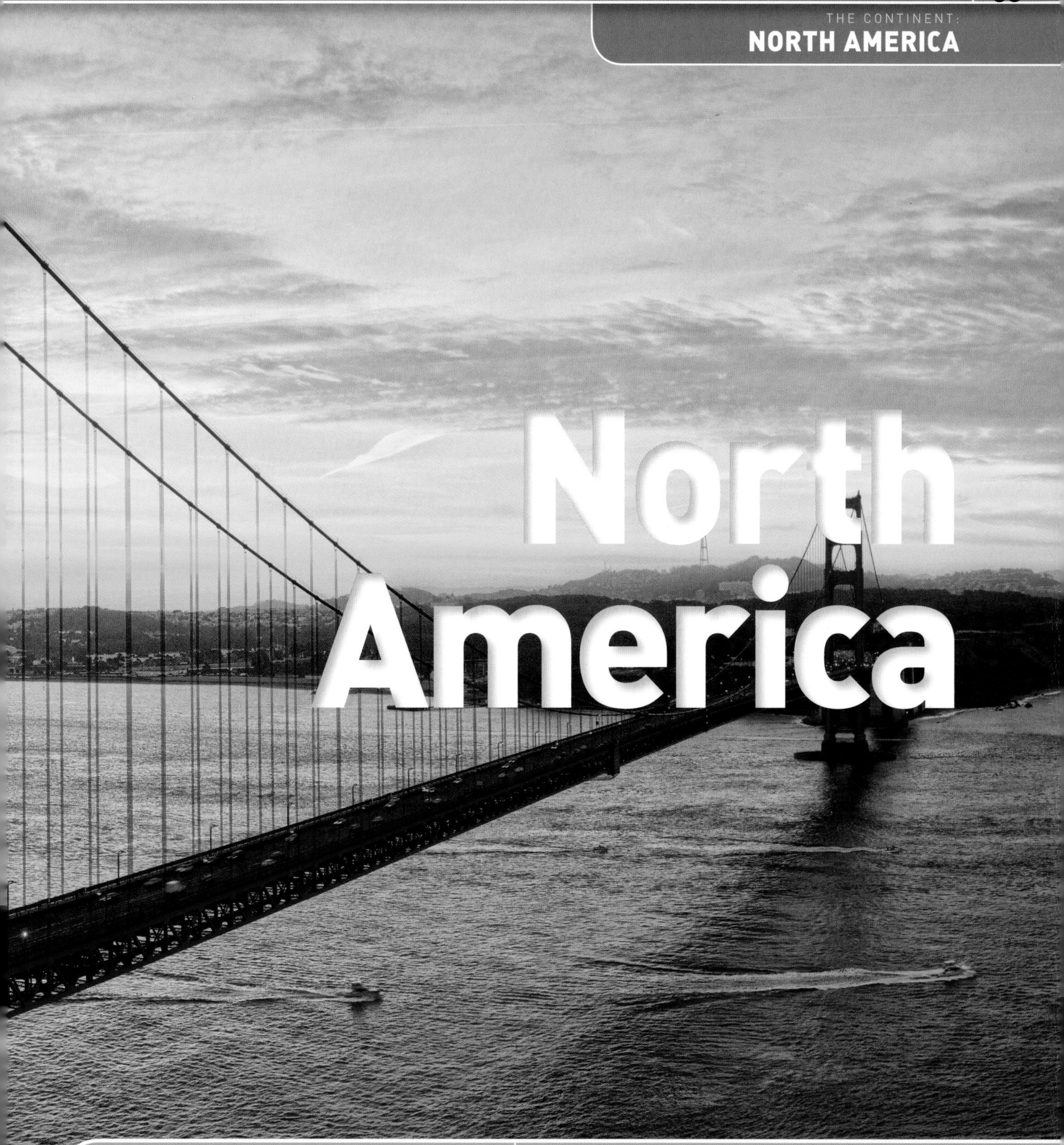

North America

PHYSICAL			POLITICAL		
Land area **9,449,000 sq mi** **(24,474,000 sq km)**	**Lowest point** **Death Valley, California** **-282 ft (-86 m)**	**Largest lake** **Lake Superior,** **U.S.-Canada** **31,700 sq mi** **(82,100 sq km)**	**Population** **556,558,000** **Number of** **independent** **countries** **23**	**Largest country** **Canada** **3,855,101 sq mi (9,984,670 sq km)** **Smallest country** **St. Kitts and Nevis** **104 sq mi (269 sq km)**	**Most populous country** **United States** **Pop. 316,158,000** **Least populous country** **St. Kitts and Nevis** **Pop. 55,000**
Highest point **Mount McKinley** **(Denali), Alaska** **20,320 ft (6,194 m)**	**Longest river** **Mississippi-Missouri,** **United States** **3,710 mi (5,970 km)**				

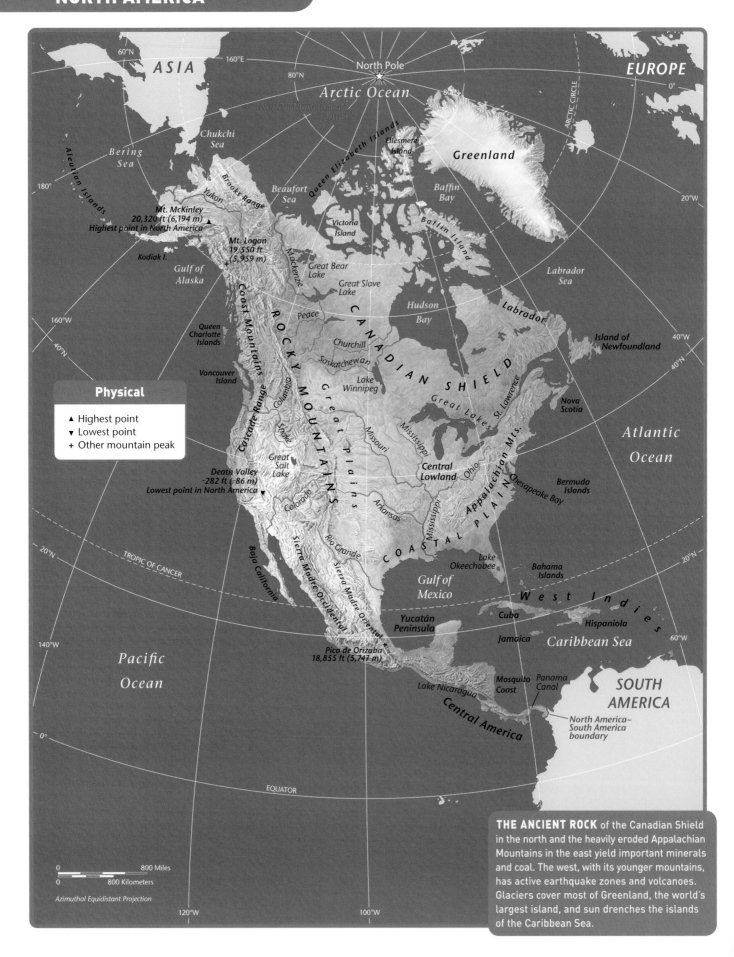

ASIA

60°N 160°E

North Pole

80°N

Arctic Ocean

North Magnetic Pole
(2014)

EUROPE

0°

ARCTIC CIRCLE

80°N

20°W

Chukchi
Sea

Bering
Sea

180°

Aleutian Islands

Mt. McKinley
20,320 ft (6,194 m)
Highest point in North America ▲

Brooks Range

Yukon

Mt. Logan
19,550 ft
+ (5,959 m)

Kodiak I.

Gulf of
Alaska

160°W

40°N

Queen
Charlotte
Islands

Vancouver
Island

Queen Elizabeth Islands

Ellesmere
Island

Greenland

Baffin
Bay

Baffin Island

Victoria
Island

Mackenzie

Great Bear
Lake

Great Slave
Lake

Peace

Hudson
Bay

CANADIAN SHIELD

Labrador
Sea

Labrador

Island of
Newfoundland

40°W

40°N

Coast Mountains

Churchill

Saskatchewan

Lake
Winnipeg

Nova
Scotia

Atlantic
Ocean

Physical

- ▲ Highest point
- ▼ Lowest point
- + Other mountain peak

Cascade Range

Columbia

Snake

ROCKY MOUNTAINS

Great Plains

Missouri

Great Lakes

St. Lawrence

Mississippi

Central
Lowland

Ohio

Appalachian Mts.

Chesapeake Bay

Bermuda
Islands

Death Valley
-282 ft (-86 m)
Lowest point in North America ▼

Great
Salt
Lake

Colorado

Arkansas

Mississippi

COASTAL PLAIN

20°N

TROPIC OF CANCER

140°W

Baja California

Sierra Madre Occidental

Rio Grande

Sierra Madre Oriental

Lake
Okeechobee

Gulf of
Mexico

Bahama
Islands

West Indies

20°N

60°W

Pacific
Ocean

Yucatán
Peninsula

Cuba

Jamaica

Hispaniola

Caribbean Sea

Pico de Orizaba
18,855 ft (5,747 m) +

0°

Lake Nicaragua

Mosquito
Coast

Panama
Canal

SOUTH
AMERICA

Central America

North America–
South America
boundary

EQUATOR

0 800 Miles
0 800 Kilometers

Azimuthal Equidistant Projection

120°W

100°W

THE ANCIENT ROCK of the Canadian Shield
in the north and the heavily eroded Appalachian
Mountains in the east yield important minerals
and coal. The west, with its younger mountains,
has active earthquake zones and volcanoes.
Glaciers cover most of Greenland, the world's
largest island, and sun drenches the islands
of the Caribbean Sea.

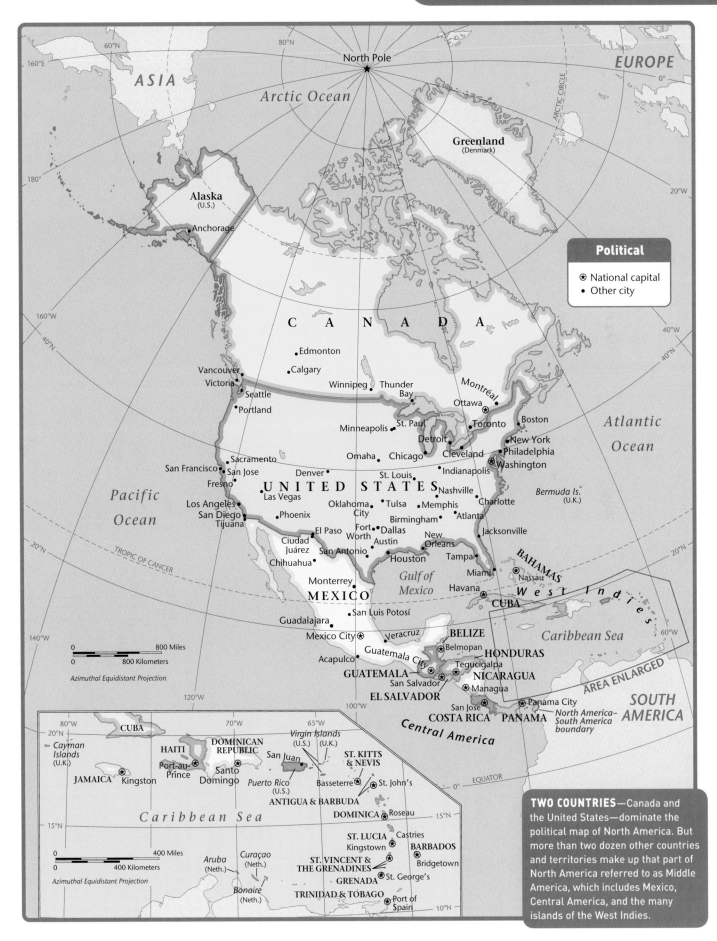

Political
⊛ National capital
• Other city

ASIA

160°E
60°N
80°N
North Pole
EUROPE
0°

Arctic Ocean

ARCTIC CIRCLE

180°
20°W

Alaska
(U.S.)
Greenland
(Denmark)

160°W
40°N
40°N
40°W

• Anchorage

C A N A D A

• Edmonton
• Calgary

Vancouver
Victoria
• Seattle
Winnipeg • Thunder Bay
Montréal
Ottawa ⊛
Boston

• Portland
Minneapolis • St. Paul
Toronto
New York

Atlantic
Ocean

Detroit
Philadelphia

Sacramento
Omaha • Chicago
Cleveland
Washington ⊛

San Francisco • San Jose
Denver
St. Louis
Indianapolis

Fresno
U N I T E D   S T A T E S
Nashville
Charlotte

Bermuda Is.
(U.K.)

Pacific
Ocean

Las Vegas
Oklahoma City • Tulsa
Memphis

Los Angeles
Phoenix
Birmingham
Atlanta

San Diego
Tijuana
El Paso
Fort Worth • Dallas
New Orleans
Jacksonville

20°N
TROPIC OF CANCER
Ciudad Juárez
San Antonio • Austin
Houston
Tampa

Chihuahua
Gulf of
Mexico
Miami
BAHAMAS
Nassau
West Indies
20°N

Monterrey
Havana ⊛
CUBA
Caribbean Sea
60°W

140°W
MEXICO
San Luis Potosí

Guadalajara
Mexico City ⊛ Veracruz
BELIZE
AREA ENLARGED

Acapulco
Guatemala City ⊛ Belmopan ⊛
HONDURAS
SOUTH
AMERICA

120°W
100°W
GUATEMALA
Tegucigalpa ⊛
NICARAGUA

San Salvador ⊛
Managua ⊛

EL SALVADOR
San José ⊛ ⊛ Panama City

COSTA RICA   PANAMA
North America–
South America
boundary

Central America
EQUATOR

0
800 Miles
0
800 Kilometers
Azimuthal Equidistant Projection

Inset map:

80°W
20°N
CUBA

70°W
65°W
Virgin Islands
(U.S.)   (U.K.)

Cayman
Islands
(U.K.)
HAITI
DOMINICAN
REPUBLIC
San Juan
ST. KITTS
& NEVIS

JAMAICA   Kingston
Port-au- ⊛
Prince
Santo
Domingo
Puerto Rico
(U.S.)
Basseterre ⊛
⊛ St. John's

15°N
ANTIGUA & BARBUDA

DOMINICA ⊛ Roseau
15°N

Caribbean Sea
ST. LUCIA ⊛ Castries
Kingstown ⊛

0
400 Miles
Aruba
(Neth.)
Curaçao
(Neth.)
ST. VINCENT &
THE GRENADINES
BARBADOS
⊛ Bridgetown

0
400 Kilometers
Azimuthal Equidistant Projection
Bonaire
(Neth.)
GRENADA ⊛ St. George's
TRINIDAD & TOBAGO
Port of
Spain
10°N

TWO COUNTRIES—Canada and the United States—dominate the political map of North America. But more than two dozen other countries and territories make up that part of North America referred to as Middle America, which includes Mexico, Central America, and the many islands of the West Indies.

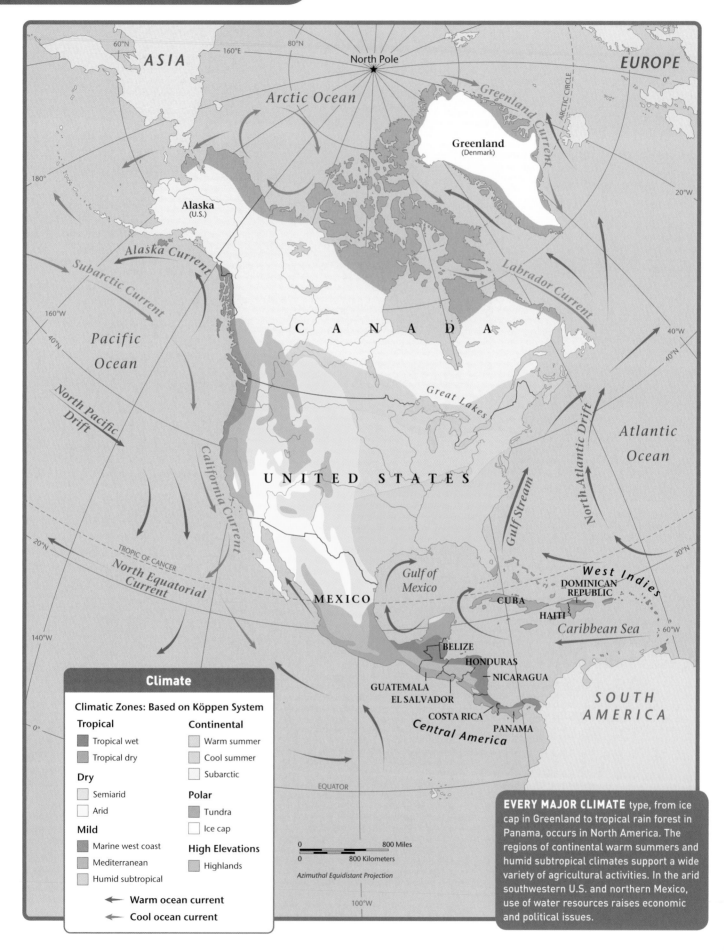

Climate

Climatic Zones: Based on Köppen System

Tropical
- Tropical wet
- Tropical dry

Dry
- Semiarid
- Arid

Mild
- Marine west coast
- Mediterranean
- Humid subtropical

Continental
- Warm summer
- Cool summer
- Subarctic

Polar
- Tundra
- Ice cap

High Elevations
- Highlands

⟵ Warm ocean current
⟵ Cool ocean current

0   800 Miles
0   800 Kilometers

Azimuthal Equidistant Projection

EVERY MAJOR CLIMATE type, from ice cap in Greenland to tropical rain forest in Panama, occurs in North America. The regions of continental warm summers and humid subtropical climates support a wide variety of agricultural activities. In the arid southwestern U.S. and northern Mexico, use of water resources raises economic and political issues.

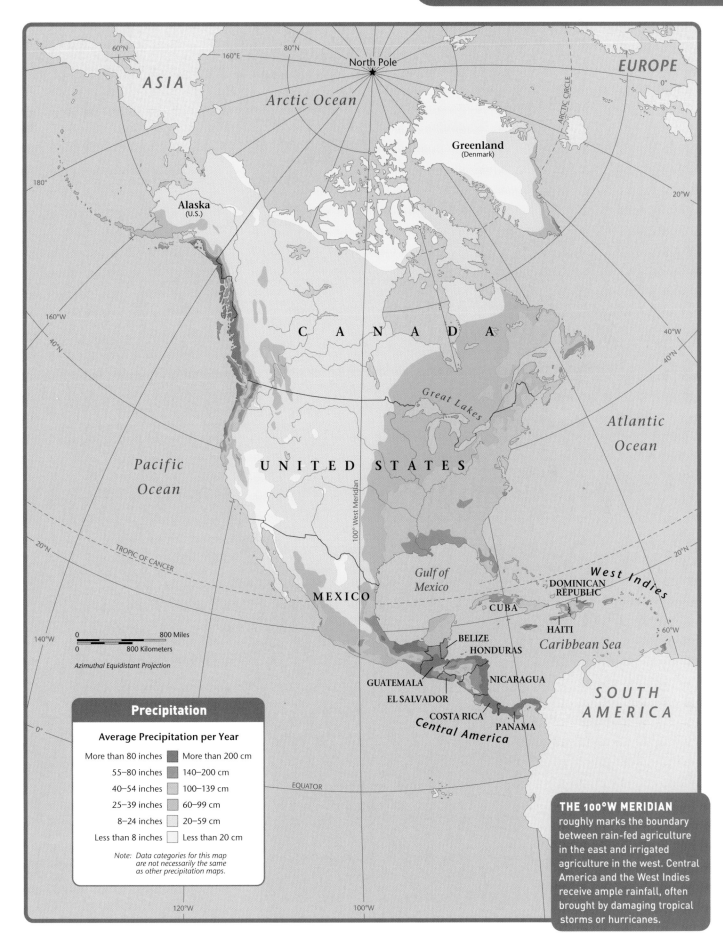

ASIA

Arctic Ocean

North Pole

EUROPE

Greenland
(Denmark)

Alaska
(U.S.)

C A N A D A

Great Lakes

Atlantic
Ocean

Pacific
Ocean

U N I T E D   S T A T E S

100° West Meridian

TROPIC OF CANCER

Gulf of
Mexico

West Indies

DOMINICAN
REPUBLIC

M E X I C O

CUBA

HAITI

Caribbean Sea

BELIZE
HONDURAS

800 Miles

800 Kilometers

Azimuthal Equidistant Projection

GUATEMALA

NICARAGUA

SOUTH
AMERICA

EL SALVADOR

COSTA RICA

PANAMA

Central America

EQUATOR

Precipitation

Average Precipitation per Year

More than 80 inches	More than 200 cm
55–80 inches	140–200 cm
40–54 inches	100–139 cm
25–39 inches	60–99 cm
8–24 inches	20–59 cm
Less than 8 inches	Less than 20 cm

*Note: Data categories for this map
are not necessarily the same
as other precipitation maps.*

THE 100°W MERIDIAN
roughly marks the boundary
between rain-fed agriculture
in the east and irrigated
agriculture in the west. Central
America and the West Indies
receive ample rainfall, often
brought by damaging tropical
storms or hurricanes.

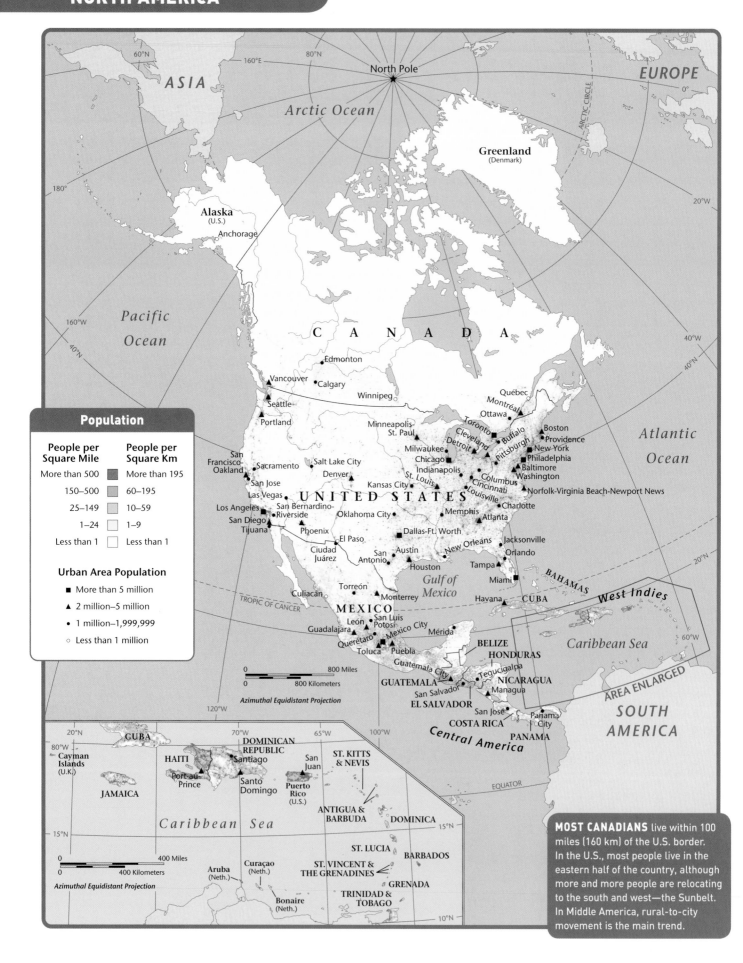

Population

People per Square Mile / **People per Square Km**

People per Square Mile	People per Square Km
More than 500	More than 195
150–500	60–195
25–149	10–59
1–24	1–9
Less than 1	Less than 1

Urban Area Population

- ■ More than 5 million
- ▲ 2 million–5 million
- ● 1 million–1,999,999
- ○ Less than 1 million

0   800 Miles
0   800 Kilometers
Azimuthal Equidistant Projection

0   400 Miles
0   400 Kilometers
Azimuthal Equidistant Projection

MOST CANADIANS live within 100 miles (160 km) of the U.S. border. In the U.S., most people live in the eastern half of the country, although more and more people are relocating to the south and west—the Sunbelt. In Middle America, rural-to-city movement is the main trend.

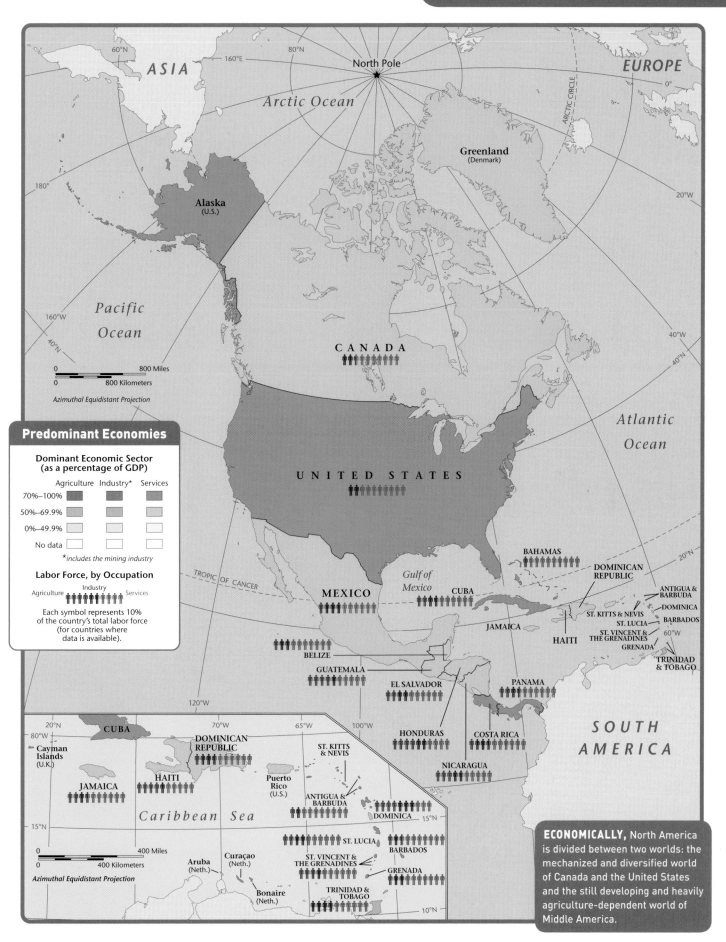

Predominant Economies

Dominant Economic Sector
(as a percentage of GDP)

	Agriculture	Industry*	Services
70%–100%			
50%–69.9%			
0%–49.9%			
No data			

*includes the mining industry

Labor Force, by Occupation

Agriculture   Industry   Services

Each symbol represents 10%
of the country's total labor force
(for countries where
data is available).

ASIA

EUROPE

Arctic Ocean

North Pole

Greenland
(Denmark)

Alaska
(U.S.)

Pacific
Ocean

CANADA

Atlantic
Ocean

UNITED STATES

BAHAMAS

DOMINICAN
REPUBLIC

ANTIGUA &
BARBUDA

DOMINICA

Gulf of
Mexico

CUBA

ST. KITTS & NEVIS

BARBADOS

MEXICO

JAMAICA

ST. LUCIA
ST. VINCENT &
THE GRENADINES

GRENADA

HAITI

TRINIDAD
& TOBAGO

BELIZE

GUATEMALA

EL SALVADOR

PANAMA

SOUTH
AMERICA

HONDURAS

COSTA RICA

NICARAGUA

TROPIC OF CANCER

Inset map:

CUBA

DOMINICAN
REPUBLIC

Cayman
Islands
(U.K.)

ST. KITTS
& NEVIS

HAITI

Puerto
Rico
(U.S.)

JAMAICA

ANTIGUA &
BARBUDA

DOMINICA

Caribbean Sea

ST. LUCIA

BARBADOS

Aruba
(Neth.)

Curaçao
(Neth.)

ST. VINCENT &
THE GRENADINES

GRENADA

Bonaire
(Neth.)

TRINIDAD &
TOBAGO

Azimuthal Equidistant Projection

0   800 Miles
0   800 Kilometers

Azimuthal Equidistant Projection

0   400 Miles
0   400 Kilometers

ECONOMICALLY, North America
is divided between two worlds: the
mechanized and diversified world
of Canada and the United States
and the still developing and heavily
agriculture-dependent world of
Middle America.

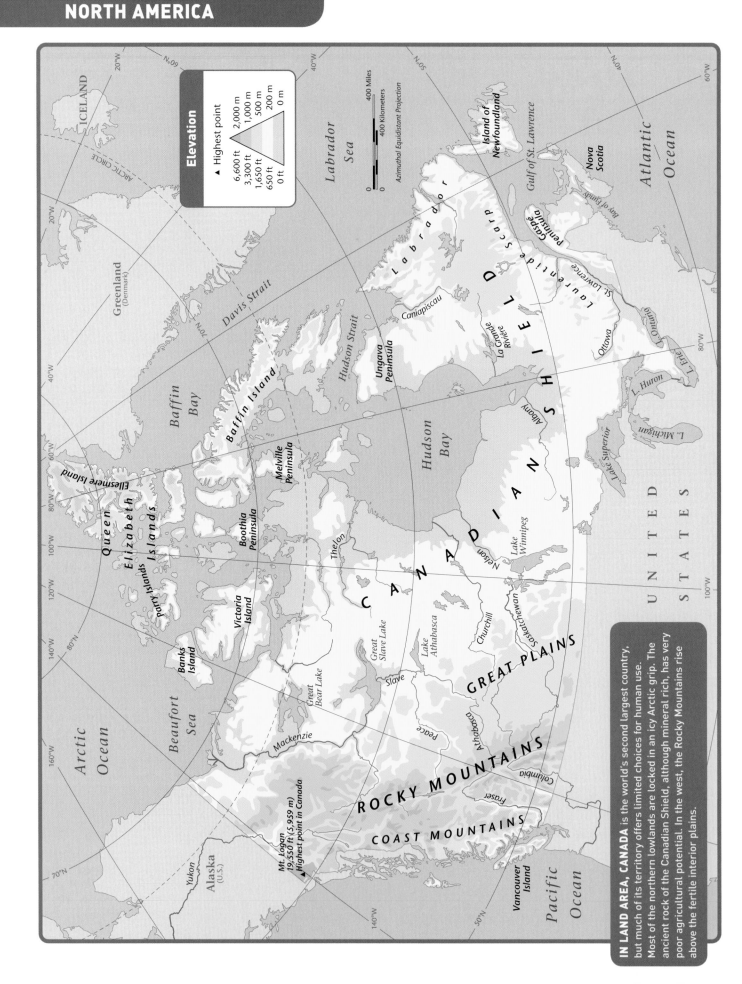

Elevation

▲ Highest point

6,600 ft — 2,000 m
3,300 ft — 1,000 m
1,650 ft — 500 m
650 ft — 200 m
0 ft — 0 m

400 Miles
400 Kilometers
Azimuthal Equidistant Projection

ICELAND

Greenland
(Denmark)

ARCTIC CIRCLE

Labrador
Sea

Island of
Newfoundland

Gulf of St. Lawrence

Nova
Scotia

Atlantic
Ocean

Bay of Fundy

Gaspé
Peninsula

St. Lawrence

Laurentide Escarpment

Davis Strait

Baffin
Bay

Baffin Island

Hudson Strait

Ungava
Peninsula

Caniapiscau

La Grande
Rivière

Labrador

Ottawa

L. Ontario

L. Erie

Ellesmere Island

Queen
Elizabeth
Islands

Parry Islands

Victoria
Island

Melville
Peninsula

Boothia
Peninsula

Thelon

Hudson
Bay

Albany

CANADIAN SHIELD

Lake
Winnipeg

Nelson

Lake Superior

Lake Michigan

L. Huron

L. Michigan

Banks
Island

Beaufort
Sea

Great
Bear Lake

Great
Slave Lake

Slave

Lake
Athabasca

Churchill

Saskatchewan

GREAT PLAINS

UNITED

STATES

Arctic
Ocean

Mackenzie

Peace

Athabasca

ROCKY MOUNTAINS

Columbia

COAST MOUNTAINS

Fraser

Yukon

Alaska
(U.S.)

Mt. Logan
19,550 ft (5,959 m)
▲ Highest point in Canada

Vancouver
Island

Pacific
Ocean

IN LAND AREA, CANADA is the world's second largest country, but much of its territory offers limited choices for human use. Most of the northern lowlands are locked in an icy Arctic grip. The ancient rock of the Canadian Shield, although mineral rich, has very poor agricultural potential. In the west, the Rocky Mountains rise above the fertile interior plains.

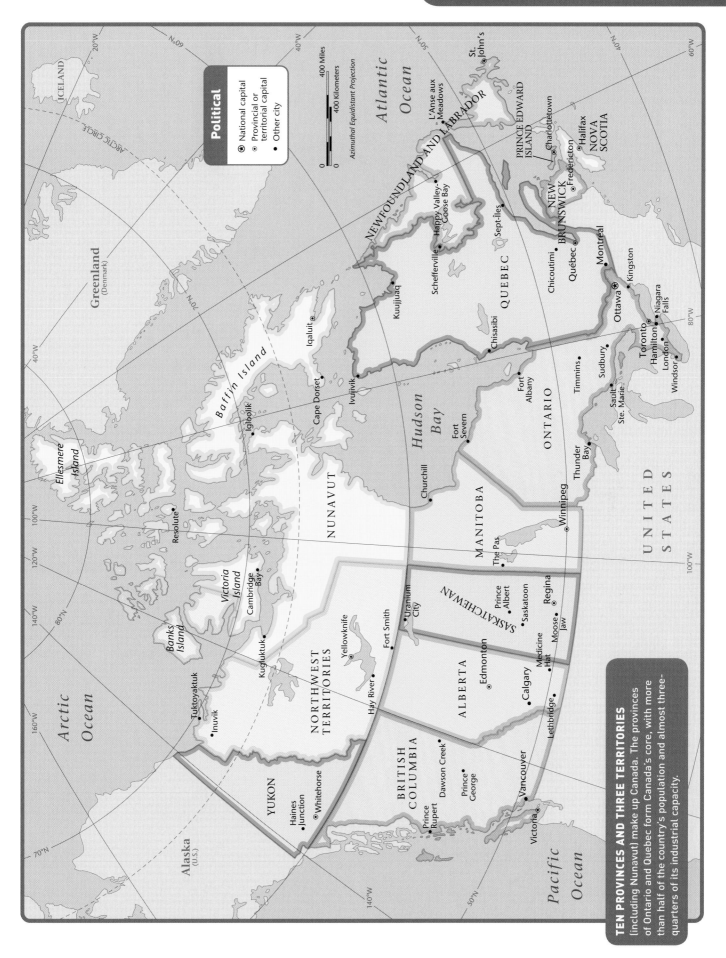

Political

⊕ National capital
◉ Provincial or territorial capital
• Other city

400 Miles
400 Kilometers
Azimuthal Equidistant Projection

ICELAND

Greenland
(Denmark)

ARCTIC CIRCLE

Ellesmere Island

Arctic Ocean

Alaska
(U.S.)

Banks Island

Victoria Island

Baffin Island

Resolute

Cambridge Bay

Kugluktuk

Tuktoyaktuk

Inuvik

NORTHWEST TERRITORIES

Yellowknife

Hay River

Fort Smith

Uranium City

Igloolik

Cape Dorset

Iqaluit

Ivujivik

NUNAVUT

Hudson Bay

Churchill

Fort Severn

Kuujjuaq

NEWFOUNDLAND AND LABRADOR

Atlantic Ocean

St. John's

L'Anse aux Meadows

Happy Valley-Goose Bay

Schefferville

Sept-Îles

Chisasibi

QUEBEC

Chicoutimi

Québec

Montréal

PRINCE EDWARD ISLAND

Charlottetown

Fredericton

NEW BRUNSWICK

Halifax

NOVA SCOTIA

Kingston

Ottawa

Niagara Falls

Toronto

Hamilton

London

Windsor

Sudbury

Sault Ste. Marie

Timmins

Fort Albany

ONTARIO

Thunder Bay

The Pas

MANITOBA

Winnipeg

UNITED STATES

SASKATCHEWAN

Prince Albert

Saskatoon

Regina

Moose Jaw

Medicine Hat

Edmonton

ALBERTA

Calgary

Lethbridge

BRITISH COLUMBIA

Dawson Creek

Prince George

Prince Rupert

Vancouver

Victoria

Pacific Ocean

YUKON

Whitehorse

Haines Junction

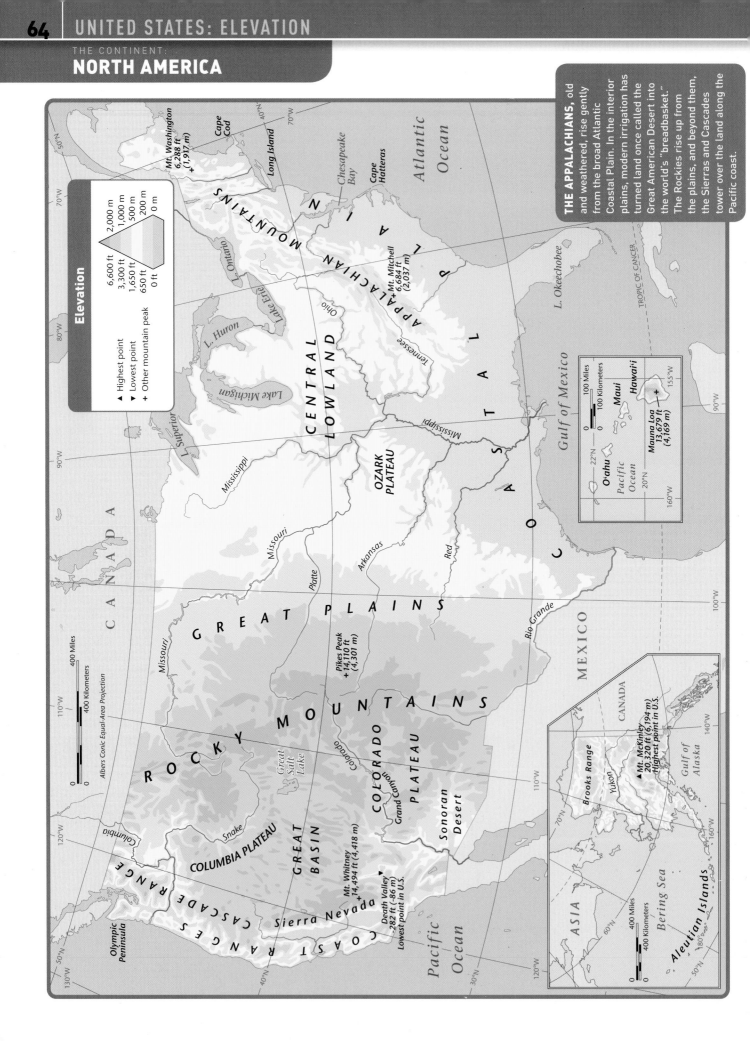

THE APPALACHIANS, old and weathered, rise gently from the broad Atlantic Coastal Plain. In the interior plains, modern irrigation has turned land once called the Great American Desert into the world's "breadbasket." The Rockies rise up from the plains, and beyond them, the Sierras and Cascades tower over the land along the Pacific coast.

Elevation

2,000 m	6,600 ft
1,000 m	3,300 ft
500 m	1,650 ft
200 m	650 ft
0 m	0 ft

▲ Highest point
▼ Lowest point
+ Other mountain peak

Mt. Washington
6,288 ft
(1,917 m)

Cape Cod

Long Island

Chesapeake Bay

Cape Hatteras

Atlantic Ocean

APPALACHIAN MOUNTAINS

Mt. Mitchell
6,684 ft
(2,037 m)

L. Ontario

Lake Erie

L. Huron

Lake Michigan

L. Superior

CENTRAL LOWLAND

Ohio

Tennessee

Mississippi

CANADA

Mississippi

Missouri

OZARK PLATEAU

Arkansas

Red

L. Okeechobee

Gulf of Mexico

COASTAL PLAIN

TROPIC OF CANCER

Platte

GREAT PLAINS

Rio Grande

MEXICO

400 Miles
400 Kilometers
Albers Conic Equal-Area Projection

Missouri

Pikes Peak
+14,110 ft
(4,301 m)

ROCKY MOUNTAINS

COLORADO PLATEAU

Sonoran Desert

Great Salt Lake

Colorado

Grand Canyon

Snake

Columbia

COLUMBIA PLATEAU

GREAT BASIN

Mt. Whitney
+14,494 ft (4,418 m)

Death Valley
-282 ft (-86 m)
Lowest point in U.S.

Sierra Nevada

COAST RANGES

CASCADE RANGE

Olympic Peninsula

Pacific Ocean

Hawai'i inset:
100 Miles
100 Kilometers
Maui
O'ahu
Hawai'i
Mauna Loa
13,679 ft
(4,169 m)
Pacific Ocean
22°N
20°N
160°W
155°W

Alaska inset:
CANADA
Brooks Range
Yukon
Mt. McKinley
20,320 ft (6,194 m)
Highest point in U.S.
Gulf of Alaska
ASIA
Bering Sea
Aleutian Islands
400 Miles
400 Kilometers
70°N
60°N
50°N
180°
160°W
140°W

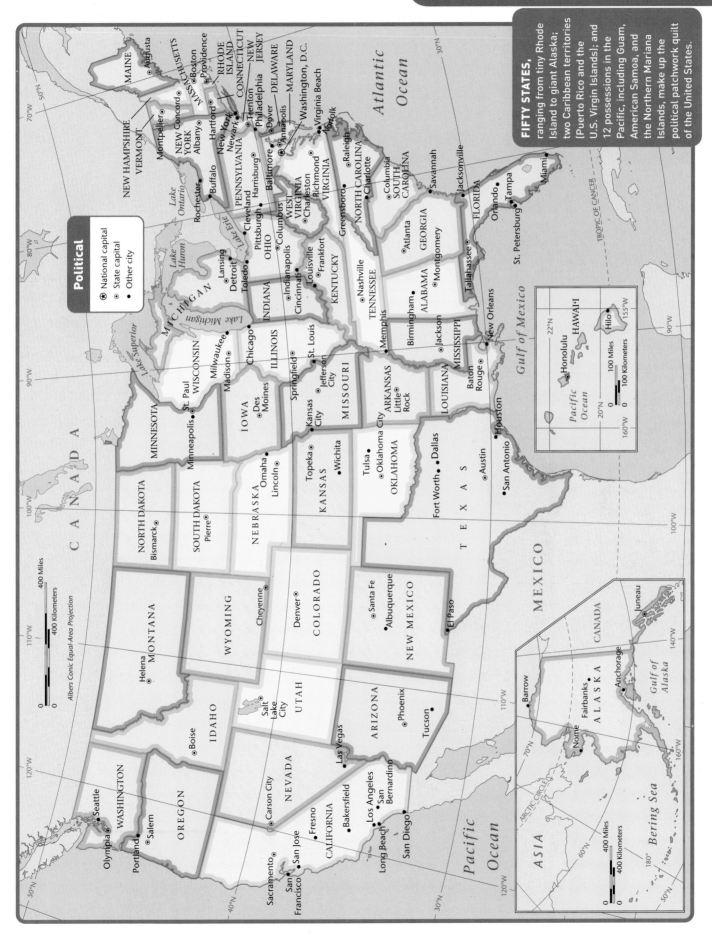

FIFTY STATES, ranging from tiny Rhode Island to giant Alaska; two Caribbean territories (Puerto Rico and the U.S. Virgin Islands); and 12 possessions in the Pacific, including Guam, American Samoa, and the Northern Mariana Islands, make up the political patchwork quilt of the United States.

Political
⊛ National capital
⊙ State capital
• Other city

Albers Conic Equal-Area Projection

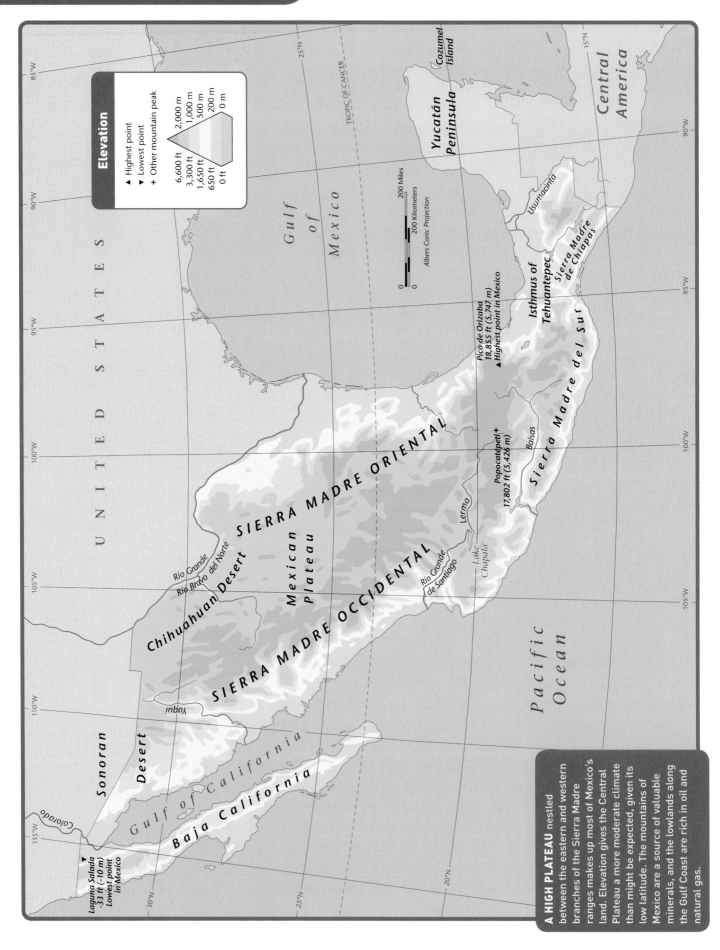

Elevation

▲ Highest point
▼ Lowest point
+ Other mountain peak

2,000 m
1,000 m
500 m
200 m
0 m

6,600 ft
3,300 ft
1,650 ft
650 ft
0 ft

UNITED STATES

Gulf of Mexico

TROPIC OF CANCER

Yucatán Peninsula

Cozumel Island

Central America

200 Miles
200 Kilometers
Albers Conic Projection

Usumacinta

Sierra Madre de Chiapas

Isthmus of Tehuantepec

Pico de Orizaba
18,855 ft (5,747 m)
▲ Highest point in Mexico

SIERRA MADRE ORIENTAL

Rio Grande
Río Bravo del Norte

Chihuahuan Desert

Mexican Plateau

SIERRA MADRE OCCIDENTAL

Rio Grande de Santiago

Lerma

Lake Chapala

Balsas

Popocatépetl +
17,802 ft (5,426 m)

Sierra Madre del Sur

Pacific Ocean

Yaqui

Sonoran Desert

Gulf of California

Baja California

Colorado

Laguna Salada
-33 ft (-10 m)
Lowest point
in Mexico

A HIGH PLATEAU nestled between the eastern and western branches of the Sierra Madre ranges makes up most of Mexico's land. Elevation gives the Central Plateau a more moderate climate than might be expected, given its low latitude. The mountains of Mexico are a source of valuable minerals, and the lowlands along the Gulf Coast are rich in oil and natural gas.

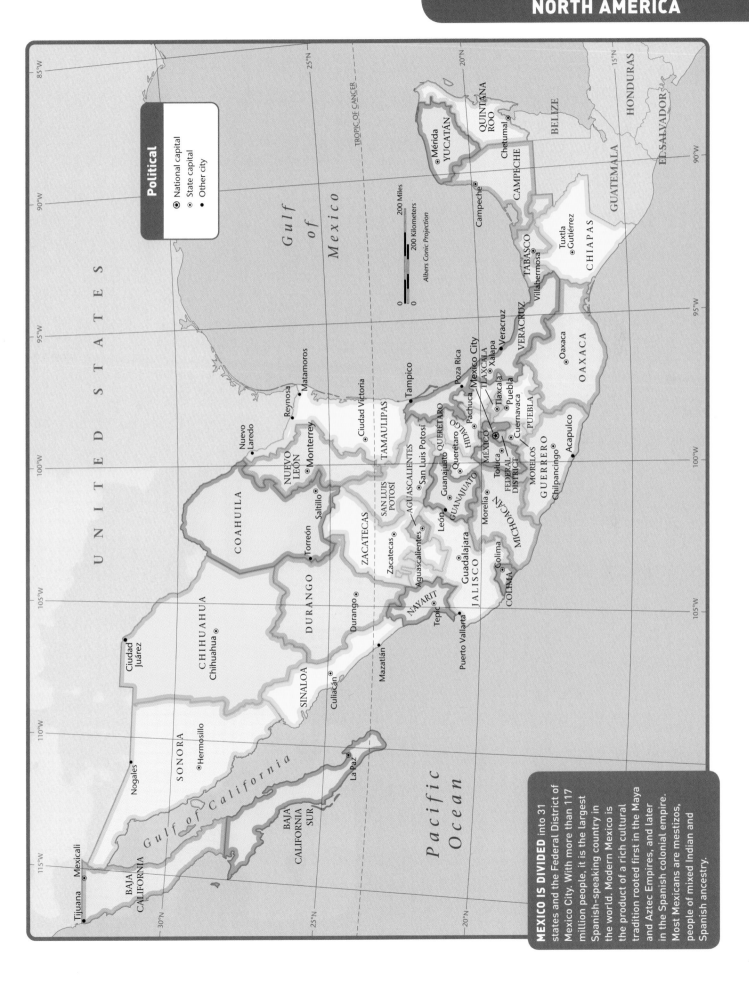

Political

⊛ National capital
⊙ State capital
• Other city

UNITED STATES

Gulf
of
Mexico

TROPIC OF CANCER

200 Miles
200 Kilometers
Albers Conic Projection

BAJA
CALIFORNIA

Tijuana
Mexicali

Nogales

Gulf of California

BAJA
CALIFORNIA
SUR

La Paz

SONORA

•Hermosillo

Ciudad
Juárez

CHIHUAHUA

Chihuahua⊙

SINALOA

Culiacán•

Mazatlán•

Durango•

DURANGO

COAHUILA

Torreón•

Saltillo⊙

NUEVO
LEÓN

Monterrey⊙

Nuevo
Laredo•

Reynosa•
Matamoros•

TAMAULIPAS

Ciudad Victoria•

Tampico•

Pacific
Ocean

Tepic⊙

NAYARIT

Puerto Vallarta•

JALISCO

Guadalajara⊙

Colima•
COLIMA

ZACATECAS

Zacatecas⊙

Aguascalientes⊙
AGUASCALIENTES

SAN LUIS
POTOSÍ

San Luis Potosí⊙

Guanajuato⊙
GUANAJUATO

León•

Morelia⊙

MICHOACÁN

QUERÉTARO

Querétaro⊙

HIDALGO

MÉXICO

Toluca⊙
FEDERAL
DISTRICT

Pachuca⊙

MORELOS

Chilpancingo⊙

GUERRERO

Acapulco•

Mexico City⊛
TLAXCALA
Tlaxcala⊙
Cuernavaca⊙
PUEBLA
Puebla⊙

Poza Rica•

VERACRUZ

Xalapa⊙
Veracruz•

OAXACA

Oaxaca•

Villahermosa⊙
TABASCO

CHIAPAS

Tuxtla
Gutiérrez⊙

Campeche⊙

CAMPECHE

Mérida⊙
YUCATÁN

QUINTANA
ROO

Chetumal⊙

BELIZE

GUATEMALA

HONDURAS

EL SALVADOR

MEXICO IS DIVIDED into 31 states and the Federal District of Mexico City. With more than 117 million people, it is the largest Spanish-speaking country in the world. Modern Mexico is the product of a rich cultural tradition rooted first in the Maya and Aztec Empires, and later in the Spanish colonial empire. Most Mexicans are mestizos, people of mixed Indian and Spanish ancestry.

Natural Hazards

The forces of nature inspire awe. They can also bring damage and destruction, especially when people locate homes and businesses in places that are at risk of experiencing violent storms, earthquakes, volcanoes, floods, wildfires, or other natural hazards. Tornadoes—violent, swirling storms with winds that can exceed 200 miles (300 km) per hour— strike the U.S. more than 800 times each year. Hurricanes, massive low-pressure storms that form over warm ocean waters, bring destructive winds and rain primarily to the Gulf of Mexico and the southeastern mainland. Melting spring snows and heavy rains trigger flooding; periods of drought make other regions vulnerable to wildfires. These and other hazards of nature are not limited to this continent. Natural hazards pose serious threats to lives and property wherever people live.

WILDFIRES. Putting lives and property at great risk, wildfires destroy millions of acres (ha) of forest each year. At the same time, fires help renew ecosystems by removing debris and encouraging seedling growth.

VOLCANOES. From deep inside Earth, molten rock, called magma, rises and breaks through the surface, sometimes quietly, but more often violently, shooting billowing ash clouds, as shown here at Mount St. Helens, in Washington State.

FLOODS. Towns located along New Jersey's coastline experienced widespread flooding as a result of the storm surge and heavy rains associated with Hurricane Sandy in October 2012.

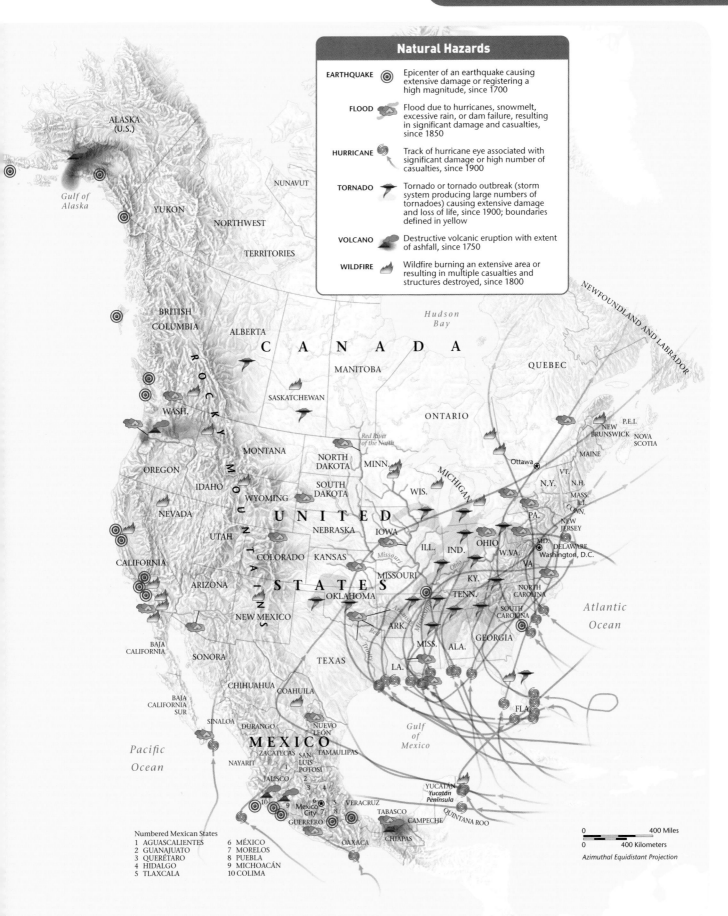

Natural Hazards

EARTHQUAKE — Epicenter of an earthquake causing extensive damage or registering a high magnitude, since 1700

FLOOD — Flood due to hurricanes, snowmelt, excessive rain, or dam failure, resulting in significant damage and casualties, since 1850

HURRICANE — Track of hurricane eye associated with significant damage or high number of casualties, since 1900

TORNADO — Tornado or tornado outbreak (storm system producing large numbers of tornadoes) causing extensive damage and loss of life, since 1900; boundaries defined in yellow

VOLCANO — Destructive volcanic eruption with extent of ashfall, since 1750

WILDFIRE — Wildfire burning an extensive area or resulting in multiple casualties and structures destroyed, since 1800

Numbered Mexican States
1 AGUASCALIENTES
2 GUANAJUATO
3 QUERÉTARO
4 HIDALGO
5 TLAXCALA
6 MÉXICO
7 MORELOS
8 PUEBLA
9 MICHOACÁN
10 COLIMA

0 — 400 Miles
0 — 400 Kilometers

Azimuthal Equidistant Projection

THE CONTINENT:
SOUTH AMERICA

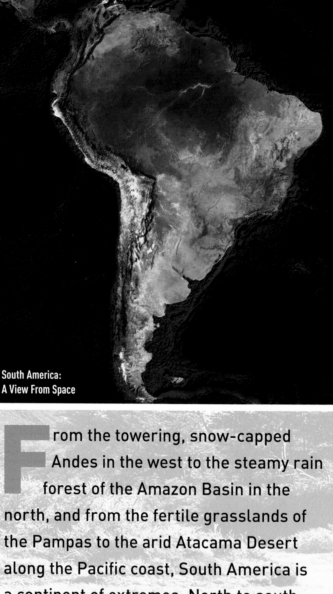

South America:
A View From Space

From the towering, snow-capped Andes in the west to the steamy rain forest of the Amazon Basin in the north, and from the fertile grasslands of the Pampas to the arid Atacama Desert along the Pacific coast, South America is a continent of extremes. North to south, the continent extends from the tropical waters of the Caribbean Sea to the wind-swept islands of Tierra del Fuego. Its longest river, the Amazon, carries more water than any other river in the world.

Snow- and ice-covered Mount Fitzroy rises above Los Glaciares National Park in Patagonia, Argentina.

South America

PHYSICAL

Land area	Lowest point	Largest lake
6,880,000 sq mi (17,819,000 sq km)	Laguna del Carbón, Argentina -344 ft (-105 m)	Lake Titicaca, Bolivia-Peru 3,200 sq mi (8,290 sq km)
Highest point Cerro Aconcagua, Argentina 22,831 ft (6,959 m)	Longest river Amazon 4,150 mi (6,679 km)	

POLITICAL

Population	Largest country	Most populous country
401,139,000	Brazil 3,300,169 sq mi (8,547,403 sq km)	Brazil Pop. 195,527,000
Number of independent countries 12	Smallest country Suriname 63,037 sq mi (163,265 sq km)	Least populous country Suriname Pop. 558,000

TWO PHYSICAL FEATURES dominate South America's landscape—the rugged Andes that stretch north to south from Colombia to Tierra del Fuego, and the Amazon Basin, the drainage area of the Amazon River and site of the world's largest tropical forest.

Caribbean Sea

Central America

Lake Maracaibo

Orinoco

Angel Falls

GUIANA HIGHLANDS

Llanos

South America–North America boundary

Malpelo I.

Negro

A M A Z O N

Amazon

Marajó I.

EQUATOR

B A S I N

Purus

Amazon

Madeira

Tapajós

Xingu

Tocantins

São Francisco

Ucayali

ANDES

Lake Titicaca

BRAZILIAN

HIGHLANDS

Atacama Desert

Pantanal

Paraguay

Gran Chaco

Iguazú Falls

TROPIC OF CAPRICORN

San Félix I.   San Ambrosio I.

Ojos del Salado
22,572 ft
(6,880 m)

Atlantic

Ocean

Paraná

Cerro Aconcagua
22,831 ft (6,959 m)
Highest point in South America

Uruguay

P A M P A S

Río de la Plata

Juan Fernández Is.

Physical

▲ Highest point
▼ Lowest point
+ Other mountain peak

Colorado

A N D E S

Pacific

Ocean

Isla Grande de Chiloé

600 Miles

600 Kilometers

P A T A G O N I A

Gulf of San Jorge

Laguna del Carbón
-344 ft (-105 m)
Lowest point in South America

Azimuthal Equidistant Projection

Falkland Islands

Strait of Magellan

Tierra del Fuego

South Georgia

Cape Horn

80°W   70°W   60°W   50°W

0°   0°

10°S   10°S

20°S   20°S

30°S   30°S

40°S   40°S

50°S   50°S

100°W   90°W   80°W   70°W   60°W   50°W   40°W   30°W   20°W

TWELVE COUNTRIES and one French territory (French Guiana) make up South America. The continent was under mainly Spanish and Portuguese control from the 16th century to the 19th century. Colonial influence is still evident in the use of Spanish and Portuguese languages and in the widespread presence of the Roman Catholic church.

Central America

Caribbean Sea

80°W

70°W

60°W

50°W

Barranquilla
Maracaibo
Caracás
Valencia
Barquisimeto

VENEZUELA

South America–North America boundary

Medellín

GUYANA

Georgetown
Paramaribo
SURINAME
Cayenne
French Guiana (France)

Bogotá

Cali

COLOMBIA

EQUATOR 0°

Quito
ECUADOR

Manaus

Belém

EQUATOR 0°

Guayaquil

P E R U

Fortaleza

Natal

Trujillo

Recife

B R A Z I L

10°S

Lima

Cusco

B O L I V I A

La Paz

Salvador (Bahia)

Goiânia
Brasília

Santa Cruz

Sucre

Belo Horizonte

PARAGUAY

Nova Iguaçu
São Paulo
Rio de Janeiro
Santos
Curitiba

TROPIC OF CAPRICORN

20°S

Asunción

San Miguel de Tucumán

Atlantic Ocean

Porto Alegre

Pacific Ocean

Córdoba

Santa Fe

Rosario

URUGUAY

Valparaíso
Santiago

Buenos Aires
La Plata
Montevideo

30°S

C H I L E

A R G E N T I N A

Mar del Plata

Political

⊛ National capital

• Other city

40°S

Stanley
Falkland Islands (U.K.)

South Georgia (U.K.)

0   600 Miles
0   600 Kilometers

Azimuthal Equidistant Projection

50°S

Punta Arenas

100°W   90°W   80°W   70°W   60°W   50°W   40°W   30°W   20°W

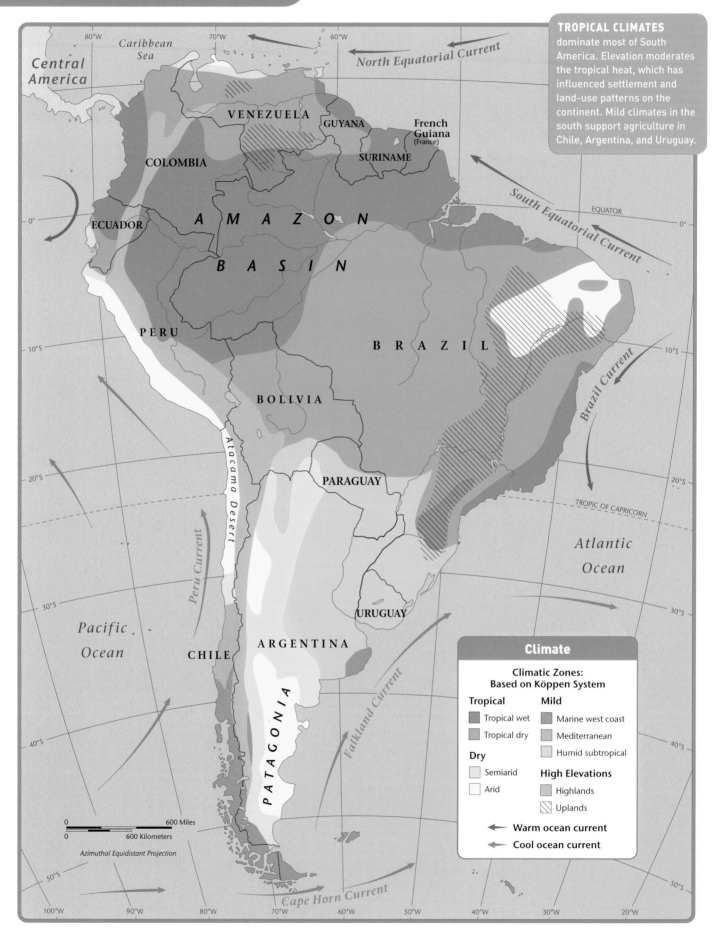

TROPICAL CLIMATES dominate most of South America. Elevation moderates the tropical heat, which has influenced settlement and land-use patterns on the continent. Mild climates in the south support agriculture in Chile, Argentina, and Uruguay.

Central America

Caribbean Sea

North Equatorial Current

VENEZUELA

GUYANA

French Guiana (France)

COLOMBIA

SURINAME

South Equatorial Current

EQUATOR

ECUADOR

A M A Z O N

B A S I N

PERU

B R A Z I L

Brazil Current

BOLIVIA

Peru Current

PARAGUAY

TROPIC OF CAPRICORN

Atacama Desert

Atlantic Ocean

URUGUAY

Pacific Ocean

CHILE

ARGENTINA

Falkland Current

P A T A G O N I A

0   600 Miles
0   600 Kilometers

Azimuthal Equidistant Projection

Cape Horn Current

Climate

Climatic Zones: Based on Köppen System

Tropical
- Tropical wet
- Tropical dry

Dry
- Semiarid
- Arid

Mild
- Marine west coast
- Mediterranean
- Humid subtropical

High Elevations
- Highlands
- Uplands

← Warm ocean current
← Cool ocean current

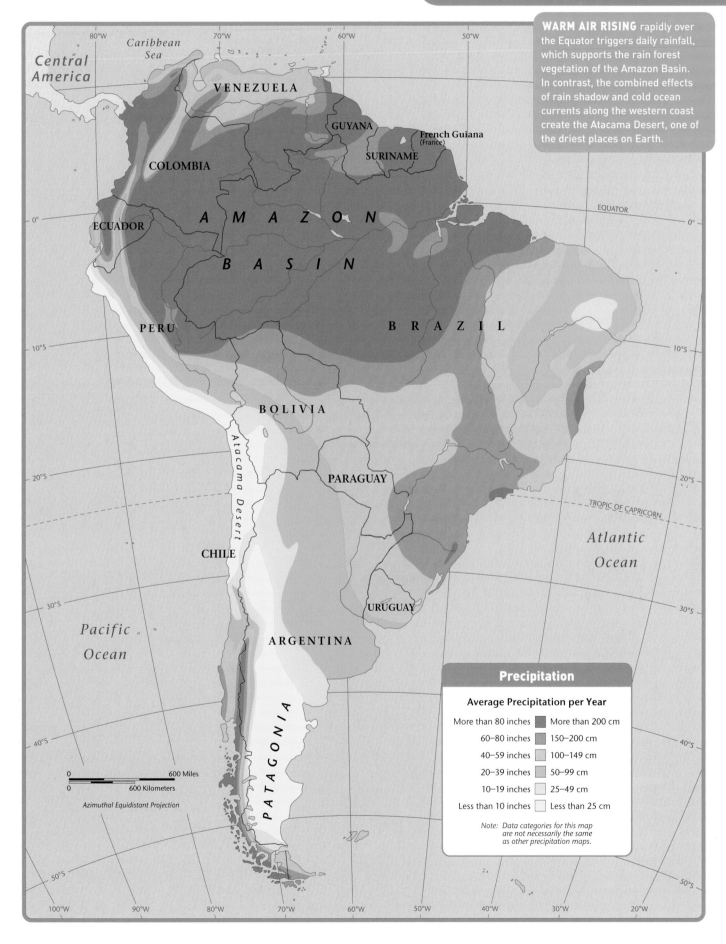

WARM AIR RISING rapidly over the Equator triggers daily rainfall, which supports the rain forest vegetation of the Amazon Basin. In contrast, the combined effects of rain shadow and cold ocean currents along the western coast create the Atacama Desert, one of the driest places on Earth.

Caribbean Sea

Central America

VENEZUELA

GUYANA

French Guiana (France)

SURINAME

COLOMBIA

A M A Z O N

EQUATOR

ECUADOR

0° 0°

B A S I N

PERU

B R A Z I L

10°S 10°S

BOLIVIA

Atacama Desert

PARAGUAY

20°S 20°S

TROPIC OF CAPRICORN

CHILE

Atlantic Ocean

URUGUAY

30°S 30°S

Pacific Ocean

ARGENTINA

P A T A G O N I A

Precipitation

Average Precipitation per Year

More than 80 inches	More than 200 cm
60–80 inches	150–200 cm
40–59 inches	100–149 cm
20–39 inches	50–99 cm
10–19 inches	25–49 cm
Less than 10 inches	Less than 25 cm

0   600 Miles
0   600 Kilometers

Azimuthal Equidistant Projection

Note: Data categories for this map are not necessarily the same as other precipitation maps.

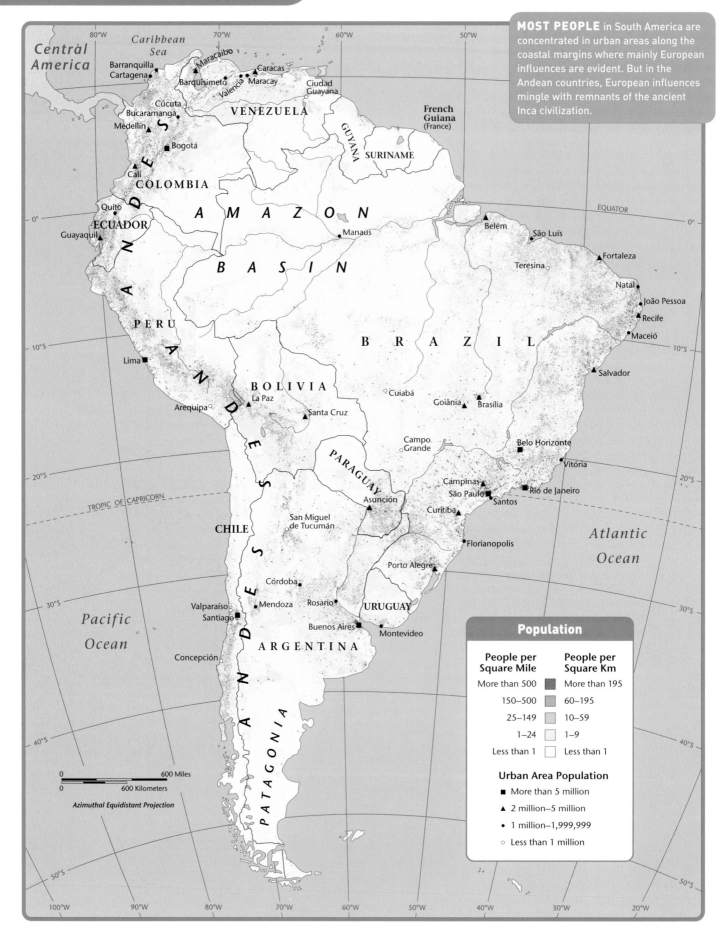

MOST PEOPLE in South America are concentrated in urban areas along the coastal margins where mainly European influences are evident. But in the Andean countries, European influences mingle with remnants of the ancient Inca civilization.

Central America

Caribbean Sea

Barranquilla
Cartagena
Maracaibo
Barquisimeto
Valencia
Caracas
Maracay
Ciudad Guayana

VENEZUELA

Cúcuta
Bucaramanga
Medellín
Bogotá

GUYANA

SURINAME

French Guiana (France)

Cali
COLOMBIA

Quito
ECUADOR
Guayaquil

A M A Z O N

B A S I N

Manaus

EQUATOR

Belém
São Luís
Teresina
Fortaleza
Natal
João Pessoa
Recife
Maceió

PERU

Lima

A
N
D
E
S

B R A Z I L

Salvador

BOLIVIA
La Paz
Arequipa
Santa Cruz

Cuiabá

Goiânia
Brasília

Campo Grande

Belo Horizonte

Vitória

PARAGUAY

Asunción

Campinas
São Paulo
Santos
Rio de Janeiro

Curitiba

CHILE

San Miguel de Tucumán

Florianopolis

Porto Alegre

Atlantic Ocean

TROPIC OF CAPRICORN

Córdoba

Valparaíso
Santiago
Mendoza
Rosario
URUGUAY
Buenos Aires
Montevideo

Pacific Ocean

A R G E N T I N A

Concepción

P A T A G O N I A

A
N
D
E
S

0   600 Miles
0   600 Kilometers
Quito
Azimuthal Equidistant Projection

Population

People per Square Mile	People per Square Km
More than 500	More than 195
150–500	60–195
25–149	10–59
1–24	1–9
Less than 1	Less than 1

Urban Area Population

■ More than 5 million

▲ 2 million–5 million

• 1 million–1,999,999

○ Less than 1 million

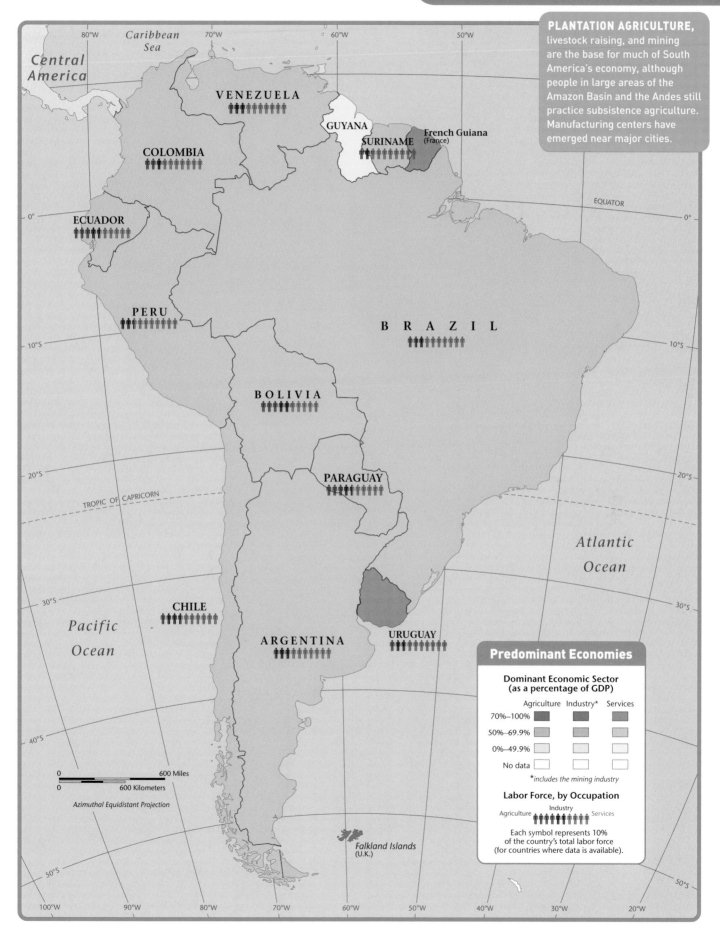

PLANTATION AGRICULTURE, livestock raising, and mining are the base for much of South America's economy, although people in large areas of the Amazon Basin and the Andes still practice subsistence agriculture. Manufacturing centers have emerged near major cities.

Predominant Economies

Dominant Economic Sector (as a percentage of GDP)

	Agriculture	Industry*	Services
70%–100%			
50%–69.9%			
0%–49.9%			
No data			

*includes the mining industry

Labor Force, by Occupation

Agriculture   Industry   Services

Each symbol represents 10% of the country's total labor force (for countries where data is available).

600 Miles
600 Kilometers
Azimuthal Equidistant Projection

Caribbean Sea
Central America
VENEZUELA
GUYANA
SURINAME
French Guiana (France)
COLOMBIA
EQUATOR
ECUADOR
PERU
BRAZIL
BOLIVIA
PARAGUAY
Atlantic Ocean
TROPIC OF CAPRICORN
CHILE
ARGENTINA
URUGUAY
Pacific Ocean
Falkland Islands (U.K.)

THE CONTINENT:
SOUTH AMERICA

TROPICAL RAIN FORESTS:

FACTS & FIGURES

○ Tropical rain forests cover 6 percent of Earth's surface, but are home to half of Earth's species.

○ Average monthly temperature is 68° to 82°F (20° to 28°C).

○ Total annual rainfall averages 5 to 33 feet (1.5 to 10 m).

○ Trees in tropical rain forests can grow up to 200 feet (60 m) in height.

○ Most nutrients in tropical rain forests are stored in the vegetation rather than in the soil, which is very poor.

○ Some of Earth's most valuable woods, such as teak, mahogany, rosewood, and sandalwood, grow in tropical rain forests.

○ Up to 25 percent of all medicines include products originating in tropical rain forests.

○ Tropical rain forests absorb carbon dioxide and release oxygen.

○ Deforestation of tropical rain forests contributes to climate change.

○ Almost half of all forest loss in the period 2000–2010 occurred in tropical forests.

○ Brazil and Indonesia had the highest net loss of forest in the 1990s but have significantly reduced their rates of loss.

Amazon Rain Forest

The Amazon rain forest, which covers approximately 2.7 million square miles (7 million sq km), is the world's largest tropical forest. Located mainly in Brazil, the Amazon rain forest accounts for more than 20 percent of all the world's tropical forests. Known in Brazil as the selva, the rain forest is a vast storehouse of biological diversity, filled with plants and animals both familiar and exotic. According to estimates, at least half of all terrestrial species are found in tropical forests, but many of these species have not yet been identified.

Tropical forests contain many valuable resources, including cacao (chocolate), nuts, spices, rare hardwoods, and plant extracts used to make medicines. Some drugs used in treating cancer and heart disease come from plants found only in tropical forests. But human intervention—logging, mining, and clearing land for crops and grazing—has put tropical forests at great risk. In Brazil, roads cut into the rain forest have opened the way for settlers, who clear away the forest only to discover soil too poor in nutrients to sustain agriculture for more than a few years. Land usually is cleared by a method called slash-and-burn, which contributes to global warming by releasing great amounts of carbon dioxide into the atmosphere.

⬣ **SLOW-MOVING,** this three-toed sloth spends most of its life in the treetops. It is one of the many unusual species of animals that make their homes in the forests of the Amazon Basin.

⬣ **SLASH-AND-BURN** is a method used in the tropics for clearing land for farms. But the soil is poor in nutrients, and good yields are short-lived.

⬣ **DENSE CANOPY OF THE RAIN FOREST** stands in sharp contrast to the silt-laden waters of one of the Amazon's many tributaries. Although seemingly endless, the forest in Brazil is decreasing in size due to mining, farming, ranching, and logging.

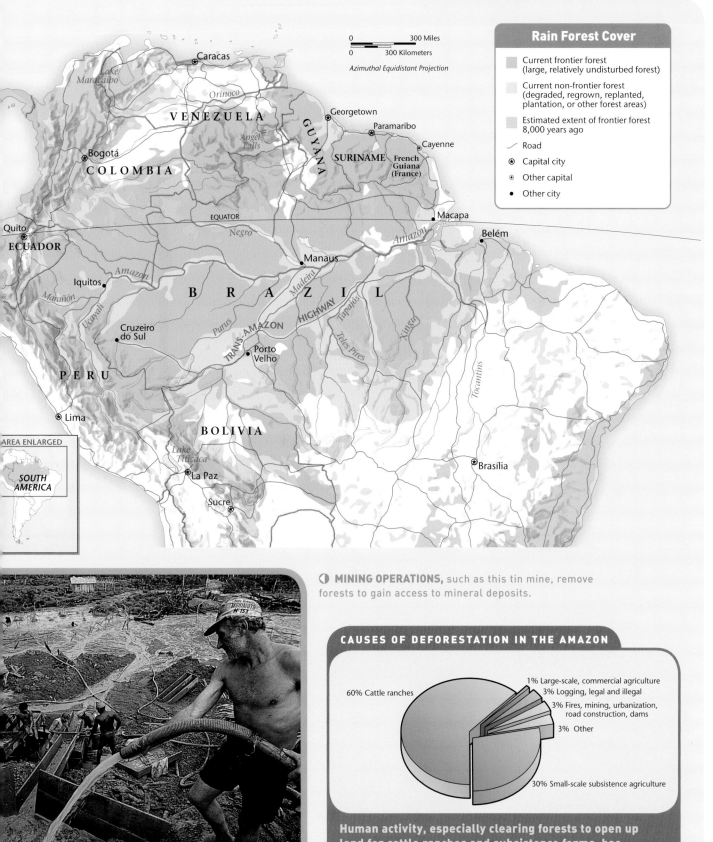

0 | 300 Miles
0 | 300 Kilometers

Azimuthal Equidistant Projection

Rain Forest Cover

Current frontier forest
(large, relatively undisturbed forest)

Current non-frontier forest
(degraded, regrown, replanted,
plantation, or other forest areas)

Estimated extent of frontier forest
8,000 years ago

Road

⊛ Capital city

⊙ Other capital

• Other city

AREA ENLARGED

SOUTH
AMERICA

◖ MINING OPERATIONS, such as this tin mine, remove
forests to gain access to mineral deposits.

CAUSES OF DEFORESTATION IN THE AMAZON

60% Cattle ranches

1% Large-scale, commercial agriculture
3% Logging, legal and illegal
3% Fires, mining, urbanization,
road construction, dams
3% Other

30% Small-scale subsistence agriculture

**Human activity, especially clearing forests to open up
land for cattle ranches and subsistence farms, has
resulted in serious loss of this valuable ecosystem.**

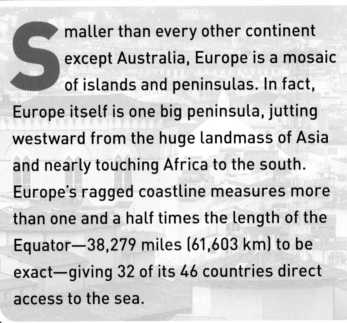

Europe:
A View From Space

Smaller than every other continent except Australia, Europe is a mosaic of islands and peninsulas. In fact, Europe itself is one big peninsula, jutting westward from the huge landmass of Asia and nearly touching Africa to the south. Europe's ragged coastline measures more than one and a half times the length of the Equator—38,279 miles (61,603 km) to be exact—giving 32 of its 46 countries direct access to the sea.

The Cathedral of Santa Maria del Fiore dominates the skyline of Florence, Italy.

Europe

PHYSICAL			POLITICAL		
Land area 3,841,000 sq mi (9,947,000 sq km)	**Lowest point** **Caspian Sea** -92 ft (-28 m)	**Largest lake entirely in Europe** **Ladoga, Russia** 6,853 sq mi (17,703 sq km)	**Population** 739,517,000 **Number of independent countries** **46 (including Russia)**	**Largest country entirely in Europe** **Ukraine** 233,090 sq mi (603,700 sq km)	**Most populous country entirely in Europe** **Germany** Pop. 80,572,000
Highest point **El'brus, Russia** 18,510 ft (5,642 m)	**Longest river** **Volga, Russia** 2,294 mi (3,692 km)			**Smallest country** **Vatican City** 0.2 sq mi (0.4 sq km)	**Least populous country** **Vatican City** Pop. 798

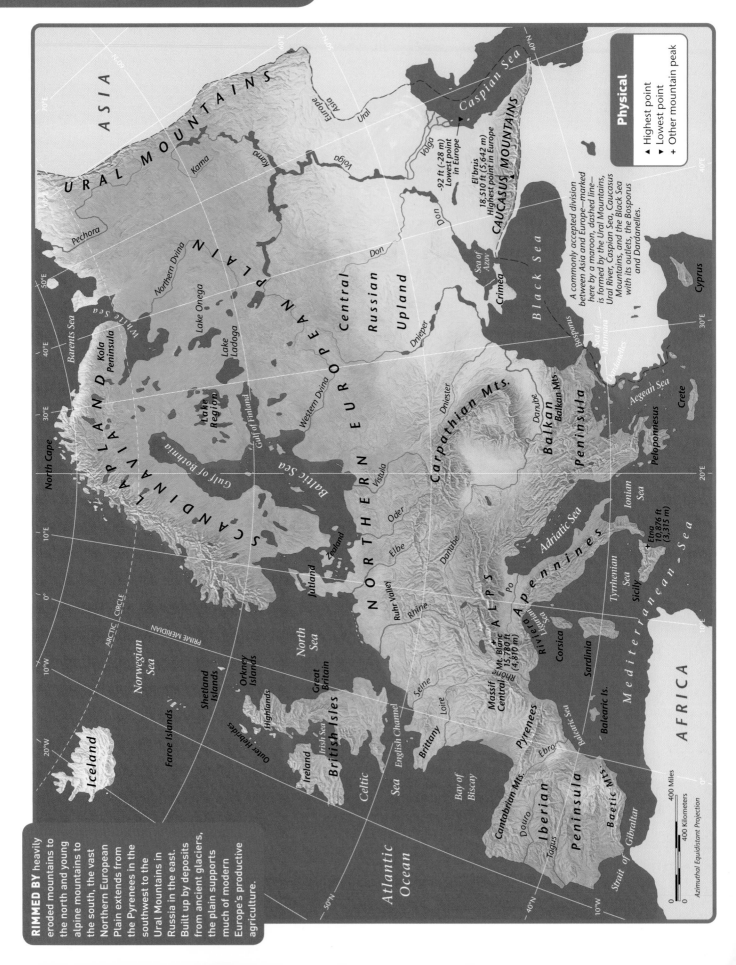

Physical
- ▲ Highest point
- ▼ Lowest point
- + Other mountain peak

A commonly accepted division between Asia and Europe—marked here by a maroon, dashed line—is formed by the Ural Mountains, Ural River, Caspian Sea, Caucasus Mountains, and the Black Sea with its outlets, the Bosporus and Dardanelles.

ASIA

URAL MOUNTAINS

Pechora

Kama

Kama

Ural

Europe
Asia

Volga

Volga

Caspian Sea

Don

-92 ft (-28 m)
Lowest point
in Europe

El'brus
18,510 ft (5,642 m)
Highest point in Europe

CAUCASUS MOUNTAINS

Sea of Azov

Crimea

Black Sea

Bosporus

Cyprus

Northern Dvina

NORTHERN EUROPEAN PLAIN

Central Russian Upland

Don

Dnieper

Sea of Marmara

Dardanelles

30°E

Barents Sea

White Sea

Lake Onega

Lake Ladoga

Western Dvina

Dniester

Carpathian Mts.

Danube

Balkan Mts.

Balkan Peninsula

Aegean Sea

Crete

Kola Peninsula

Lake Region

SCANDINAVIAN UPLAND

Gulf of Finland

Gulf of Bothnia

Baltic Sea

Vistula

Oder

Elbe

Danube

Po

Adriatic Sea

Apennines

Ionian Sea

Peloponnesus

North Cape

40°E

30°E

20°E

Zealand

Jutland

Ruhr Valley

Rhine

Etna
10,876 ft
(3,315 m)

Tyrrhenian Sea

Sicily

ALPS

Ligurian Sea

Norwegian Sea

Iceland

Faroe Islands

Shetland Islands

Orkney Islands

Outer Hebrides

Highlands

Great Britain

North Sea

Seine

Mt. Blanc
15,780 ft
(4,810 m)

Massif Central

Rhône

Riviera

Corsica

Sardinia

Mediterranean Sea

AFRICA

ARCTIC CIRCLE

PRIME MERIDIAN

Ireland

British Isles

Irish Sea

Celtic Sea

English Channel

Brittany

Loire

Bay of Biscay

Pyrenees

Ebro

Balearic Sea

Balearic Is.

Cantabrian Mts.

Douro

Iberian Peninsula

Baetic Mts.

Tagus

Strait of Gibraltar

Atlantic Ocean

20°W

10°W

0°

10°E

50°N

40°N

400 Miles

400 Kilometers

Azimuthal Equidistant Projection

RIMMED BY heavily eroded mountains to the north and young alpine mountains to the south, the vast Northern European Plain extends from the Pyrenees in the southwest to the Ural Mountains in Russia in the east. Built up by deposits from ancient glaciers, the plain supports much of modern Europe's productive agriculture.

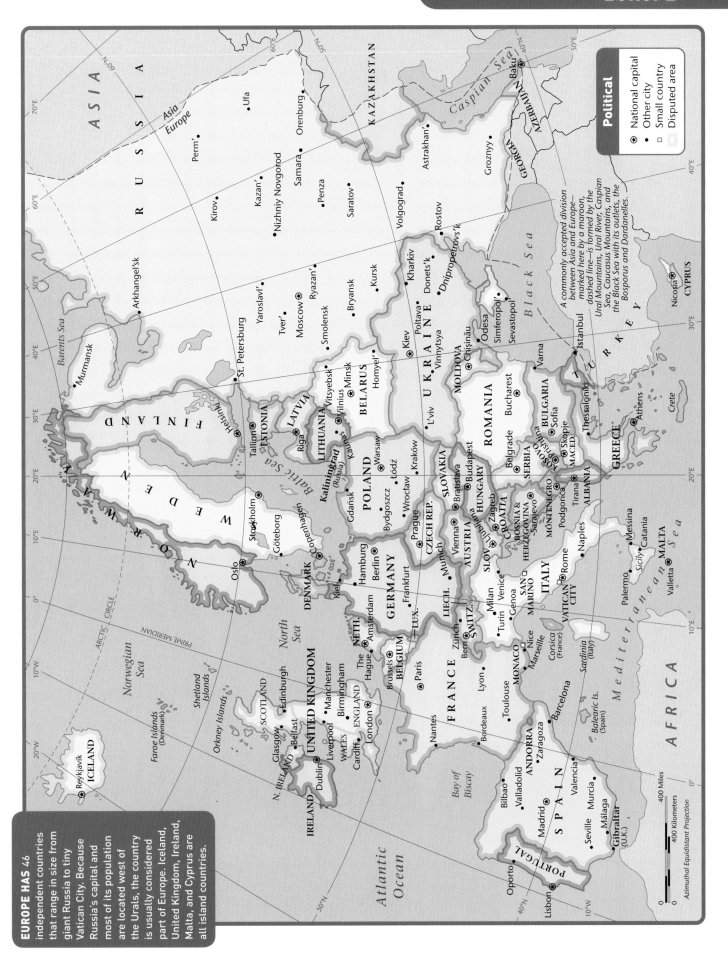

Political

- ⊛ National capital
- • Other city
- □ Small country
- ▢ Disputed area

A commonly accepted division between Asia and Europe—marked here by a maroon, dashed line—is formed by the Ural Mountains, Ural River, Caspian Sea, Caucasus Mountains, and the Black Sea with its outlets, the Bosporus and Dardanelles.

EUROPE HAS 46 independent countries that range in size from giant Russia to tiny Vatican City. Because Russia's capital and most of its population are located west of the Urals, the country is usually considered part of Europe. Iceland, United Kingdom, Ireland, Malta, and Cyprus are all island countries.

400 Miles
400 Kilometers

Azimuthal Equidistant Projection

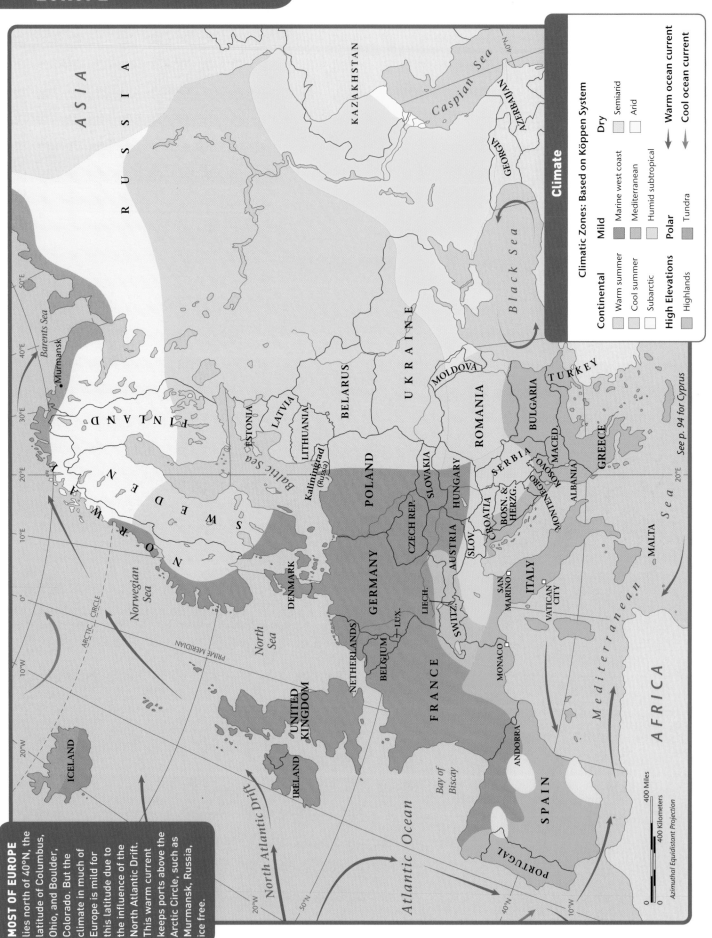

MOST OF EUROPE lies north of 40°N, the latitude of Columbus, Ohio, and Boulder, Colorado. But the climate in much of Europe is mild for this latitude due to the influence of the North Atlantic Drift. This warm current keeps ports above the Arctic Circle, such as Murmansk, Russia, ice free.

Climate

Climatic Zones: Based on Köppen System

Continental
- Warm summer
- Cool summer
- Subarctic

Mild
- Marine west coast
- Mediterranean
- Humid subtropical

Dry
- Semiarid
- Arid

Polar
- Tundra

High Elevations
- Highlands

→ Warm ocean current
→ Cool ocean current

See p. 94 for Cyprus

400 Miles
400 Kilometers

Azimuthal Equidistant Projection

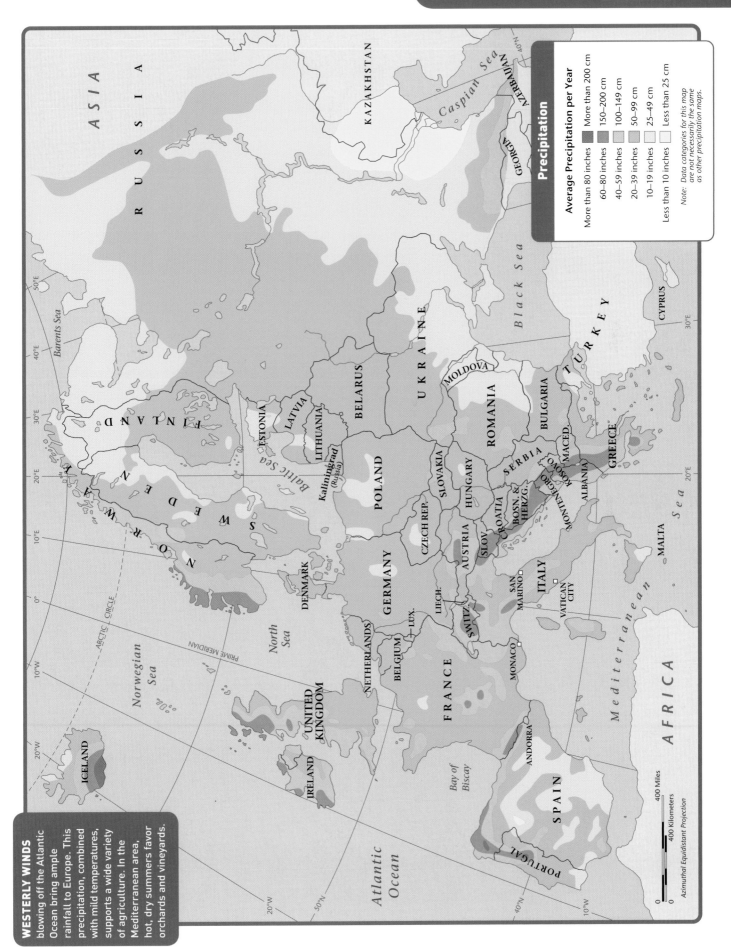

Precipitation

Average Precipitation per Year

More than 80 inches	More than 200 cm
60–80 inches	150–200 cm
40–59 inches	100–149 cm
20–39 inches	50–99 cm
10–19 inches	25–49 cm
Less than 10 inches	Less than 25 cm

Note: Data categories for this map are not necessarily the same as other precipitation maps.

WESTERLY WINDS blowing off the Atlantic Ocean bring ample rainfall to Europe. This precipitation, combined with mild temperatures, supports a wide variety of agriculture. In the Mediterranean area, hot, dry summers favor orchards and vineyards.

400 Miles

400 Kilometers

Azimuthal Equidistant Projection

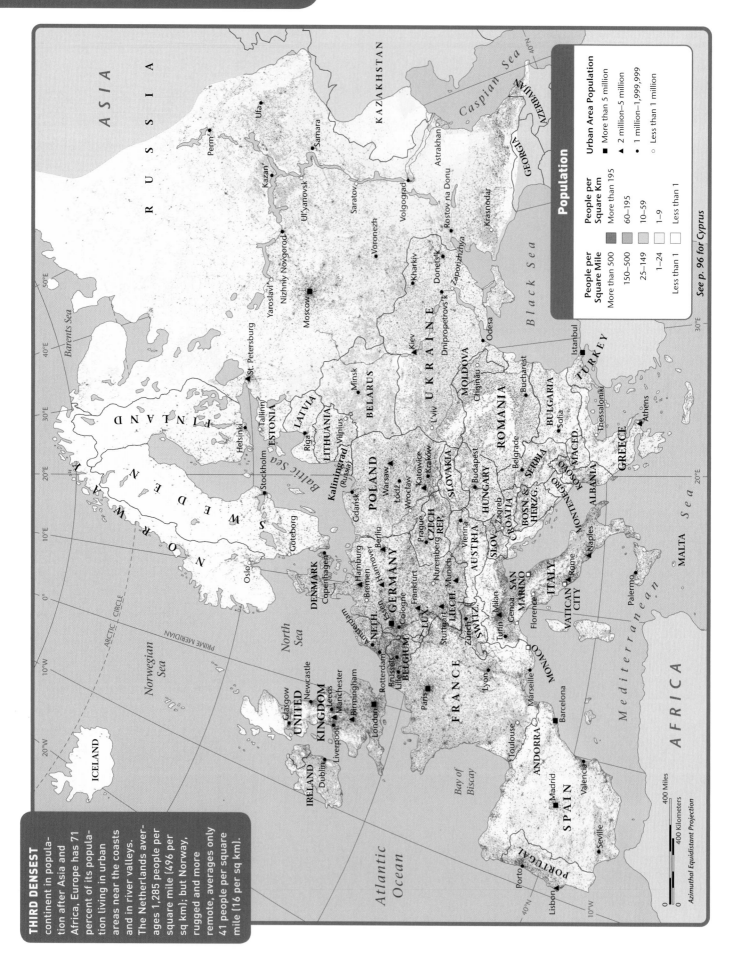

THIRD DENSEST

continent in population after Asia and Africa, Europe has 71 percent of its population living in urban areas near the coasts and in river valleys. The Netherlands averages 1,285 people per square mile (496 per sq km); but Norway, rugged and more remote, averages only 41 people per square mile (16 per sq km).

Population

People per Square Mile	People per Square Km
More than 500	More than 195
150–500	60–195
25–149	10–59
1–24	1–9
Less than 1	Less than 1

Urban Area Population

- ■ More than 5 million
- ▲ 2 million–5 million
- ● 1 million–1,999,999
- ○ Less than 1 million

See p. 96 for Cyprus

Azimuthal Equidistant Projection

400 Miles
400 Kilometers

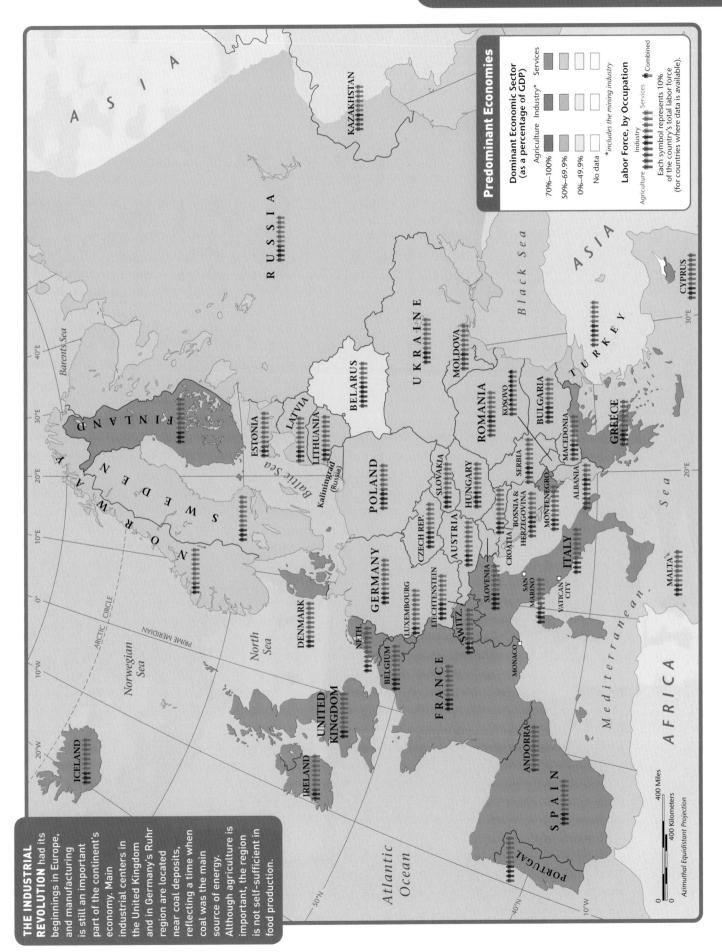

Predominant Economies

Dominant Economic Sector
(as a percentage of GDP)

Agriculture Industry* Services

70%–100%
50%–69.9%
0%–49.9%
No data

*includes the mining industry

Labor Force, by Occupation

Industry
Agriculture   Services   Combined

Each symbol represents 10%
of the country's total labor force
(for countries where data is available).

THE INDUSTRIAL REVOLUTION had its beginnings in Europe, and manufacturing is still an important part of the continent's economy. Main industrial centers in the United Kingdom and in Germany's Ruhr region are located near coal deposits, reflecting a time when coal was the main source of energy. Although agriculture is important, the region is not self-sufficient in food production.

EUROPEAN WATERWAYS:

FACTS & FIGURES

○ More than 25,000 miles (40,000 km) of inland waterways link cities of Europe to a network of trade, both within the continent and around the world.

○ The Rhine and Danube Rivers have been important to trade and commerce since the time of the Roman Empire.

○ The Rhine and Danube Rivers were linked by a canal in 1992, opening up water travel from the North Sea to the Black Sea, a distance of 2,175 miles (3,500 km).

○ The Upper Middle Rhine Valley has been named a UNESCO World Heritage site for its natural beauty and its many historic castles.

○ The Danube is the second longest river in Europe (after the Volga), draining 10 percent of the entire European continent.

○ More than 49.5 million tons (45 million MT) of goods are transported on the Danube River.

○ The Rhine River empties into the North Sea at Rotterdam in the Netherlands. In 2008, work began to expand the port's deep-water facilities to accommodate increasingly larger container ships.

European Waterways

The physical landscape of Europe is crossed by many rivers that link the countries, people, and economies to the seas that border the continent. Fourteen of Europe's countries are landlocked (have no direct access to open waters), but the rivers and canals that make up Europe's network of waterways give even these countries access to global shipping routes.

⊖ HEIDELBURG CASTLE stands above the Rhine River in Germany, attracting millions of tourists each year.

Among these many waterways, the Rhine-Main-Danube system supports commercial and recreational traffic all the way from Rotterdam on the North Sea to Constanta on the Black Sea. Rotterdam, Europe's largest port as well as a major world port, handles 495 million tons (450 million MT) of goods each year. And Constanta is the largest port on the Black Sea.

The Rhine-Main-Danube waterway boasts a rich historical and cultural tradition. During Roman times, the rivers were used to transport supplies to armies along the northern border of the empire. Cities, such as Cologne, Vienna, and Budapest, emerged as cultural centers with churches, cathedrals, opera houses, and palaces that today attract tourists from around the world. And the Middle Rhine is famous for castles perched high above the banks of the river, where traders were once required to pay tolls to travel on the waterways.

◖ COLOGNE CATHEDRAL, begun in 1248, rises above the city of Cologne, Germany, on the banks of the Rhine River.

⊖ IRON GATE: The face of the Dacian king Decebalus is carved into the rocks above the Iron Gates gorges on the Danube River between Romania and Serbia.

SELECTED EUROPEAN RIVERS

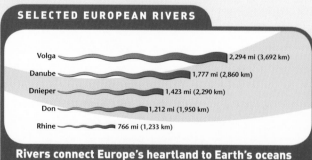

Volga — 2,294 mi (3,692 km)
Danube — 1,777 mi (2,860 km)
Dnieper — 1,423 mi (2,290 km)
Don — 1,212 mi (1,950 km)
Rhine — 766 mi (1,233 km)

Rivers connect Europe's heartland to Earth's oceans and seas, linking people, cities, and commerce to the global economy.

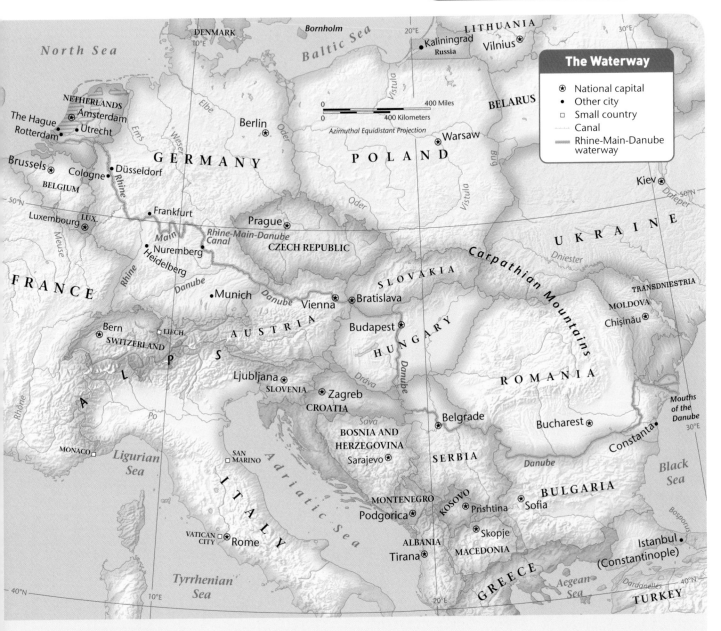

THE RHINE-MAIN-DANUBE CANAL, completed in 1992, connects the Rhine, Main, and Danube Rivers to create a continuous waterway from the North Sea to the Black Sea, which gives access to Turkey's Dardanelles and to the ports of Asia. The canal is 106 miles (171 km) long and makes navigation by large barges and riverboats possible for the full length of the waterway.

A CITY DIVIDED, Budapest, Hungary, lies on both sides of the Danube River. Once two separate towns, Buda and Pest were united in 1872. The country's Parliament Building, an important city landmark, stretches 880 feet (268 m) along the Pest side of the river.

Asia:
A View From Space

From the frozen shores of the Arctic Ocean to the equatorial islands of Indonesia, Asia stretches across 90 degrees of latitude. From the Ural Mountains to the Pacific Ocean, it covers more than 150 degrees of longitude. Here, three of history's great culture hearths emerged in the valleys of the Tigris and Euphrates, the Indus, and the Yellow (Huang) Rivers. Today, Asia is home to 60 percent of Earth's people and some of the world's fastest growing economies.

The Taj Mahal in Agra, India

Asia

PHYSICAL

Land area
17,208,000 sq mi
(44,570,000 sq km)

Highest point
Mount Everest,
China-Nepal
29,035 ft (8,850 m)

Lowest point
Dead Sea, Israel-Jordan
-1,385 ft (-422 m)

Longest river
Yangtze (Chang), China
3,880 mi (6,244 km)

**Largest lake
entirely in Asia**
Lake Baikal
12,200 sq mi
(31,500 sq km)

POLITICAL

Population
4,302,088,000

**Number of
independent
countries**
46 (excluding
Russia)

**Largest country
entirely in Asia**
China
3,705,405 sq mi (9,596,960 sq km)

Smallest country
Maldives
115 sq mi (298 sq km)

Most populous country
China
Pop. 1,357,372,000

Least populous country
Maldives
Pop. 360,000

THE CONTINENT:
ASIA

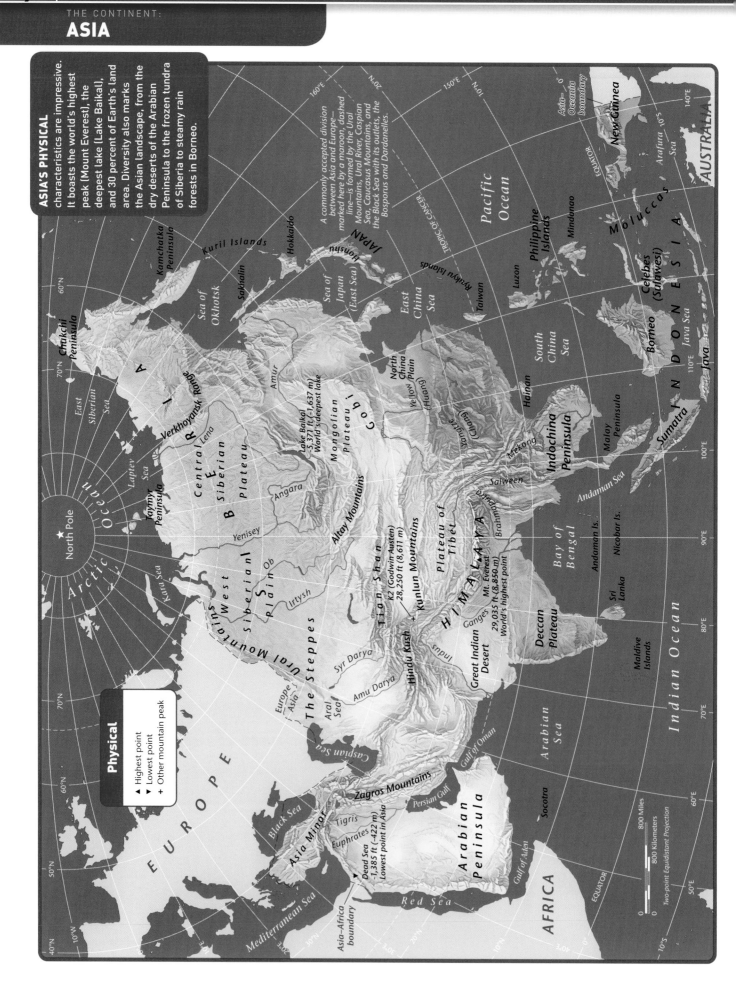

ASIA'S PHYSICAL

characteristics are impressive. It boasts the world's highest peak (Mount Everest), the deepest lake (Lake Baikal), and 30 percent of Earth's land area. Diversity also marks the Asian landscape, from the dry deserts of the Arabian Peninsula to the frozen tundra of Siberia to steamy rain forests in Borneo.

A commonly accepted division between Asia and Europe—marked here by a maroon, dashed line—is formed by the Ural Mountains, Ural River, Caspian Sea, Caucasus Mountains, and the Black Sea with its outlets, the Bosporus and Dardanelles.

Physical
◄ Highest point
► Lowest point
+ Other mountain peak

Pacific Ocean

AUSTRALIA

New Guinea

Asia–Oceania boundary

Moluccas

Philippine Islands

Mindanao

Celebes (Sulawesi)

Luzon

Borneo

Java Sea

INDONESIA

Sumatra

Java

South China Sea

Hainan

Taiwan

Ryukyu Islands

Malay Peninsula

Indochina Peninsula

East China Sea

Mekong

Salween

Andaman Sea

Andaman Is.

Nicobar Is.

Yangtze (Chang)

Yangtze

North China Plain

Yellow Plain

Huang (Huang)

JAPAN

Honshu

Hokkaido

Sea of Japan (East Sea)

Sakhalin

Kuril Islands

Kamchatka Peninsula

Sea of Okhotsk

Amur

Brahmaputra

Irrawaddy

HIMALAYA

Ganges

Mt. Everest 29,035 ft (8,850 m) World's highest point

Plateau of Tibet

Kunlun Mountains

K2 (Godwin Austen) 28,250 ft (8,611 m)

+

Tian Shan

Altay Mountains

Mongolian Plateau

Gobi

Lake Baikal -5,371 ft (-1,637 m) World's deepest lake

Central Siberian Plateau

Lena

Angara

Yenisey

Verkhoyansk Range

Taymyr Peninsula

Chukchi Peninsula

East Siberian Sea

Laptev Sea

Kara Sea

Arctic Ocean

North Pole ★

SIBERIA

West Siberian Plain

Ob

Irtysh

Ural Mountains

The Steppes

Aral Sea

Syr Darya

Amu Darya

Europe Asia

Hindu Kush

Indus

Deccan Plateau

Bay of Bengal

Sri Lanka

Maldive Islands

Indian Ocean

Great Indian Desert

Zagros Mountains

Caspian Sea

Tigris

Euphrates

Asia Minor

Black Sea

Dead Sea -1,385 ft (-422 m) Lowest point in Asia

Persian Gulf

Gulf of Oman

Arabian Sea

Socotra

Gulf of Aden

Arabian Peninsula

Red Sea

Mediterranean Sea

EUROPE

Asia–Africa boundary

AFRICA

EQUATOR

TROPIC OF CANCER

Arafura Sea

Java

Nicobar Is.

800 Miles
800 Kilometers
Two-point Equidistant Projection

160°E 150°E 140°E 100°E 90°E 80°E 70°E 60°E 50°E

70°N 60°N 50°N 40°N 70°N 60°N

20°N 10°N 0° EQUATOR 10°S

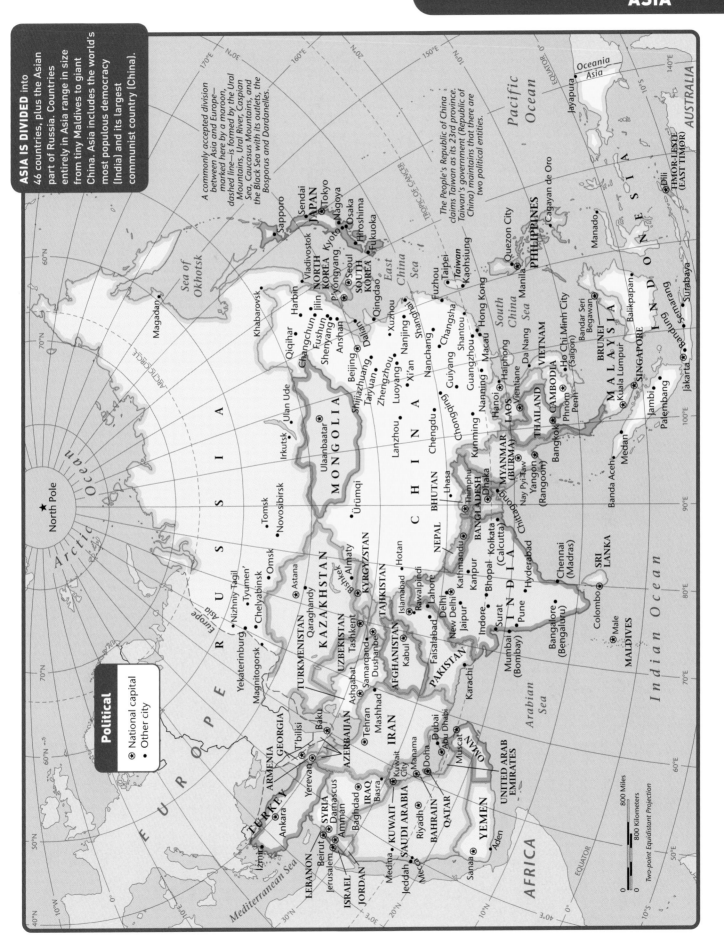

ASIA IS DIVIDED into 46 countries, plus the Asian part of Russia. Countries entirely in Asia range in size from tiny Maldives to giant China. Asia includes the world's most populous democracy (India) and its largest communist country (China).

A commonly accepted division between Asia and Europe—marked here by a maroon, dashed line—is formed by the Ural Mountains, Ural River, Caspian Sea, Caucasus Mountains, and the Black Sea with its outlets, the Bosporus and Dardanelles.

The People's Republic of China claims Taiwan as its 23rd province. Taiwan's government (Republic of China) maintains that there are two political entities.

Political
⊛ National capital
• Other city

Two-point Equidistant Projection

800 Miles
800 Kilometers

North Pole

Arctic Ocean

Magadan

Sea of Okhotsk

Khabarovsk

Vladivostok

Sapporo
Sendai
JAPAN Tokyo
NORTH Kyoto Nagoya
KOREA Osaka
P'yongyang Hiroshima
Seoul Fukuoka
SOUTH
KOREA
Qingdao

East China Sea

Fuzhou
Taipei
Taiwan
Kaohsiung

Pacific Ocean

Oceania
Asia

Jayapura

AUSTRALIA

Cagayan de Oro

Quezon City
PHILIPPINES Manila

Manado

Dili
TIMOR-LESTE (EAST TIMOR)

Harbin
Qiqihar
Changchun Jilin
Fushun
Shenyang
Anshan
Dalian
Beijing

Ulan Ude

Irkutsk

M O N G O L I A

Ulaanbaatar

Xuzhou
Nanjing
Shanghai
Zhengzhou
Luoyang Xi'an
Shijiazhuang
Taiyuan

Nanchang
Changsha
Guiyang
Chongqing

Fuzhou
Shantou
Guangzhou
Hong Kong
Macau

South China Sea

Haiphong
Da Nang
VIETNAM
Ho Chi Minh City (Saigon)

Bandar Seri Begawan
BRUNEI

Balikpapan

Tomsk
Novosibirsk

Ürümqi

C H I N A

Lanzhou
Chengdu
Kunming
Nanning
Hanoi
Vientiane
LAOS

Semarang
Surabaya

I N D O N E S I A

Jambi
Palembang
Jakarta
Bandung

M A L A Y S I A
Kuala Lumpur
SINGAPORE

Medan
Banda Aceh

R U S S I A

Omsk

Astana

Yekaterinburg
Nizhniy Tagil
Tyumen'
Chelyabinsk
Magnitogorsk

Europe Asia

Qaraghandy

K A Z A K H S T A N

Bishkek Almaty
KYRGYZSTAN
Tashkent
TAJIKISTAN
UZBEKISTAN
Hotan
Dushanbe
Samarqand

Lhasa
BHUTAN
Thimphu
NEPAL
Kathmandu
Kanpur

MYANMAR (BURMA)
Nay Pyi Taw
Yangon (Rangoon)

THAILAND
Bangkok

CAMBODIA
Phnom Penh

BANGLADESH
Dhaka
Chittagong

Bhopal
Kolkata (Calcutta)

TURKMENISTAN
Ashgabat
Mashhad
AFGHANISTAN
Kabul
Faisalabad
Islamabad
Rawalpindi
Lahore
Delhi
New Delhi
PAKISTAN
Jaipur
Karachi

I N D I A
Indore
Surat
Hyderabad
Pune

Bangalore (Bengaluru)

Chennai (Madras)

SRI LANKA
Colombo
Male
MALDIVES

Indian Ocean

Mumbai (Bombay)

Tehran
IRAN
Baku
AZERBAIJAN
T'bilisi
GEORGIA
ARMENIA
Yerevan
Dubai
Abu Dhabi
OMAN
Muscat

UNITED ARAB EMIRATES

Arabian Sea

Kuwait City
KUWAIT
Manama
Doha
QATAR
BAHRAIN
Riyadh
SAUDI ARABIA

TURKEY
Izmir
Ankara
SYRIA
Beirut
LEBANON Damascus
Jerusalem Amman
ISRAEL **JORDAN**
IRAQ
Baghdad
Basra

Medina
Mecca
Jeddah

Sanaa
YEMEN
Aden

AFRICA

Mediterranean Sea

ARCTIC CIRCLE

TROPIC OF CANCER

EQUATOR

E U R O P E

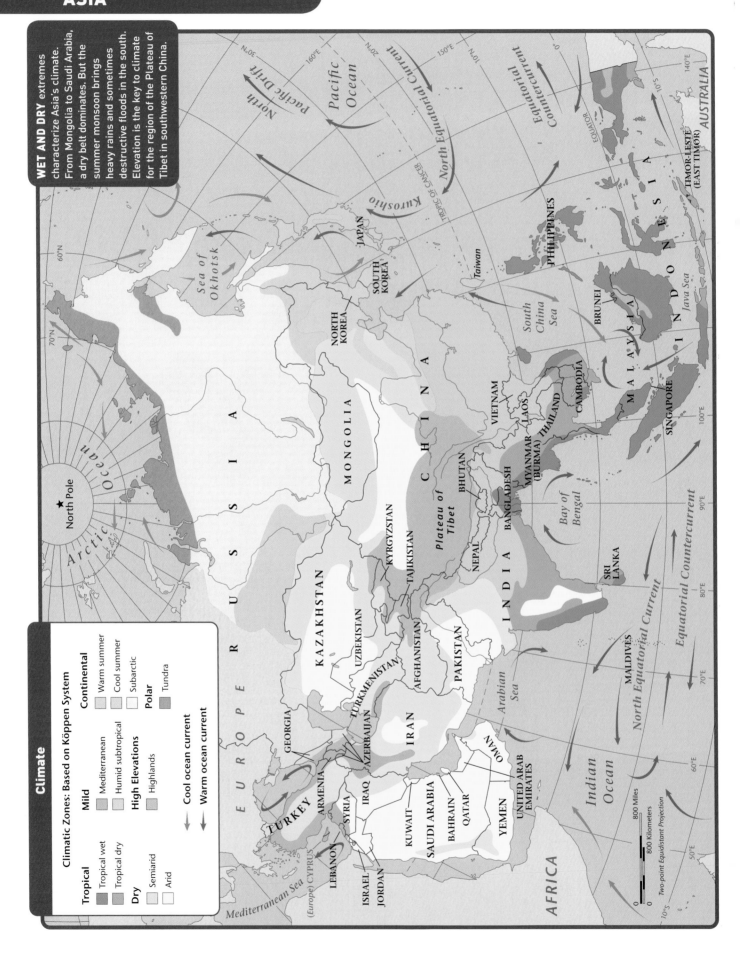

WET AND DRY extremes characterize Asia's climate. From Mongolia to Saudi Arabia, a dry belt dominates. But the summer monsoon brings heavy rains and sometimes destructive floods in the south. Elevation is the key to climate for the region of the Plateau of Tibet in southwestern China.

Climate

Climatic Zones: Based on Köppen System

Tropical
- Tropical wet
- Tropical dry

Dry
- Semiarid
- Arid

Mild
- Mediterranean
- Humid subtropical

High Elevations
- Highlands

Continental
- Warm summer
- Cool summer
- Subarctic

Polar
- Tundra

→ Cool ocean current
→ Warm ocean current

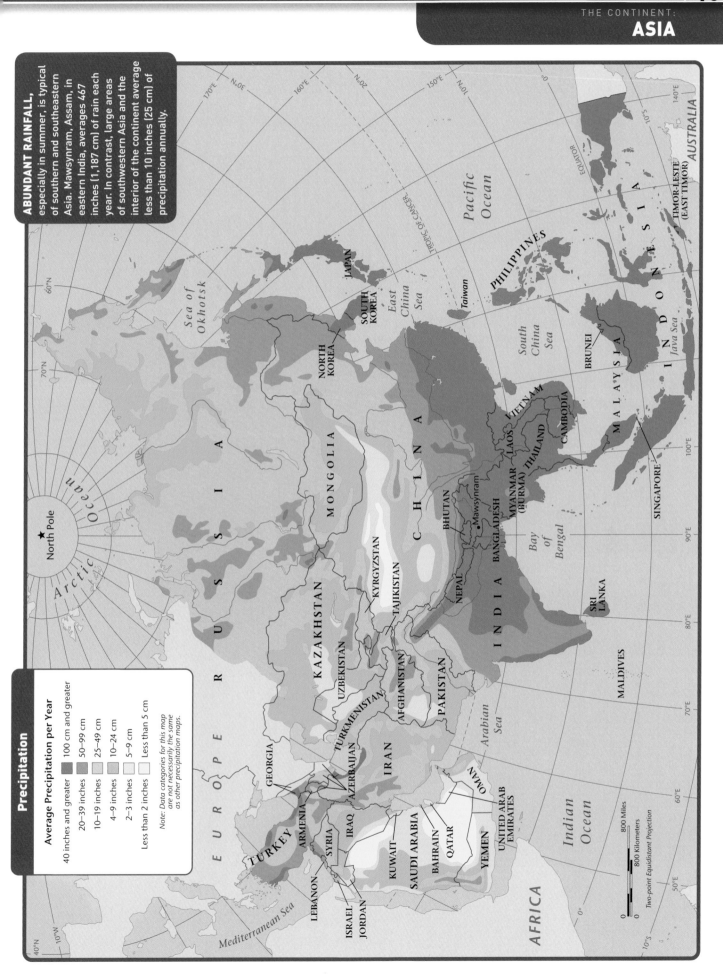

ABUNDANT RAINFALL, especially in summer, is typical of southern and southeastern Asia. Mawsynram, Assam, in eastern India, averages 467 inches (1,187 cm) of rain each year. In contrast, large areas of southwestern Asia and the interior of the continent average less than 10 inches (25 cm) of precipitation annually.

Precipitation

Average Precipitation per Year

- 40 inches and greater — 100 cm and greater
- 20–39 inches — 50–99 cm
- 10–19 inches — 25–49 cm
- 4–9 inches — 10–24 cm
- 2–3 inches — 5–9 cm
- Less than 2 inches — Less than 5 cm

Note: Data categories for this map are not necessarily the same as other precipitation maps.

800 Miles
800 Kilometers
Two-point Equidistant Projection

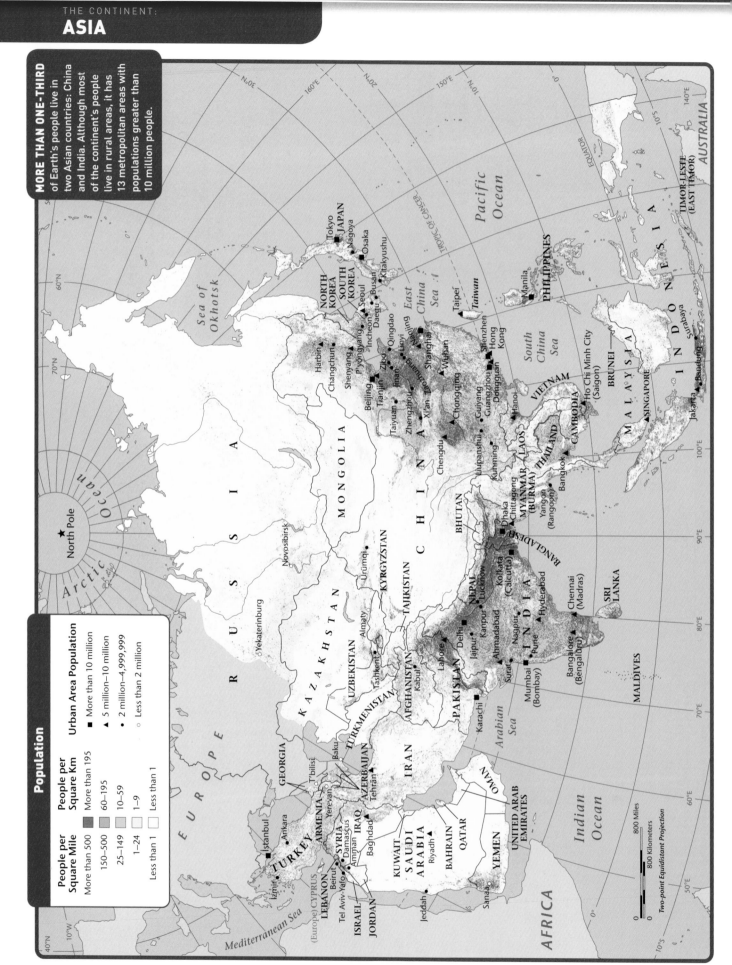

MORE THAN ONE-THIRD of Earth's people live in two Asian countries: China and India. Although most of the continent's people live in rural areas, it has 13 metropolitan areas with populations greater than 10 million people.

Population

People per Square Mile

	More than 500
	150–500
	25–149
	1–24
	Less than 1

People per Square Km

	More than 195
	60–195
	10–59
	1–9
	Less than 1

Urban Area Population

- ■ More than 10 million
- ▲ 5 million–10 million
- ● 2 million–4,999,999
- ○ Less than 2 million

800 Miles
800 Kilometers
Two-point Equidistant Projection

NOMADIC HERDING, farming, and other subsistence activities define the economic lifestyle of the majority of Asia's people. But Asia also includes some of the world's industrial giants, such as Japan and South Korea.

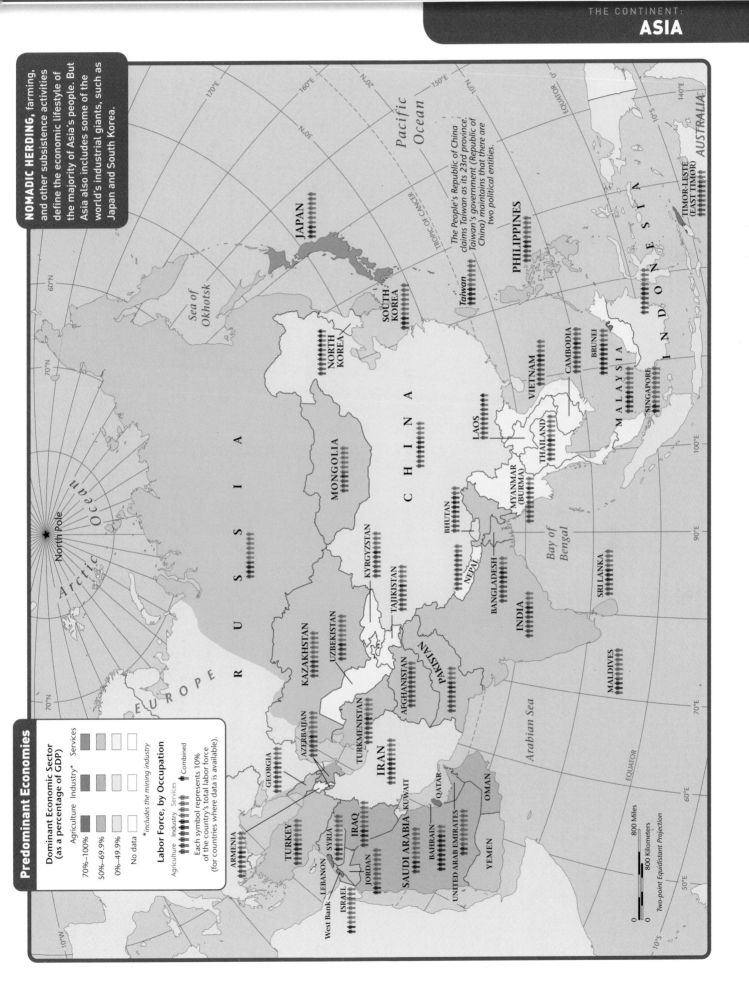

The People's Republic of China claims Taiwan as its 23rd province. Taiwan's government (Republic of China) maintains that there are two political entities.

Predominant Economies

Dominant Economic Sector
(as a percentage of GDP)

Agriculture Industry* Services

70%–100%

50%–69.9%

0%–49.9%

No data

*includes the mining industry

Labor Force, by Occupation

Agriculture Industry Services Combined

Each symbol represents 10% of the country's total labor force (for countries where data is available).

800 Miles

800 Kilometers

Two-point Equidistant Projection

GLOBAL CONTAINER PORTS:

FACTS & FIGURES

Largest World Container Ports
(by volume – million tons; 2011 data)

Shanghai	590.4 MT
Singapore	531.2 FT
Tianjin	459.9 MT
Rotterdam	434.6 MT
Guangzhou	431.0 MT
Qingdao	372.0 MT
Ningbo	348.9 MT
Qinhuangdao	284.6 MT
Busan	281.5 RT

MT=Metric Ton; FT=Freight Ton; RT=Revenue Ton

Leading U.S. Waterborne Trade
Partners (exports by volume – metric
tons; 2012 data)

China	92,451,000
Japan	42,019,000
Mexico	38,962,000
Netherlands	28,514,000
Brazil	25,382,000
South Korea	23,514,000
Canada	22,092,000
Turkey	19,255,000
United Kingdom	16,772,000

Leading U.S. Waterborne Trade
Partners (imports by volume – metric
tons; 2012 data)

Saudi Arabia	69,519,000
Mexico	66,362,000
Venezuela	56,989,000
China	54,799,000
Canada	50,561,000
Russia	34,514,000
Brazil	31,660,000
Colombia	31,187,000

Largest Container Shipping Companies
(by world market share, 2013 data)

APM-Maersk (Denmark)	14.6%
Mediterranean Shipping Co. (Italy)	13.3%
CMA CGM (France)	8.5%
Evergreen Line (Taiwan)	4.8%
COSCO Container (China)	4.4%
Hapag-Lloyd (Germany)	4.1%
American Presidential Lines (USA)	3.6%
Hanjin Shipping (Korea/Germany)	3.5%
China Shipping Container Line	3.3%

East Asia Ports

Since the mid-20th century the world's economy has expanded to a truly global scale, made possible, in large part, by the growth of containerized shipping. The first container ship, a converted oil tanker, set sail from Newark, New Jersey, in 1956 carrying 58 containers. Today, almost 5,000 container vessels move manufactured goods cheaply and efficiently among ports around the world.

Container ships range in size up to 1,300 feet (396 m) long and 180 feet (55 m) wide—bigger than four football fields. The capacity of a container ship is measured in TEUs—a unit of measure equivalent to a 20-foot (6-m) standard container. A large container vessel can carry more than 10,000 20-foot containers, each loaded with as much as 100 tons (91 MT) of cargo. Container ports are equipped with giant cranes, more than 400 feet (122 m) tall and weighing as much as 2,000 tons (1,814 MT), that can move 30 to 40 containers on and off a ship each hour. With eight of the world's busiest container ports, containerized shipping has played an important role in Asia's economic boom.

⬤ **WAIGAOQIAO TERMINAL,** Shanghai Port's largest container terminal, appears as a colorful mosaic when viewed from above. Shanghai leads all container ports in tonnage handled, moving some 650 million tons (590 million MT) of goods and material each year.

⬤ **SHIPPING CONTAINERS** are stacked high above trucks moving through the busy port of Busan, which opened in 2004, 280 miles (450 km) southeast of Seoul, South Korea.

⬤ **OLD MEETS NEW** in the harbor of Ho Chi Minh City, Vietnam. Vendors steer their traditional sampan near a giant container vessel in this newly built Southeast Asian container port.

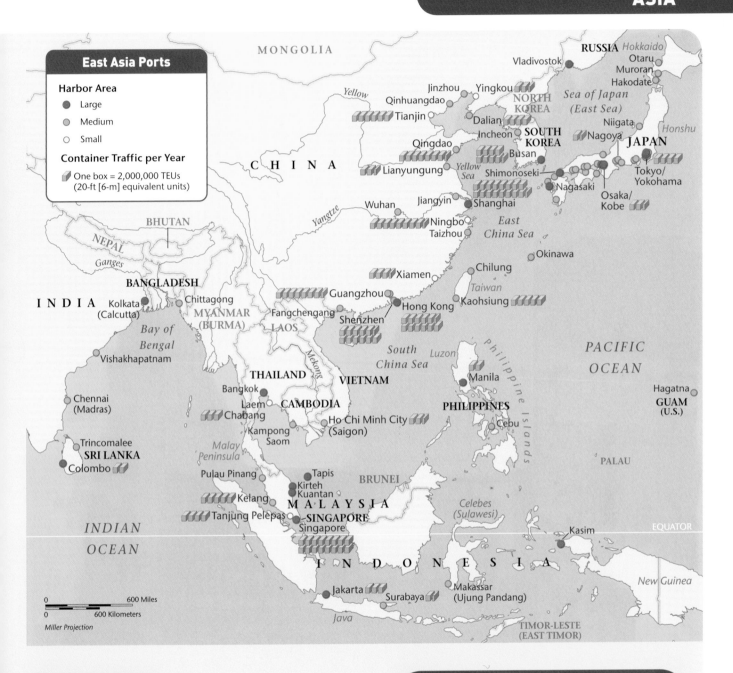

East Asia Ports

Harbor Area
- ● Large
- ● Medium
- ○ Small

Container Traffic per Year
One box = 2,000,000 TEUs
(20-ft [6-m] equivalent units)

MONGOLIA

RUSSIA   *Hokkaido*
Vladivostok   Otaru
Muroran
Jinzhou   Yingkou   Hakodate
Qinhuangdao   NORTH   *Sea of Japan*
Tianjin   KOREA   *(East Sea)*
Dalian   Niigata
Yellow   Incheon   SOUTH   Nagoya   *Honshu*
CHINA   KOREA   JAPAN
Qingdao   Busan   Tokyo/
Lianyungung   Shimoneseki   Yokohama
Yellow   Nagasaki   Osaka/
Sea   Kobe
Wuhan   Jiangyin
Yangtze   Shanghai   *East*
BHUTAN   Ningbo   *China Sea*
NEPAL   Taizhou
Ganges   Okinawa
BANGLADESH   Xiamen   Chilung
INDIA   Kolkata   *Taiwan*
(Calcutta)   Chittagong   Guangzhou   Kaohsiung
MYANMAR   Fangchengang   Hong Kong
(BURMA)   LAOS   Shenzhen
Bay of   South   *Luzon*   PACIFIC
Bengal   *China Sea*   OCEAN
Vishakhapatnam   Manila   Hagatna
THAILAND   VIETNAM   GUAM
Chennai   Bangkok   PHILIPPINES   (U.S.)
(Madras)   Laem   CAMBODIA
Chabang   Ho Chi Minh City   Cebu
Trincomalee   Kampong   (Saigon)
SRI LANKA   Saom   PALAU
Colombo   *Malay*
Peninsula   Tapis   BRUNEI   *Celebes*
Pulau Pinang   Kirteh   *(Sulawesi)*
Kelang   Kuantan   EQUATOR
INDIAN   Tanjung Pelepas   MALAYSIA   Kasim
OCEAN   SINGAPORE
Singapore   INDONESIA
New Guinea
Jakarta   Makassar
Surabaya   (Ujung Pandang)
Java   TIMOR-LESTE
(EAST TIMOR)

0   600 Miles
0   600 Kilometers
Miller Projection

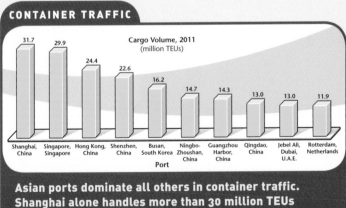

CONTAINER TRAFFIC

Cargo Volume, 2011
(million TEUs)

Port	million TEUs
Shanghai, China	31.7
Singapore, Singapore	29.9
Hong Kong, China	24.4
Shenzhen, China	22.6
Busan, South Korea	16.2
Ningbo-Zhoushan, China	14.7
Guangzhou Harbor, China	14.3
Qingdao, China	13.0
Jebel Ali, Dubai, U.A.E.	13.0
Rotterdam, Netherlands	11.9

Asian ports dominate all others in container traffic. Shanghai alone handles more than 30 million TEUs (20-foot-/6-meter-equivalent units) of cargo each year.

⬤ **CONTAINER CRANES** line this waterway in Hong Kong, one of the world's busiest international container ports.

THE CONTINENT:
AFRICA

Africa:
A View From Space

rom space, Africa appears divided into three regions: the north, dominated by the Sahara, the largest hot desert in the world; a central green band of rain forests and tropical grasslands; and more dry land to the south. Africa may actually be dividing: the Great Rift Valley, running from the Red Sea through the volcanic Afar Triangle to the southern lake district, may split apart the continent.

PHYSICAL

Land area 11,608,000 sq mi (30,065,000 sq km)	**Lowest point** Lake Assai, Djibouti -512 ft (-156 m)	**Largest lake** Victoria 26,800 sq mi (69,500 sq km)
Highest point Kilimanjaro, Tanzania 19,340 ft (5,895 m)	**Longest river** Nile 4,160 mi (6,695 km)	

POLITICAL

Population 1,099,579,000 **Number of independent countries** 54	**Largest country** Algeria 919,595 sq mi (2,381,741 sq km)	**Most populous country** Nigeria Pop. 173,615,000
	Smallest country Seychelles 176 sq mi (455 sq km)	**Least populous country** Seychelles Pop. 93,000

THE CONTINENT:
AFRICA

Africa

An elephant and calf walk in Amboseli National Park, Kenya.

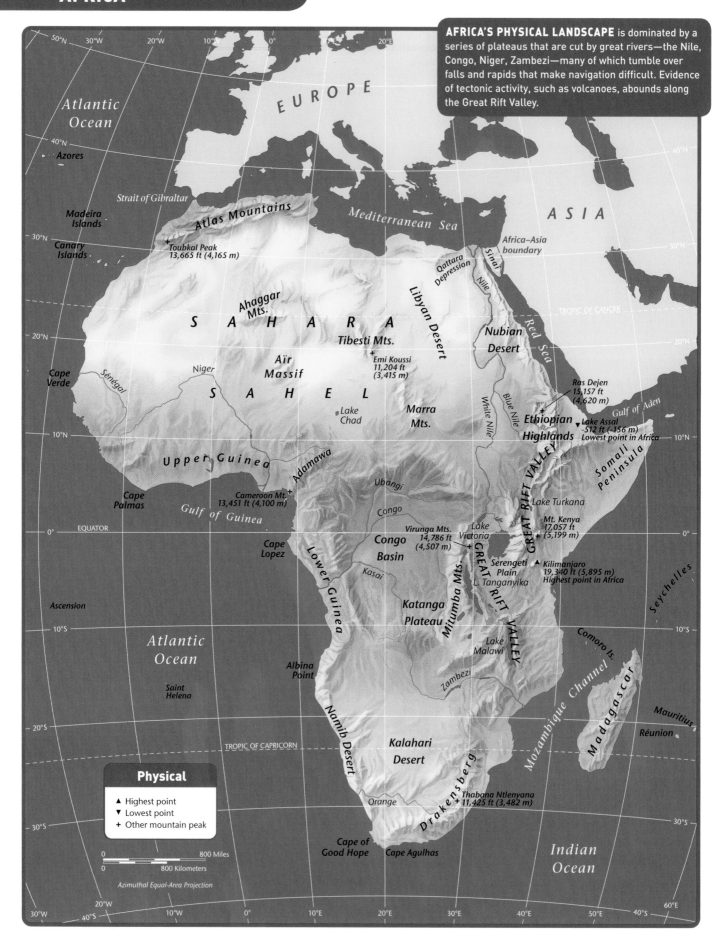

AFRICA'S PHYSICAL LANDSCAPE is dominated by a series of plateaus that are cut by great rivers—the Nile, Congo, Niger, Zambezi—many of which tumble over falls and rapids that make navigation difficult. Evidence of tectonic activity, such as volcanoes, abounds along the Great Rift Valley.

EUROPE

ASIA

Atlantic Ocean

Azores

Madeira Islands

Canary Islands

Cape Verde

Strait of Gibraltar

Atlas Mountains

Toubkal Peak
13,665 ft (4,165 m)

Mediterranean Sea

Africa–Asia boundary

Sinai

Qattara Depression

Nile

TROPIC OF CANCER

Ahaggar Mts.

S A H A R A

Libyan Desert

Nubian Desert

Red Sea

Tibesti Mts.

Aïr Massif

Emi Koussi
11,204 ft
(3,415 m)

S A H E L

Niger

Sénégal

Lake Chad

Marra Mts.

White Nile

Blue Nile

Ethiopian Highlands

Ras Dejen
15,157 ft
(4,620 m)

Lake Assal
-512 ft (-156 m)
Lowest point in Africa

Gulf of Aden

Somali Peninsula

Upper Guinea

Adamawa

Cape Palmas

Cameroon Mt.
13,451 ft (4,100 m)

Gulf of Guinea

Ubangi

Congo

Virunga Mts.
14,786 ft
(4,507 m)

Lake Victoria

Lake Turkana

GREAT RIFT VALLEY

Mt. Kenya
17,057 ft
(5,199 m)

EQUATOR

Cape Lopez

Lower Guinea

Kasai

Congo Basin

Serengeti Plain

L. Tanganyika

GREAT RIFT VALLEY

Kilimanjaro
19,340 ft (5,895 m)
Highest point in Africa

Seychelles

Ascension

Katanga Plateau

Mitumba Mts.

Lake Malawi

Comoro Is.

Mozambique Channel

Madagascar

Mauritius

Réunion

Atlantic Ocean

Albina Point

Saint Helena

Namib Desert

Zambezi

TROPIC OF CAPRICORN

Kalahari Desert

Drakensberg

Thabana Ntlenyana
11,425 ft (3,482 m)

Orange

Cape of Good Hope

Cape Agulhas

Indian Ocean

Physical

▲ Highest point
▼ Lowest point
+ Other mountain peak

0   800 Miles
0   800 Kilometers

Azimuthal Equal-Area Projection

THE CONTINENT:
AFRICA

BOUNDARIES DRAWN by colonial powers at the 1884 Berlin Conference cut across culture and language divisions. These imposed borders contribute to much of the turmoil that has plagued African countries as they have moved from the colonial era to independence.

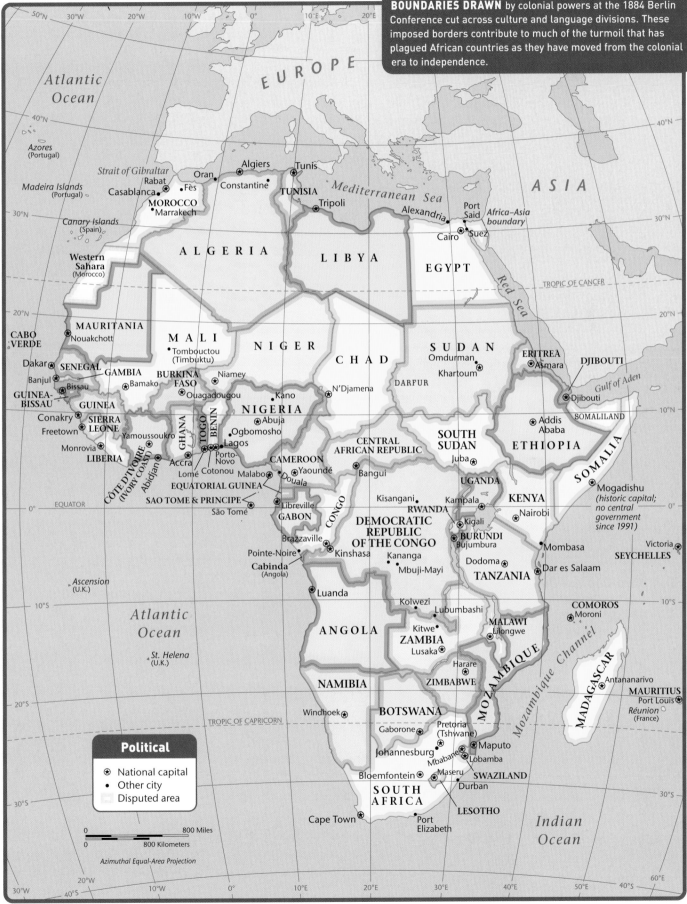

Atlantic Ocean

EUROPE

ASIA

Azores (Portugal)

Madeira Islands (Portugal)

Strait of Gibraltar
Rabat
Oran
Algiers
Tunis
Casablanca · Fès
MOROCCO
· Marrakech
Constantine
TUNISIA
Mediterranean Sea
Tripoli
Alexandria
Port Said
Africa–Asia boundary
Cairo · Suez

Canary Islands (Spain)

Western Sahara (Morocco)

ALGERIA
LIBYA
EGYPT

TROPIC OF CANCER

Red Sea

MAURITANIA
Nouakchott
MALI
· Tombouctou (Timbuktu)
NIGER
CHAD
SUDAN
Omdurman ·
Khartoum ·
ERITREA
· Asmara
DJIBOUTI
Gulf of Aden

CABO VERDE

Dakar ·
SENEGAL
GAMBIA
Banjul ·
Bamako ·
Niamey ·
BURKINA FASO
Ouagadougou ·
N'Djamena ·
DARFUR
SOUTH SUDAN
· Djibouti
SOMALILAND

Bissau
GUINEA-BISSAU
GUINEA
Conakry ·
SIERRA LEONE
Freetown ·
Monrovia ·
LIBERIA
Yamoussoukro ·
CÔTE D'IVOIRE (IVORY COAST)
Abidjan ·
Accra ·
GHANA
TOGO
BENIN
Lomé Cotonou
Porto-Novo
Lagos
· Ogbomosho
Kano ·
NIGERIA
· Abuja
CAMEROON
Malabo ·
Yaoundé ·
Douala ·
CENTRAL AFRICAN REPUBLIC
Bangui ·
Juba ·
ETHIOPIA
Addis Ababa ·
SOMALIA
· Mogadishu *(historic capital; no central government since 1991)*

SAO TOME & PRINCIPE
São Tomé ·
EQUATORIAL GUINEA
Libreville ·
GABON
CONGO
Brazzaville ·
Kisangani ·
DEMOCRATIC REPUBLIC OF THE CONGO
RWANDA
Kigali ·
BURUNDI
Bujumbura ·
UGANDA
Kampala ·
KENYA
Nairobi ·
· Mombasa

EQUATOR

Pointe-Noire ·
Kinshasa ·
Kananga ·
· Mbuji-Mayi
Dodoma ·
TANZANIA
Dar es Salaam ·
SEYCHELLES
Victoria ·

Cabinda *(Angola)*

Luanda ·
Kolwezi ·
Lubumbashi ·
Kitwe ·
ZAMBIA
Lusaka ·
MALAWI
Lilongwe ·
COMOROS
· Moroni

ANGOLA

Ascension (U.K.)

Atlantic Ocean

St. Helena (U.K.)

Harare ·
ZIMBABWE
MOZAMBIQUE
Mozambique Channel
MADAGASCAR
Antananarivo ·
MAURITIUS
Port Louis ·
Réunion (France)

NAMIBIA
BOTSWANA
Windhoek ·
TROPIC OF CAPRICORN
Gaborone ·
Pretoria (Tshwane) ·
Maputo ·
Johannesburg ·
Mbabane ·
Lobamba ·
Bloemfontein ·
Maseru ·
SWAZILAND
SOUTH AFRICA
LESOTHO
Durban ·
Cape Town ·
Port Elizabeth ·

Indian Ocean

Political

- ⊛ National capital
- · Other city
- ☐ Disputed area

0 ———— 800 Miles
0 ———— 800 Kilometers

Azimuthal Equal-Area Projection

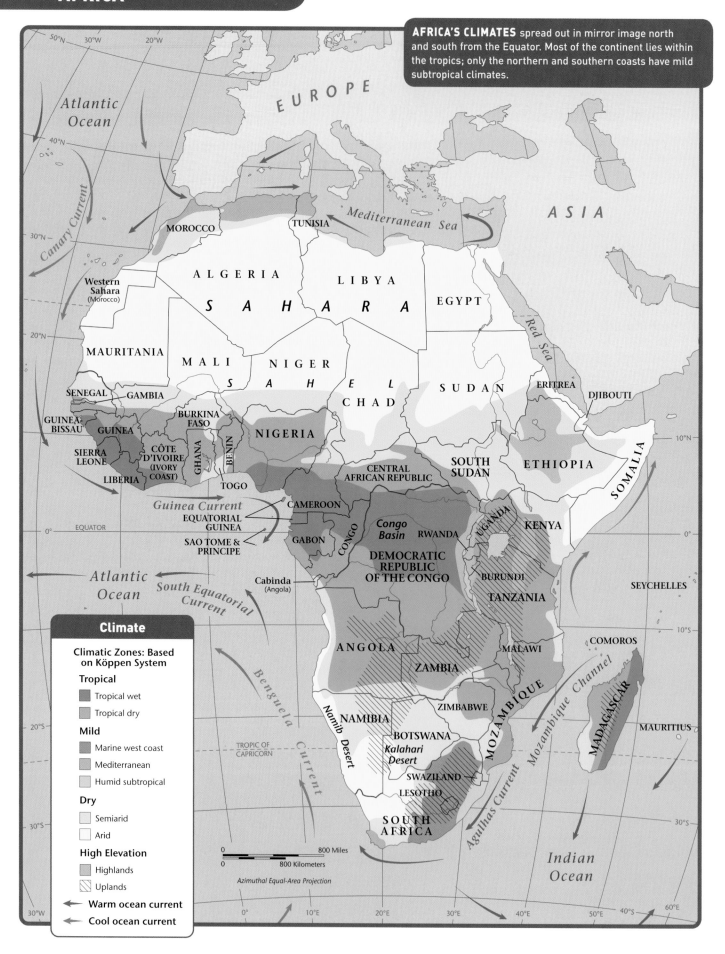

AFRICA'S CLIMATES spread out in mirror image north and south from the Equator. Most of the continent lies within the tropics; only the northern and southern coasts have mild subtropical climates.

Climate

Climatic Zones: Based on Köppen System

Tropical
- Tropical wet
- Tropical dry

Mild
- Marine west coast
- Mediterranean
- Humid subtropical

Dry
- Semiarid
- Arid

High Elevation
- Highlands
- Uplands

← Warm ocean current
← Cool ocean current

Map labels:

EUROPE

Atlantic Ocean

ASIA

Canary Current

Mediterranean Sea

MOROCCO
TUNISIA
Western Sahara (Morocco)
ALGERIA
LIBYA
EGYPT
Red Sea
SAHARA
MAURITANIA
MALI
NIGER
SAHEL
CHAD
SUDAN
ERITREA
DJIBOUTI
SENEGAL
GAMBIA
GUINEA-BISSAU
GUINEA
BURKINA FASO
NIGERIA
SOUTH SUDAN
ETHIOPIA
SOMALIA
SIERRA LEONE
CÔTE D'IVOIRE (IVORY COAST)
GHANA
BENIN
TOGO
CENTRAL AFRICAN REPUBLIC
LIBERIA
CAMEROON
EQUATORIAL GUINEA
SAO TOME & PRINCIPE
GABON
CONGO
Congo Basin
RWANDA
UGANDA
KENYA
EQUATOR
Guinea Current
Atlantic Ocean
South Equatorial Current
Cabinda (Angola)
DEMOCRATIC REPUBLIC OF THE CONGO
BURUNDI
TANZANIA
SEYCHELLES
COMOROS
Benguela Current
ANGOLA
ZAMBIA
MALAWI
MOZAMBIQUE
Mozambique Channel
MADAGASCAR
MAURITIUS
ZIMBABWE
NAMIBIA
Namib Desert
BOTSWANA
Kalahari Desert
TROPIC OF CAPRICORN
SWAZILAND
Agulhas Current
LESOTHO
SOUTH AFRICA
Indian Ocean

0   800 Miles
0   800 Kilometers
Azimuthal Equal-Area Projection

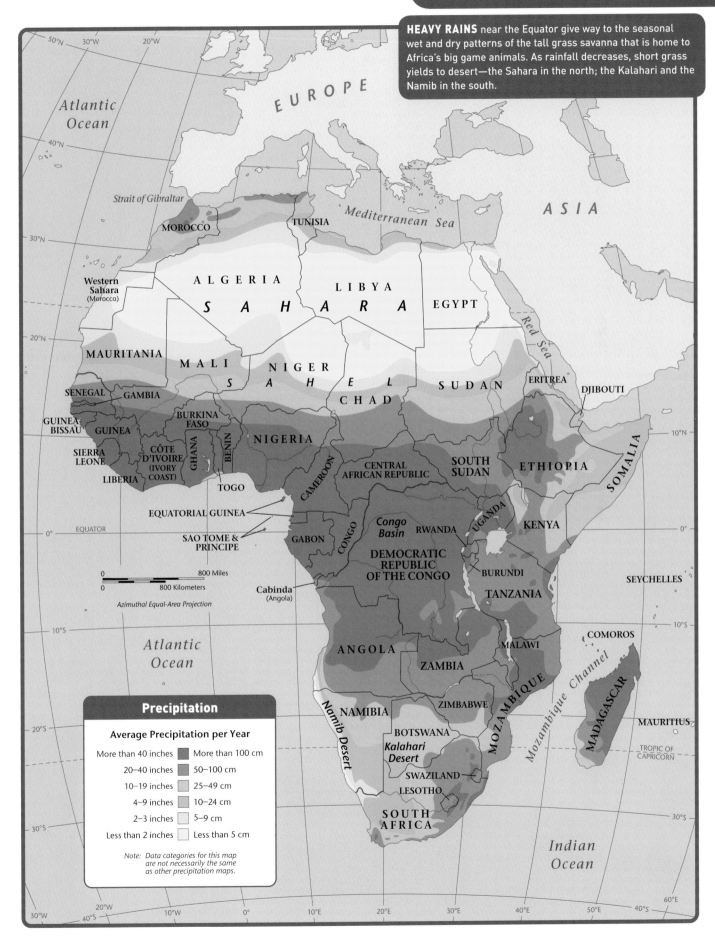

HEAVY RAINS near the Equator give way to the seasonal wet and dry patterns of the tall grass savanna that is home to Africa's big game animals. As rainfall decreases, short grass yields to desert—the Sahara in the north; the Kalahari and the Namib in the south.

Precipitation

Average Precipitation per Year

More than 40 inches	More than 100 cm
20–40 inches	50–100 cm
10–19 inches	25–49 cm
4–9 inches	10–24 cm
2–3 inches	5–9 cm
Less than 2 inches	Less than 5 cm

Note: Data categories for this map are not necessarily the same as other precipitation maps.

0 — 800 Miles
0 — 800 Kilometers
Azimuthal Equal-Area Projection

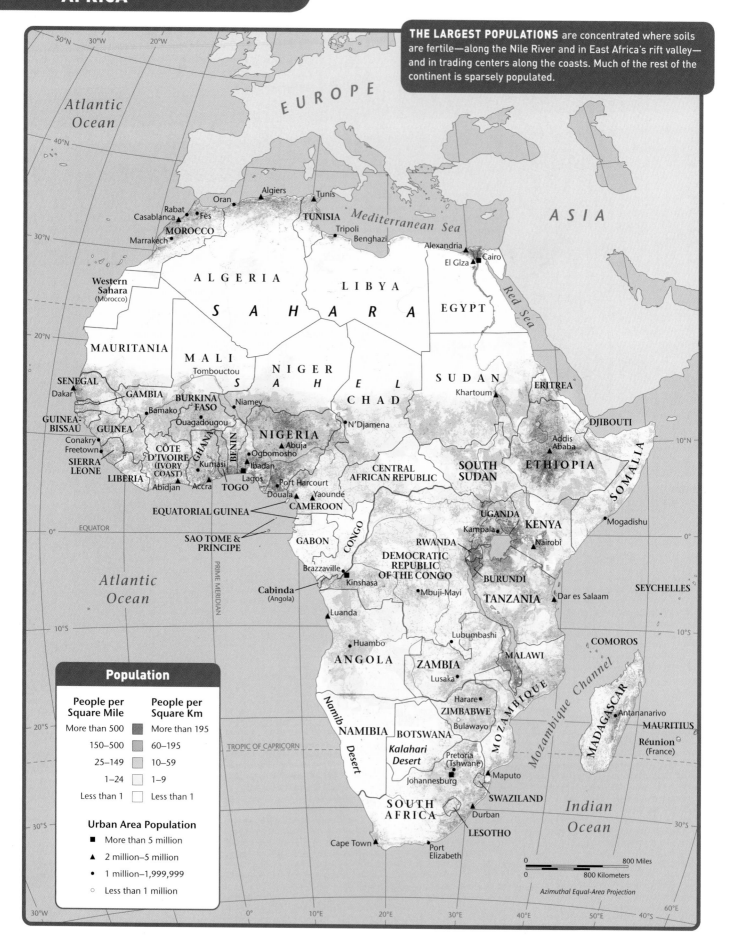

THE LARGEST POPULATIONS are concentrated where soils are fertile—along the Nile River and in East Africa's rift valley—and in trading centers along the coasts. Much of the rest of the continent is sparsely populated.

Population

People per Square Mile / **People per Square Km**

People per Square Mile	People per Square Km
More than 500	More than 195
150–500	60–195
25–149	10–59
1–24	1–9
Less than 1	Less than 1

Urban Area Population

- ■ More than 5 million
- ▲ 2 million–5 million
- • 1 million–1,999,999
- ○ Less than 1 million

Azimuthal Equal-Area Projection

800 Miles
800 Kilometers

AFRICA'S ECONOMY depends heavily on the export of cash crops, such as coffee, cacao (chocolate), peanuts, and palm oil; of minerals, including precious metals, such as gold and platinum; of gemstones, especially diamonds; and of industrial metals, such as chromite and manganese. Manufacturing is limited.

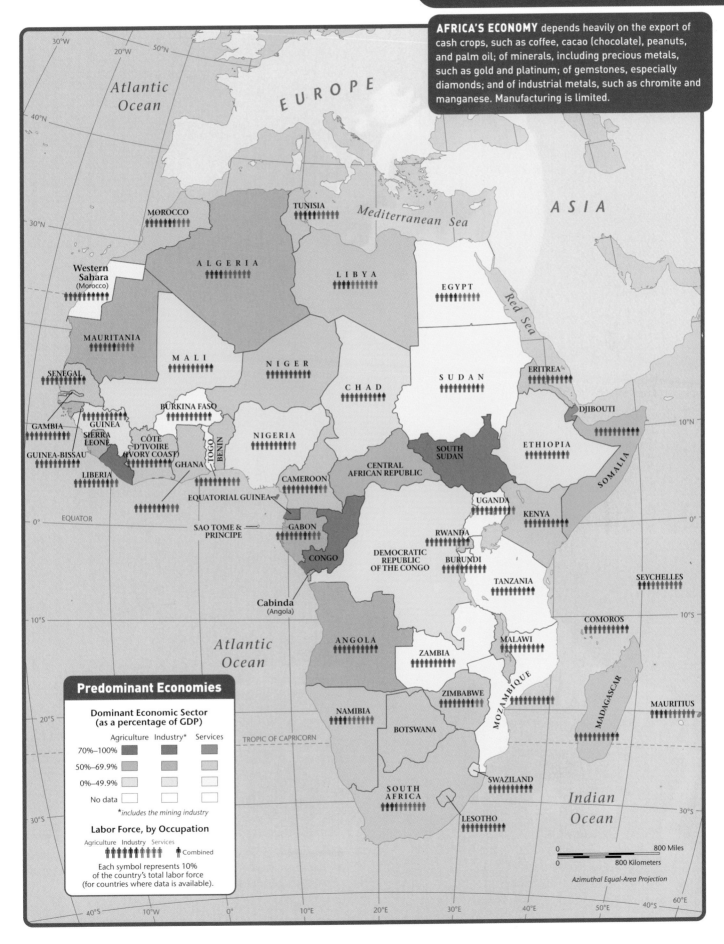

Predominant Economies

Dominant Economic Sector
(as a percentage of GDP)

	Agriculture	Industry*	Services
70%–100%			
50%–69.9%			
0%–49.9%			
No data			

*includes the mining industry

Labor Force, by Occupation

Agriculture Industry Services   Combined

Each symbol represents 10% of the country's total labor force (for countries where data is available).

0   800 Miles
0   800 Kilometers

Azimuthal Equal-Area Projection

PROTECTED AREAS:

FACTS & FIGURES

Annual forest loss (2000–2010):
Global: 32,123,700 acres (13 million ha)

Africa: 8,401,583 acres (3.4 million ha)

Main causes: subsistence and commercial agriculture, logging, fuelwood collection

Highest annual rate of loss (2005–2010):

Togo	5.75%
Nigeria	4.00%
Uganda	2.72%
Ghana	2.19%

Threatened species (2013):

Mammals	739
Birds	744
Reptiles	355
Fish	1,906
Plants	2,474

Selected species at risk:
African elephants, black rhinoceros, eastern chimpanzees, gazelles, hippopotamus, lemurs, mountain gorillas, mountain zebras

Land protected in Africa (2010):
1,086,186 square miles (2,813,208 sq km)

Land protected in North Africa (2010): 4.0%

Land protected in Sub-Saharan Africa (2010): 11.8%

Countries with highest percent of land protected (2010):

Zambia	36.04%
Botswana	30.93%
Zimbabwe	28.01%
Tanzania	27.53%

Protected Areas

Africa is home to many different animals. Some are familiar, such as the giraffe and rhinoceros; others are rare. All are part of Earth's valuable storehouse of biodiversity, but many are at risk due to a variety of pressures. Natural changes, such as periodic drought, may put stress on both plant and animal populations, but human activity is the main threat. Africa's human population is growing on average at a rate of 2.6 percent each year. Converting land for agricultural use, hunting animals for food, and cutting trees for fuel, as well as expanding commercial logging and building roads, have led to loss of natural habitat for many of Africa's animals. Some, such as the mountain gorilla, are even at risk of extinction.

To reverse this trend of biodiversity loss, many countries have created protected areas (see map at right), which include nature reserves, wilderness areas, and national parks. Protected areas allow animals to live in a natural environment. They also provide a source of income for African countries, many of which are very poor, as tourists come on photo safaris to view these unique animals.

ENDANGERED. A silverback mountain gorilla in Rwanda watches intently. Native to the Virunga Mountains of central Africa, fewer than 700 mountain gorillas remain in the wild.

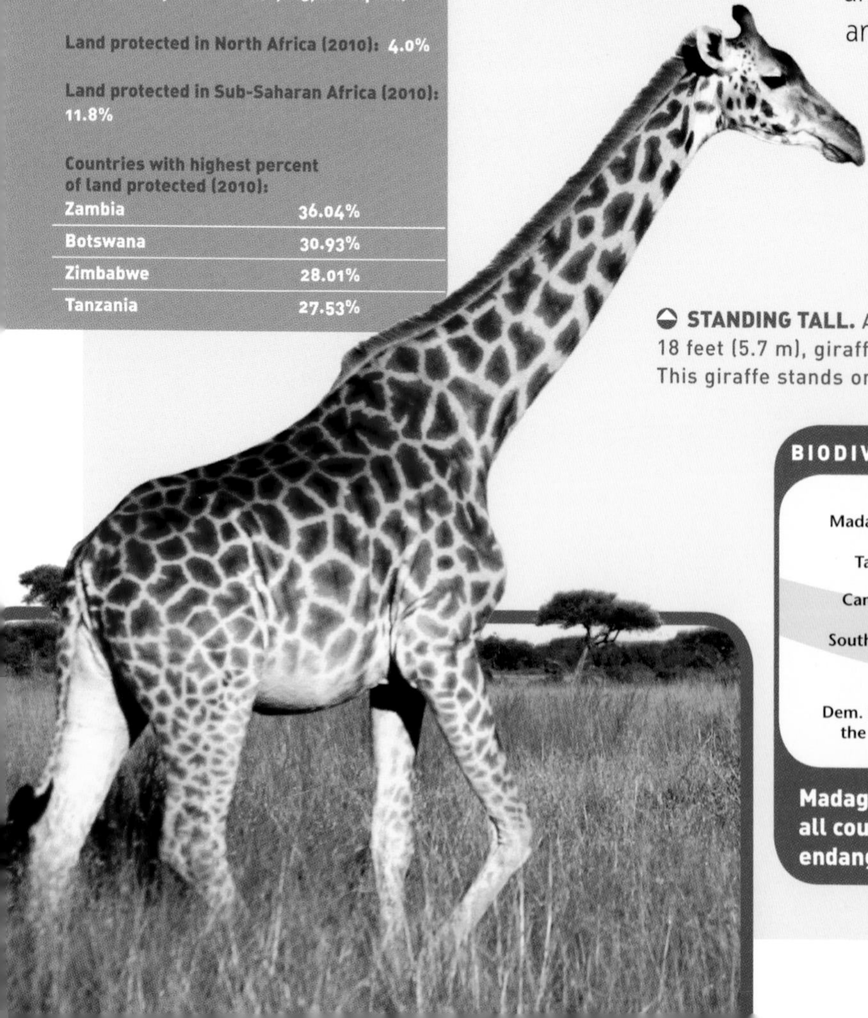

STANDING TALL. At an average height of more than 18 feet (5.7 m), giraffes are the world's tallest mammal. This giraffe stands on the grassy plain of Kenya's Masai Mara.

BIODIVERSITY THREATENED

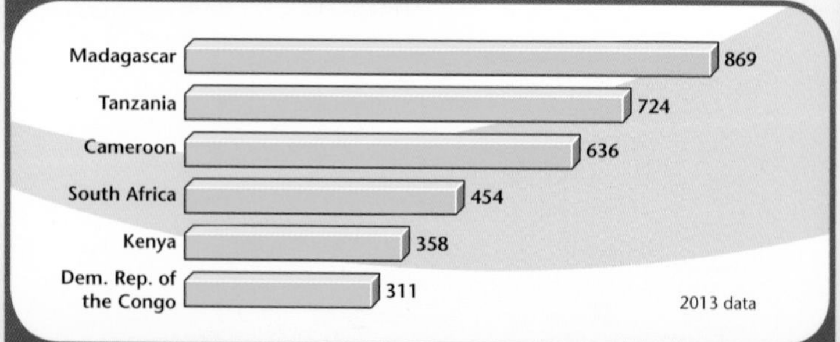

Madagascar	869
Tanzania	724
Cameroon	636
South Africa	454
Kenya	358
Dem. Rep. of the Congo	311

2013 data

Madagascar, an island country off the southeast coast, leads all countries in Africa in number of species that are critically endangered, endangered, or vulnerable.

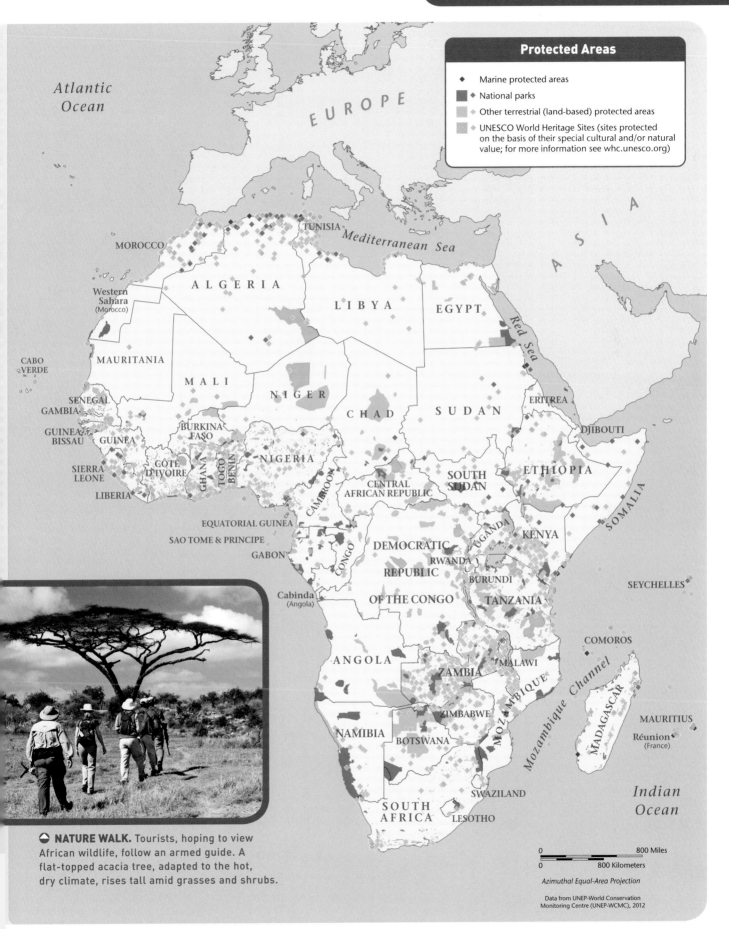

Atlantic Ocean

EUROPE

Protected Areas

- ◆ Marine protected areas
- ◆ National parks
- ◆ Other terrestrial (land-based) protected areas
- ◆ UNESCO World Heritage Sites (sites protected on the basis of their special cultural and/or natural value; for more information see whc.unesco.org)

ASIA

Mediterranean Sea

MOROCCO
TUNISIA
ALGERIA
LIBYA
EGYPT
Western Sahara (Morocco)
Red Sea
CABO VERDE
MAURITANIA
MALI
NIGER
CHAD
SUDAN
ERITREA
SENEGAL
GAMBIA
BURKINA FASO
NIGERIA
DJIBOUTI
GUINEA BISSAU
GUINEA
CÔTE D'IVOIRE
GHANA
TOGO
BENIN
CAMEROON
CENTRAL AFRICAN REPUBLIC
SOUTH SUDAN
ETHIOPIA
SIERRA LEONE
LIBERIA
EQUATORIAL GUINEA
SAO TOME & PRINCIPE
GABON
CONGO
DEMOCRATIC REPUBLIC OF THE CONGO
UGANDA
RWANDA
BURUNDI
KENYA
SOMALIA
SEYCHELLES
Cabinda (Angola)
TANZANIA
COMOROS
ANGOLA
ZAMBIA
MALAWI
MADAGASCAR
MAURITIUS
Réunion (France)
NAMIBIA
ZIMBABWE
BOTSWANA
MOZAMBIQUE
Mozambique Channel
SWAZILAND
SOUTH AFRICA
LESOTHO

Indian Ocean

🔺 **NATURE WALK.** Tourists, hoping to view African wildlife, follow an armed guide. A flat-topped acacia tree, adapted to the hot, dry climate, rises tall amid grasses and shrubs.

0 — 800 Miles
0 — 800 Kilometers

Azimuthal Equal-Area Projection

Data from UNEP-World Conservation Monitoring Centre (UNEP-WCMC), 2012

THE REGION:
AUSTRALIA & OCEANIA

Australia:
A View From Space

Smallest of Earth's great landmasses, Australia is the only one that is both a continent and a country. It is part of the greater region of Oceania, which includes New Zealand, the eastern part of New Guinea, and hundreds of smaller islands scattered across the Pacific Ocean. Although Hawai'i is politically part of the United States, geographically and culturally it is part of Oceania.

The opera house in Sydney, Australia

Australia & Oceania

PHYSICAL			POLITICAL		
Area and population totals are for the independent countries in the region only.	Highest point **Mount Wilhelm, Papua New Guinea** 14,793 ft (4,509 m)	Longest river **Murray-Darling, Australia** 2,310 mi (3,718 km)	Population 37,916,000	Largest country **Australia** 2,970,000 sq mi (7,692,000 sq km)	Most populous country **Australia** Pop. 23,106,000
			Number of independent countries 14	Smallest country **Nauru** 8 sq mi (21 sq km)	Least populous country **Nauru** Pop. 11,000
Land area 3,278,062 sq mi (8,490,180 sq km)	Lowest point **Lake Eyre, Australia** -52 ft (-16 m)	Largest lake **Lake Eyre, Australia** 3,430 sq mi (8,884 sq km)			

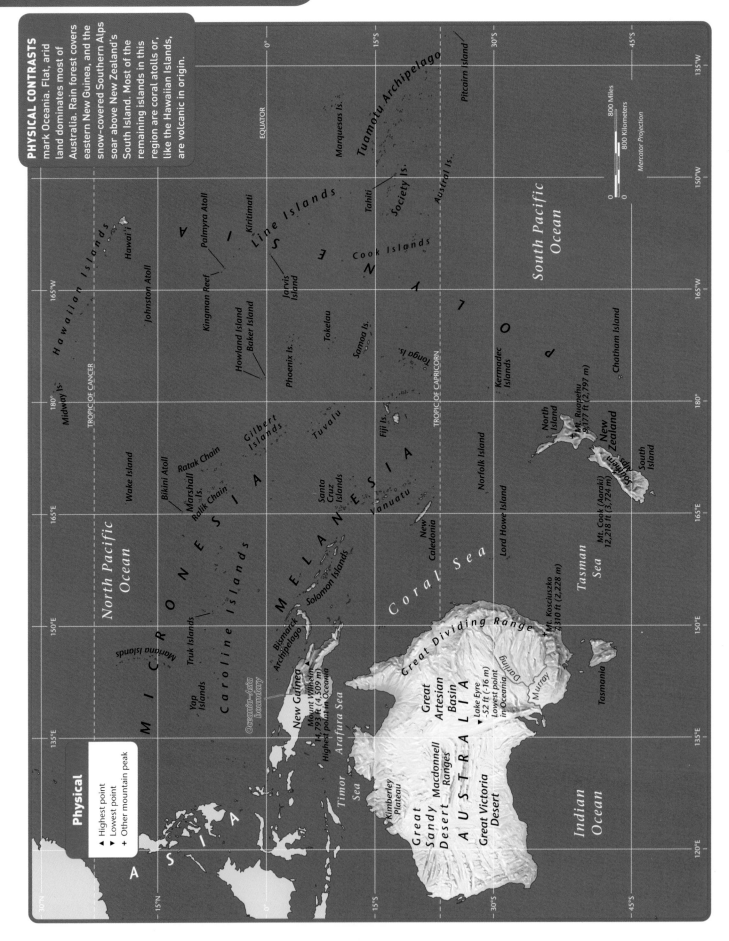

PHYSICAL CONTRASTS mark Oceania. Flat, arid land dominates most of Australia. Rain forest covers eastern New Guinea, and the snow-covered Southern Alps soar above New Zealand's South Island. Most of the remaining islands in this region are coral atolls or, like the Hawaiian Islands, are volcanic in origin.

Physical
- ◄ Highest point
- ► Lowest point
- + Other mountain peak

Mercator Projection

800 Miles
800 Kilometers

0°

EQUATOR

TROPIC OF CANCER

TROPIC OF CAPRICORN

South Pacific Ocean

North Pacific Ocean

Indian Ocean

Tasman Sea

Coral Sea

Arafura Sea

Timor Sea

MICRONESIA

MELANESIA

POLYNESIA

Tuamotu Archipelago

Pitcairn Island

Marquesas Is.

Society Is.
Tahiti
Austral Is.

Line Islands
Kiritimati
Palmyra Atoll

Cook Islands

Jarvis Island

Kingman Reef

Howland Island
Baker Island

Phoenix Is.

Tokelau

Samoa Is.

Tonga Is.

Tuvalu

Fiji Is.

Gilbert Islands

Wake Island

Bikini Atoll
Ratak Chain
Marshall Is.
Ralik Chain

Hawaiian Islands
Hawai'i
Johnston Atoll
Midway Is.

Mariana Islands

Yap Islands

Truk Islands

Caroline Islands

Santa Cruz Islands

Vanuatu

New Caledonia

Solomon Islands

Bismarck Archipelago

New Guinea
Mount Wilhelm
14,793 ft (4,509 m)
Highest point in Oceania

Oceania-Asia Boundary

Norfolk Island

Kermadec Islands

Lord Howe Island

New Zealand
North Island
Mt. Ruapehu
9,177 ft (2,797 m)
South Island
Southern Alps
Mt. Cook (Aoraki)
12,218 ft (3,724 m)

Chatham Island

Tasmania

AUSTRALIA
Great Dividing Range
Mt. Kosciuszko
7,310 ft (2,228 m)

Great Artesian Basin

Lake Eyre
-52 ft (-16 m)
Lowest point in Oceania

Darling
Murray

Great Sandy Desert
Macdonnell Ranges

Kimberley Plateau

Great Victoria Desert

ASIA

30°N
15°N
0°
15°S
30°S
45°S

135°E
150°E
165°E
180°
165°W
150°W
135°W
120°E

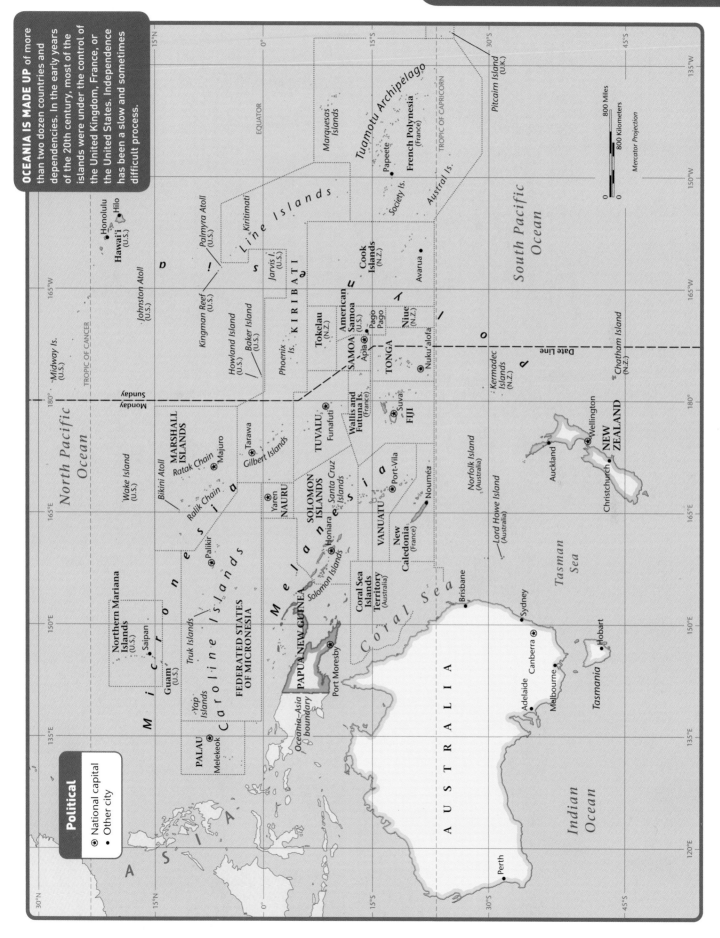

OCEANIA IS MADE UP of more than two dozen countries and dependencies. In the early years of the 20th century, most of the islands were under the control of the United Kingdom, France, or the United States. Independence has been a slow and sometimes difficult process.

Political
- ⊛ National capital
- • Other city

15°N

0°

EQUATOR

TROPIC OF CANCER

TROPIC OF CAPRICORN

Mercator Projection

800 Miles
800 Kilometers

North Pacific Ocean

South Pacific Ocean

Indian Ocean

Tasman Sea

Coral Sea

Date Line

Monday Sunday

Honolulu
Hilo
Hawai'i (U.S.)

Midway Is. (U.S.)

Wake Island (U.S.)

Johnston Atoll (U.S.)

Palmyra Atoll (U.S.)

Kingman Reef (U.S.)

Kiritimati

Line Islands

Jarvis I. (U.S.)

Howland Island (U.S.)
Baker Island (U.S.)

Phoenix Is.

KIRIBATI

Tokelau (N.Z.)

American Samoa (U.S.)
Pago Pago

SAMOA
Apia

Niue (N.Z.)

TONGA
Nuku'alofa

Marquesas Islands

Tuamotu Archipelago

Papeete
French Polynesia (France)

Society Is.

Austral Is.

Cook Islands (N.Z.)
Avarua

Pitcairn Island (U.K.)

Chatham Island (N.Z.)

NEW ZEALAND
Wellington
Auckland
Christchurch

Kermadec Islands (N.Z.)

Norfolk Island (Australia)

Lord Howe Island (Australia)

Wallis and Futuna Is. (France)
Suva
FIJI

TUVALU
Funafuti

SOLOMON ISLANDS
Honiara
Santa Cruz Islands

VANUATU
Port-Vila

New Caledonia (France)
Nouméa

Northern Mariana Islands (U.S.)
Saipan

Guam (U.S.)

Truk Islands

MARSHALL ISLANDS
Ratak Chain
Majuro
Bikini Atoll
Ralik Chain

Tarawa

Gilbert Islands

NAURU
Yaren

Caroline Islands

Yap Islands

FEDERATED STATES OF MICRONESIA
Palikir

PALAU
Melekeok

Micronesia

Melanesia

Polynesia

PAPUA NEW GUINEA
Port Moresby

Solomon Islands

Coral Sea Islands Territory (Australia)

Oceania-Asia boundary

ASIA

AUSTRALIA

Brisbane
Sydney
Canberra ⊛
Adelaide
Melbourne
Hobart
Tasmania

Perth

South Pacific Ocean

180°

165°E

150°E

135°E

120°E

165°W

150°W

135°W

30°N

15°N

0°

15°S

30°S

45°S

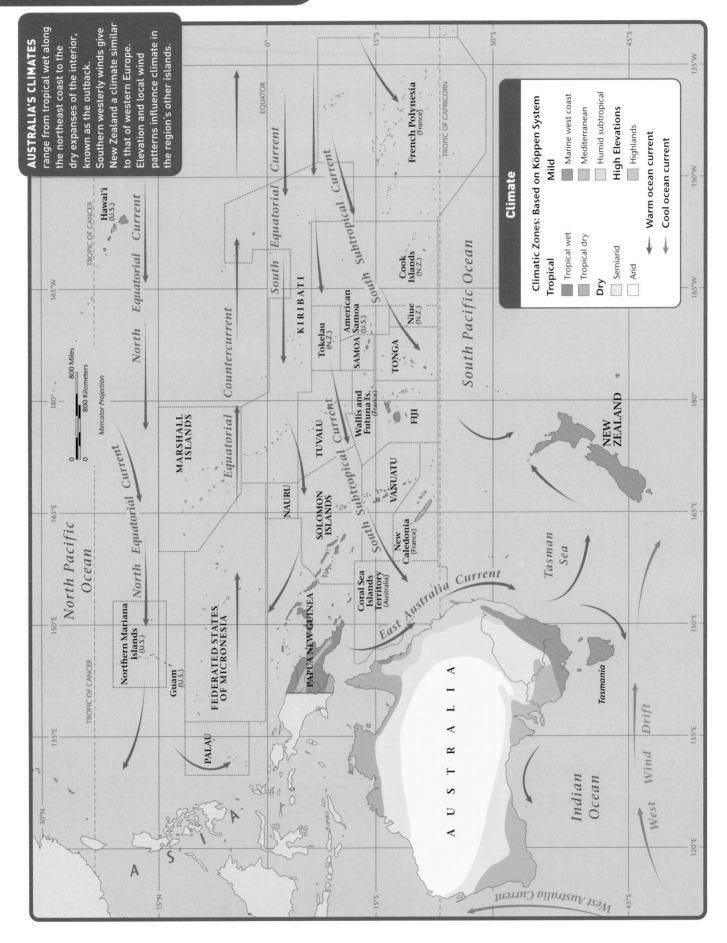

Climate

Climatic Zones: Based on Köppen System

Tropical
- Tropical wet
- Tropical dry

Dry
- Semiarid
- Arid

Mild
- Marine west coast
- Mediterranean
- Humid subtropical

High Elevations
- Highlands

→ Warm ocean current
→ Cool ocean current

800 Miles
800 Kilometers
Mercator Projection

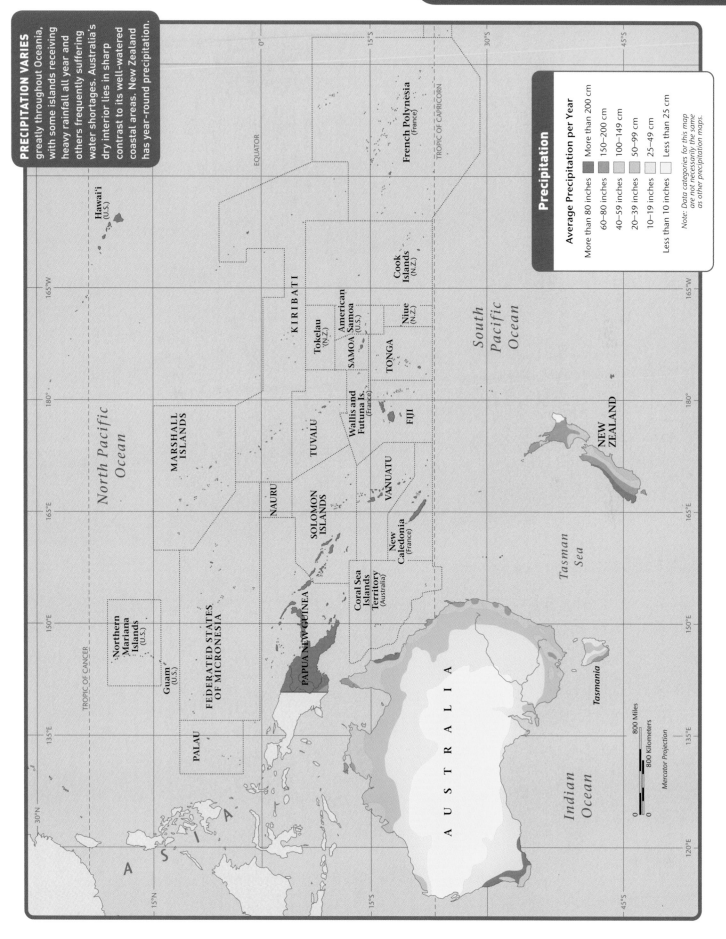

PRECIPITATION VARIES greatly throughout Oceania, with some islands receiving heavy rainfall all year and others frequently suffering water shortages. Australia's dry interior lies in sharp contrast to its well-watered coastal areas. New Zealand has year-round precipitation.

Precipitation

Average Precipitation per Year

■	More than 80 inches	More than 200 cm
■	60–80 inches	150–200 cm
■	40–59 inches	100–149 cm
■	20–39 inches	50–99 cm
■	10–19 inches	25–49 cm
□	Less than 10 inches	Less than 25 cm

Note: Data categories for this map are not necessarily the same as other precipitation maps.

Hawai'i (U.S.)

North Pacific Ocean

MARSHALL ISLANDS

KIRIBATI

Tokelau (N.Z.)

American Samoa (U.S.)

SAMOA

Niue (N.Z.)

TONGA

French Polynesia (France)

Cook Islands (N.Z.)

South Pacific Ocean

TUVALU

Wallis and Futuna Is. (France)

FIJI

NAURU

SOLOMON ISLANDS

VANUATU

New Caledonia (France)

NEW ZEALAND

Tasman Sea

Northern Mariana Islands (U.S.)

Guam (U.S.)

FEDERATED STATES OF MICRONESIA

PAPUA NEW GUINEA

Coral Sea Islands Territory (Australia)

PALAU

A S I A

AUSTRALIA

Tasmania

Indian Ocean

EQUATOR

TROPIC OF CAPRICORN

TROPIC OF CANCER

800 Miles

800 Kilometers

Mercator Projection

THE REGION:
AUSTRALIA & OCEANIA

PEOPLE OF EUROPEAN ancestry make up the majority of the population in Australia and New Zealand, but each country has a significant indigenous population—Aborigines and Maoris (Polynesians), respectively. The various island groups are populated by Polynesians, Melanesians, and Micronesians, as well as by immigrants primarily from Europe and Asia.

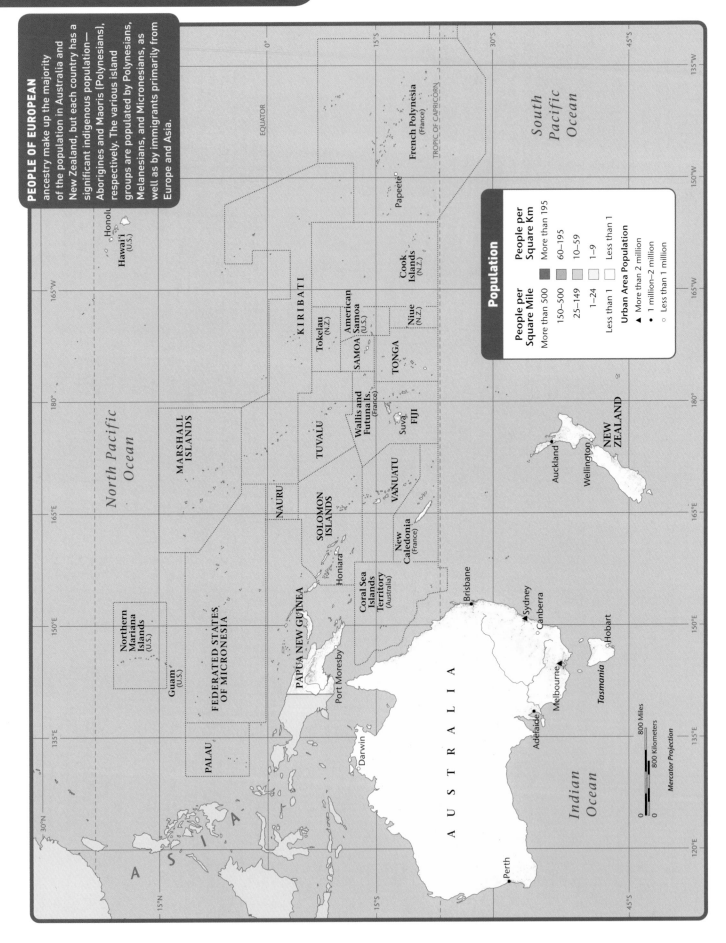

Population

People per Square Mile
- More than 500
- 150–500
- 25–149
- 1–24
- Less than 1

People per Square Km
- More than 195
- 60–195
- 10–59
- 1–9
- Less than 1

Urban Area Population
- ▲ More than 2 million
- ● 1 million–2 million
- ○ Less than 1 million

Mercator Projection

0   800 Miles
0   800 Kilometers

PRIMARY ECONOMIC products make up much of the market in Oceania. New Zealand and Australia account for more than two-thirds of world wool exports and more than one-fifth of beef exports. Plantation agriculture, fishing, tourism, or mining form the economic base in most of the small island countries. For example, New Caledonia is a leading exporter of nickel, and Fiji exports sugar and gold.

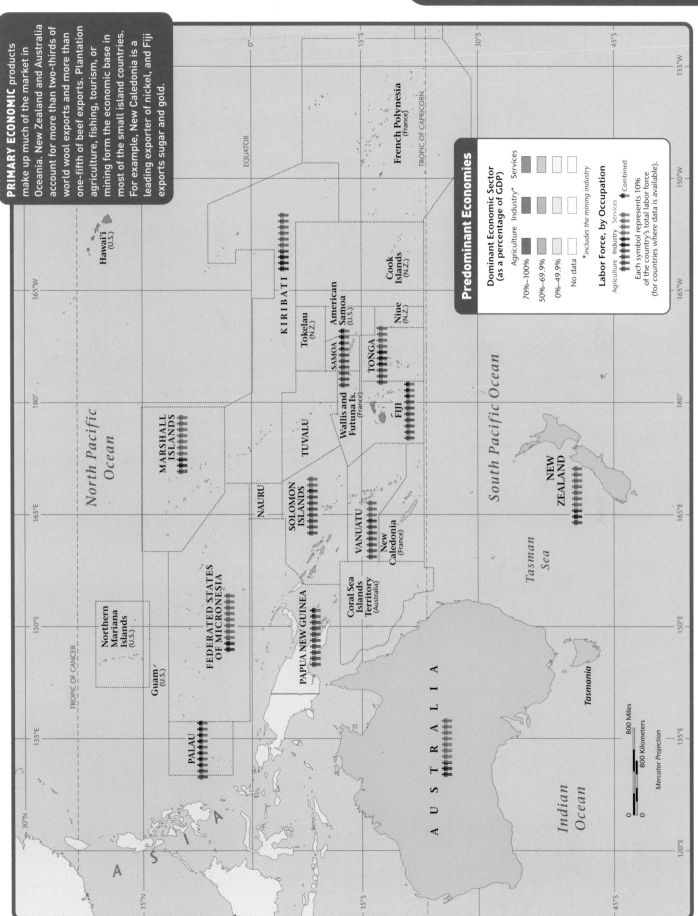

Predominant Economies

Dominant Economic Sector
(as a percentage of GDP)

Agriculture   Industry*   Services

- 70%–100%
- 50%–69.9%
- 0%–49.9%
- No data

*Includes the mining industry

Labor Force, by Occupation

Agriculture   Industry   Services   Combined

Each symbol represents 10% of the country's total labor force (for countries where data is available).

CORAL REEFS:

SELECTED FACTS

Most coral reefs are between 5,000 and 10,000 years old, but some may have begun growing as much as 50 million years ago.

TYPES OF REEFS

FRINGING REEFS form near coastlines of islands and continents.

BARRIER REEFS form parallel to coastlines but are separated by deep lagoons.

ATOLLS form as rings of coral surrounding protected lagoons.

PATCH REEFS grow from a continental shelf to form isolated reefs.

GROWING CONDITIONS

Corals grow best in

- the **TROPICS** (30°N to 30°S) where **SUNLIGHT** is consistent year-round.
- **SHALLOW, WARM WATER,** ranging in temperature from 70° to 85°F (21° to 29°C).
- **CLEAR, CLEAN WATER** that is free of pollutants or sediments that may block sunlight or smother the coral.
- **SALTWATER** where there is a constant salt-to-water ratio.

Great Barrier Reef

Stretching like intricate necklaces along the edges of landmasses in the warm ocean waters of the tropics, coral reefs form one of nature's most complex ecosystems. Corals are tiny marine animals that thrive in shallow coastal waters of the tropics. One type of coral, called a "hard coral," produces a limestone skeleton. When the tiny animal dies, its stone-like skeleton is left behind. The accumulation of millions of these skeletons over thousands of years has produced the large reef formations found in many coastal waters of the tropics.

Most coral reefs are found between 30 degrees N and 30 degrees S latitude in waters with a temperature between 70 and 85 degrees Fahrenheit (21° and 29°C). It is estimated that Earth's coral reefs cover 110,000 square miles (284,900 sq km). Coral reefs are important because they form a habitat for marine animals such as fish, sea turtles, lobsters, and starfish. They also protect fragile coastlines from damaging ocean waves and may be a source of valuable medicines.

The world's largest coral reef, the Great Barrier Reef, lies off the northeast coast of Australia (see large map). This reef, which is made up of more than 400 different types of coral and is home to more than 1,500 species of fish, is a popular tourist destination. People visit to snorkel and dive along the reef and view the great diversity of marine life living among the corals.

◒ **ANEMONE FISH** swim among the waving polyps of one of the reef's sea anemones. These fish are specially adapted to live safely among the venom-filled tentacles that can inject a paralyzing neurotoxin into unsuspecting prey when disturbed.

◖ **BRILLIANTLY COLORED CORALS** and the fish that live among them attract divers and snorkelers to the Great Barrier Reef every year.

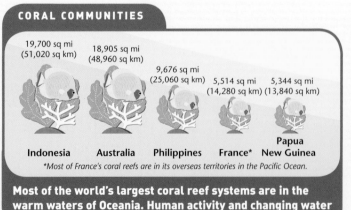

CORAL COMMUNITIES

19,700 sq mi (51,020 sq km)	18,905 sq mi (48,960 sq km)	9,676 sq mi (25,060 sq km)	5,514 sq mi (14,280 sq km)	5,344 sq mi (13,840 sq km)
Indonesia	Australia	Philippines	France*	Papua New Guinea

*Most of France's coral reefs are in its overseas territories in the Pacific Ocean.

Most of the world's largest coral reef systems are in the warm waters of Oceania. Human activity and changing water temperatures put some reefs at risk.

THE REGION:
AUSTRALIA & OCEANIA

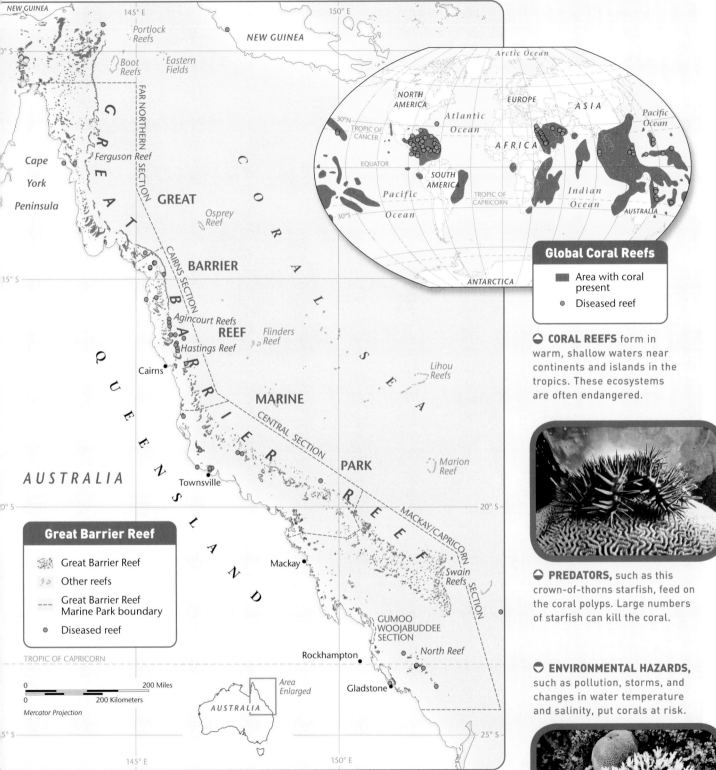

NEW GUINEA
145° E
Portlock Reefs
NEW GUINEA
150° E

Boot Reefs
Eastern Fields

GREAT

FAR NORTHERN SECTION

Cape York Peninsula
Ferguson Reef

GREAT

C O R A L

Osprey Reef

15° S

BARRIER

CAIRNS SECTION

Agincourt Reefs
REEF
Flinders Reef
Hastings Reef
Cairns

S E A

Lihou Reefs

MARINE

CENTRAL SECTION

PARK

Marion Reef

AUSTRALIA

Q U E E N S L A N D

Townsville

20° S

MACKAY/CAPRICORN

Great Barrier Reef

- Great Barrier Reef
- Other reefs
- Great Barrier Reef Marine Park boundary
- Diseased reef

Mackay

Swain Reefs

SECTION

GUMOO WOOJABUDDEE SECTION

TROPIC OF CAPRICORN

Rockhampton
North Reef

0   200 Miles
0   200 Kilometers

Gladstone

Mercator Projection

Area Enlarged
AUSTRALIA

145° E   150° E

Global Coral Reefs

Arctic Ocean
NORTH AMERICA
EUROPE
ASIA
30°N
Atlantic Ocean
TROPIC OF CANCER
AFRICA
Pacific Ocean
EQUATOR
SOUTH AMERICA
Pacific Ocean
TROPIC OF CAPRICORN
Indian Ocean
AUSTRALIA
30°S
ANTARCTICA

- Area with coral present
- Diseased reef

◒ **CORAL REEFS** form in warm, shallow waters near continents and islands in the tropics. These ecosystems are often endangered.

◒ **PREDATORS,** such as this crown-of-thorns starfish, feed on the coral polyps. Large numbers of starfish can kill the coral.

◒ **ENVIRONMENTAL HAZARDS,** such as pollution, storms, and changes in water temperature and salinity, put corals at risk.

◒ **THE GREAT BARRIER REEF** stretches along the northeast coast of Australia for 1,429 miles (2,300 km), from the tip of the Cape York Peninsula to just north of Brisbane in the state of Queensland. The reef is actually a collection of more than 3,000 individual reef systems and is home to many different species of fish, mollusks, rays, dolphins, reptiles, and birds. There are even giant clams more than 120 years old. In addition, the reef is habitat for several endangered species, including the dugong (sea cow) and the green sea turtle. UNESCO recognized the Great Barrier Reef as a World Heritage site in 1981.

Antarctica:
A View From Space

About 180 million years ago Antarctica broke away from the ancient super-continent Gondwana. Slowly the continent drifted to its present location at the southernmost point on Earth. Antarctica has no permanent human population, but it does have many unique types of wildlife. Seals, whales, and birds such as penguins, albatrosses, petrels, and terns have adapted to the continent's bitter-cold climate and long, dark winters.

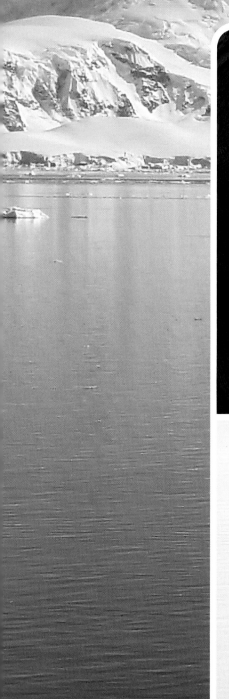

Gentoo penguins nest and raise their young in large colonies along the coastal margins of Antarctica.

PHYSICAL

Land area
5,100,000 sq mi
(13,209,000 sq km)

Highest point
Vinson Massif
16,066 ft (4,897 m)

Lowest point
Bentley Subglacial Trench
-8,383 ft (-2,555 m)

Coldest place
Annual average temperature
Ridge A
-94°F (-74°C)

Average precipitation on the polar plateau
Less than 2 in (5 cm) per year

POLITICAL

Population
There are no indigenous inhabitants, but there are both permanent and summer-only staffed research stations.

Number of independent countries
0

Number of countries claiming land
7

Number of countries operating year-round research stations
20

Number of year-round research stations
42

Antarctica

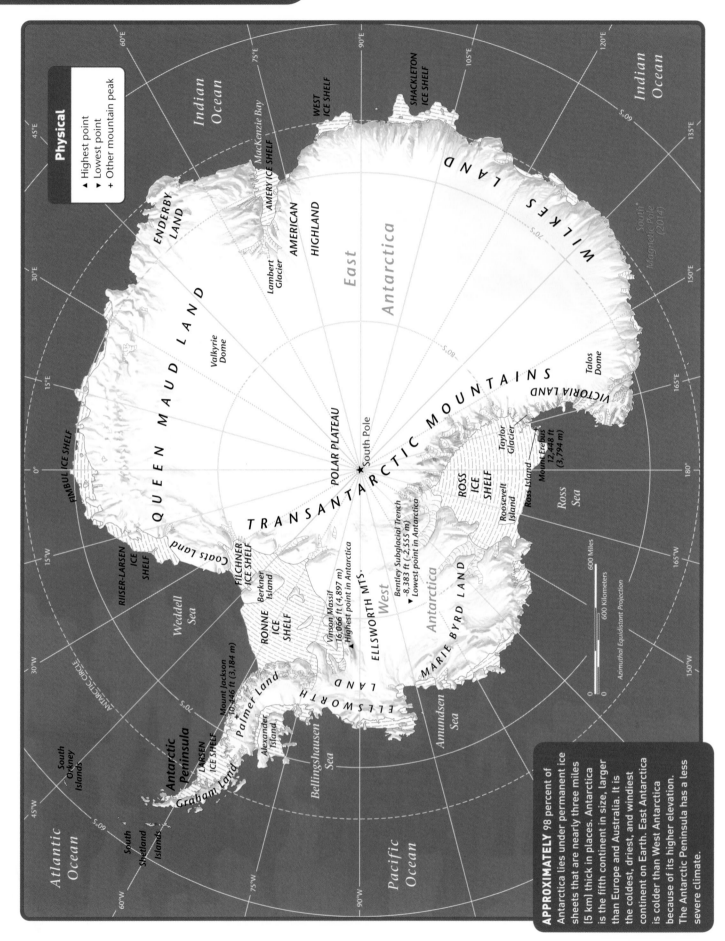

Physical

▲ Highest point
▼ Lowest point
+ Other mountain peak

Indian Ocean

Indian Ocean

WEST ICE SHELF

SHACKLETON ICE SHELF

MacKenzie Bay

AMERY ICE SHELF

ENDERBY LAND

AMERICAN HIGHLAND

Lambert Glacier

East Antarctica

WILKES LAND

South Magnetic Pole (2014)

QUEEN MAUD LAND

Valkyrie Dome

VICTORIA LAND

Talos Dome

POLAR PLATEAU

TRANSANTARCTIC MOUNTAINS

South Pole

Taylor Glacier

Mount Erebus 12,448 ft (3,794 m)

Ross Island

FIMBUL ICE SHELF

ROSS ICE SHELF

Roosevelt Island

Ross Sea

RIISER-LARSEN ICE SHELF

Coats Land

FILCHNER ICE SHELF

Berkner Island

Bentley Subglacial Trench
-8,383 ft (-2,555 m)
Lowest point in Antarctica ▼

Weddell Sea

RONNE ICE SHELF

Vinson Massif
16,066 ft (4,897 m)
Highest point in Antarctica ▲

ELLSWORTH MTS.

West Antarctica

MARIE BYRD LAND

600 Miles

600 Kilometers

Azimuthal Equidistant Projection

ELLSWORTH LAND

Mount Jackson
10,446 ft (3,184 m)

Palmer Land

Antarctic Peninsula

LARSEN ICE SHELF

Alexander Island

Bellingshausen Sea

Amundsen Sea

South Orkney Islands

Atlantic Ocean

South Shetland Islands

Graham Land

Pacific Ocean

APPROXIMATELY 98 percent of Antarctica lies under permanent ice sheets that are nearly three miles (5 km) thick in places. Antarctica is the fifth continent in size, larger than Europe and Australia. It is the coldest, driest, and windiest continent on Earth. East Antarctica is colder than West Antarctica because of its higher elevation. The Antarctic Peninsula has a less severe climate.

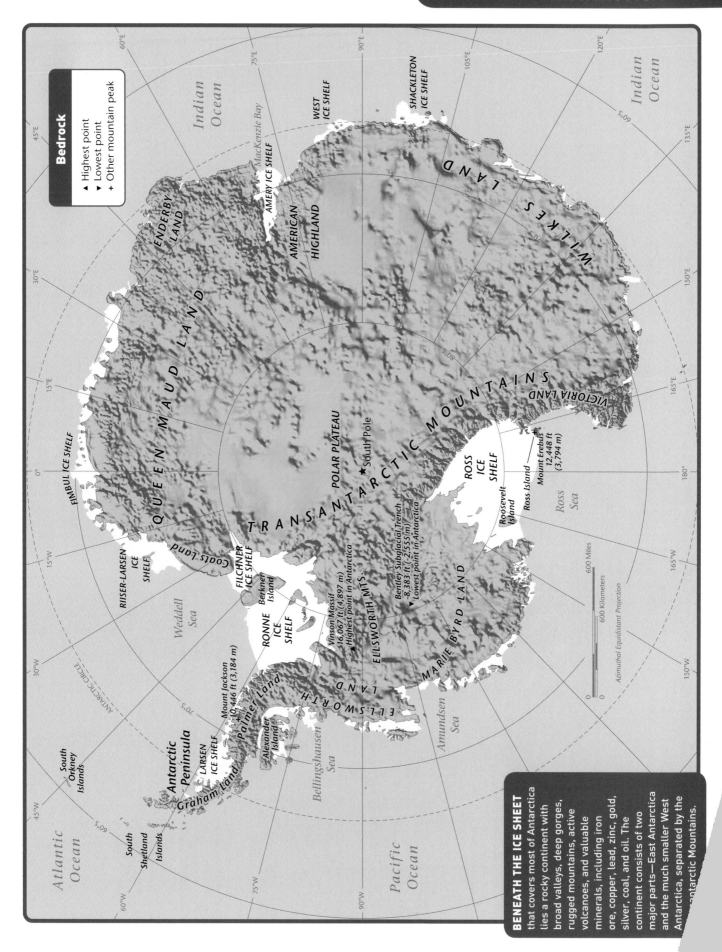

Bedrock

▲ Highest point
▼ Lowest point
+ Other mountain peak

Indian Ocean

Indian Ocean

60°E

75°E

90°E

105°E

120°E

135°E

150°E

165°E

45°E

30°E

15°E

SHACKLETON ICE SHELF

WEST ICE SHELF

MacKenzie Bay

AMERY ICE SHELF

ENDERBY LAND

AMERICAN HIGHLAND

WILKES LAND

QUEEN MAUD LAND

POLAR PLATEAU

★ South Pole

80°S

VICTORIA LAND

T R A N S A N T A R C T I C   M O U N T A I N S

EIMBUL ICE SHELF

RIISER-LARSEN ICE SHELF

Coats Land

FILCHNER ICE SHELF

Berkner Island

RONNE ICE SHELF

Vinson Massif
16,067 ft (4,897 m)
▲ Highest point in Antarctica

ELLSWORTH MTS.

Bentley Subglacial Trench
-8,383 ft (-2,555 m)
▼ Lowest point in Antarctica

MARIE BYRD LAND

ROSS ICE SHELF

Roosevelt Island

Ross Island

Mount Erebus
12,448 ft
(3,794 m)

Ross Sea

RODDS

0°

15°W

30°W

45°W

60°W

75°W

90°W

150°W

165°W

180°

Weddell Sea

ELLSWORTH LAND

Bellingshausen Sea

Amundsen Sea

Pacific Ocean

Atlantic Ocean

South Orkney Islands

South Shetland Islands

Antarctic Peninsula

Graham Land

LARSEN ICE SHELF

Palmer Land

Alexander Island

Mount Jackson
+ 10,446 ft (3,184 m)

ANTARCTIC CIRCLE

70°S

60°S

600 Miles

600 Kilometers

Azimuthal Equidistant Projection

BENEATH THE ICE SHEET
that covers most of Antarctica
lies a rocky continent with
broad valleys, deep gorges,
rugged mountains, active
volcanoes, and valuable
minerals, including iron
ore, copper, lead, zinc, gold,
silver, coal, and oil. The
continent consists of two
major parts—East Antarctica
and the much smaller West
Antarctica, separated by the
ntarctic Mountains.

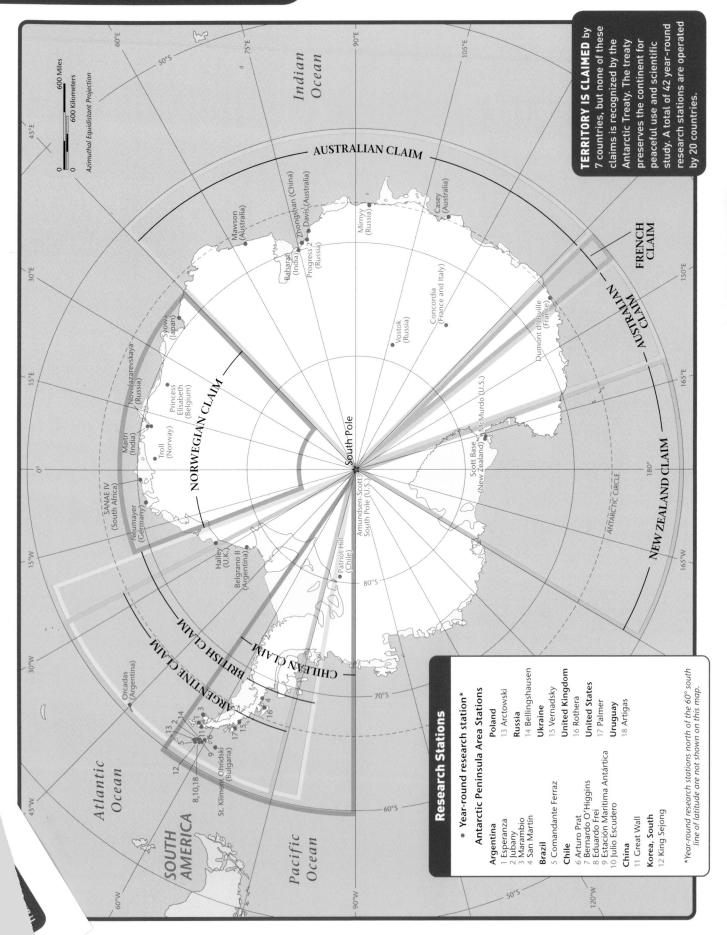

TERRITORY IS CLAIMED by 7 countries, but none of these claims is recognized by the Antarctic Treaty. The treaty preserves the continent for peaceful use and scientific study. A total of 42 year-round research stations are operated by 20 countries.

600 Miles
600 Kilometers
Azimuthal Equidistant Projection

Indian Ocean

AUSTRALIAN CLAIM

Casey (Australia)
Mirnyy (Russia)
Davis (Australia)
Zhongshan (China)
Progress 2 (Russia)
Baharati (India)
Mawson (Australia)

FRENCH CLAIM

Concordia (France and Italy)
Vostok (Russia)
Dumont d'Urville (France)

AUSTRALIAN CLAIM

Syowa (Japan)
Novolazarevskaya (Russia)
Princess Elisabeth (Belgium)

NORWEGIAN CLAIM

Maitri (India)
Troll (Norway)
SANAE IV (South Africa)
Neumayer (Germany)

McMurdo (U.S.)
Scott Base (New Zealand)

South Pole
Amundsen-Scott South Pole (U.S.)

NEW ZEALAND CLAIM

Halley (U.K.)
Belgrano II (Argentina)
Patriot Hill (Chile)

ANTARCTIC CIRCLE

80°S

CHILEAN CLAIM

BRITISH CLAIM

ARGENTINE CLAIM

70°S

Orcadas (Argentina)

13 2 14
3
16 4
15
17
5 11 7 1
9
6
St. Kliment Ohridski (Bulgaria)
12
8,10,18

60°S

Atlantic Ocean

SOUTH AMERICA

Pacific Ocean

50°S

Research Stations

• **Year-round research station***
Antarctic Peninsula Area Stations

Argentina
1 Esperanza
2 Jubany
3 Marambio
4 San Martín

Brazil
5 Comandante Ferraz

Chile
6 Arturo Prat
7 Bernardo O'Higgins
8 Eduardo Frei
9 Estación Marítima Antártica
10 Julio Escudero

China
11 Great Wall

Korea, South
12 King Sejong

Poland
13 Arctowski

Russia
14 Bellingshausen

Ukraine
15 Vernadsky

United Kingdom
16 Rothera

United States
17 Palmer

Uruguay
18 Artigas

Year-round research stations north of the 60° south line of latitude are not shown on this map.

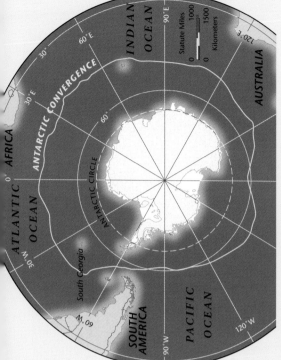

Extreme Environment

Antarctica, located at Earth's southern-most point, is one of the planet's most extreme environments. This ice-covered landmass experiences average temperatures ranging from a mild 22.5°F (-5.3°C) on the Antarctic Peninsula to a bitter -67.2°F (-55.1°C) on the high interior plateau. During the Antarctic winter, pack ice (frozen sea water) forms around the continent, making it even colder. The waters surrounding Antarctica are colder and less salty than Earth's major oceans. This results in a marine boundary called the Antarctic Convergence where the water temperature changes sharply in a short distance (see graph below, right). The mixing of waters along the convergence creates a zone extremely rich in nutrients—especially krill, which supports seals, penguins, whales, and other marine life that have adapted to the continent's extreme conditions.

◖ **THE ANTARCTIC CONVERGENCE** (approximately 55° S–60° S) is an important climate and marine boundary where cold, slightly less saline Antarctic waters meet the southern extremes of the Atlantic, Pacific, and Indian Oceans. The waters south of the Antarctic Convergence are sometimes referred to as the Southern Ocean.

FROZEN CONTINENT

FACTS & FIGURES

○ One of the largest icebergs ever—roughly the size of the state of Connecticut—broke free from the Ross Ice Shelf in 2000.

○ The lowest temperature ever recorded in Antarctica—minus 128.6°F (-89.2°C)—was at Russia's Vostok station in East Antarctica.

○ At the beginning of the Antarctic winter, sea ice advances at a rate of 40,000 square miles (100,000 sq km) each day.

○ It is estimated that if all of Antarctica's ice were to melt, the global ocean level would rise more than 200 feet (60 m). The continent itself would rise more than 1,600 feet (500 m) because of lost weight—a process known as isostasy.

ANTARCTIC CONVERGENCE

Sea Water Temperature - Degrees F (C)

■ Temperature

(Data recorded by the *National Geographic Explorer* ship on November 29, 2011.)

Cape Horn

Antarctica

Latitude

Waters surrounding Antarctica south of the Antarctic Convergence are marked by a sharp change in temperature and salinity as well as different marine life.

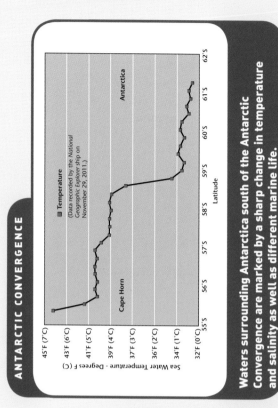

◖ **THE EMPEROR PENGUIN,** tallest of these flightless birds, is the only large animal that remains in Antarctica through the long, dark winter.

◖ **THE ALBATROSS** is the largest of all sea birds. Found mainly north of the Antarctic Convergence, the albatross often stays at sea for more than five years at a time.

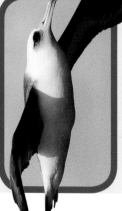

◖ **ANTARCTIC KRILL,** small shrimp-like creatures that thrive in the cold Antarctic waters, are critical to the food chain around the continent.

Flags & Stats

The following pages provide a quick glance at flags, facts, and figures for all 195 independent countries recognized by the National Geographic Society in 2013. An independent country has a national government that is accepted as the highest legal authority over its land and people.

The flags shown are national flags recognized by the United Nations. The statistical data offer a brief overview of each country. Area figures include land as well as surface areas for inland bodies of water. The languages listed are either those most commonly spoken within a country or the official language(s).

Argentina
CONTINENT: South America
AREA: 1,073,518 sq mi (2,780,400 sq km)
POPULATION: 41,267,000
CAPITAL: Buenos Aires 13,528,000
LANGUAGE: Spanish, English, Italian, German, French

Bahamas
CONTINENT: North America
AREA: 5,382 sq mi (13,939 sq km)
POPULATION: 350,000
CAPITAL: Nassau 254,000
LANGUAGE: English, Creole

Belgium
CONTINENT: Europe
AREA: 11,787 sq mi (30,528 sq km)
POPULATION: 11,164,000
CAPITAL: Brussels 1,949,000
LANGUAGE: Flemish (Dutch), French, German

Armenia
CONTINENT: Asia
AREA: 11,484 sq mi (29,743 sq km)
POPULATION: 3,048,000
CAPITAL: Yerevan 1,116,000
LANGUAGE: Armenian

Bahrain
CONTINENT: Asia
AREA: 277 sq mi (717 sq km)
POPULATION: 1,131,000
CAPITAL: Manama 262,000
LANGUAGE: Arabic, English, Persian (Farsi), Urdu

Belize
CONTINENT: North America
AREA: 8,867 sq mi (22,965 sq km)
POPULATION: 334,000
CAPITAL: Belmopan 14,000
LANGUAGE: Spanish, Creole, Maya dialects, English, Garifuna (Carib), German

Afghanistan
CONTINENT: Asia
AREA: 251,773 sq mi (652,090 sq km)
POPULATION: 30,552,000*
CAPITAL: Kabul 3,097,000
LANGUAGE: Dari (Afghan Persian), Pashto, Turkic languages

Andorra
CONTINENT: Europe
AREA: 181 sq mi (468 sq km)
POPULATION: 74,000
CAPITAL: Andorra la Vella 23,000
LANGUAGE: Catalan, French, Castilian, Portuguese

Australia
REGION: Australia/Oceania
AREA: 2,970,000 sq mi (7,692,000 sq km)
POPULATION: 23,106,000
CAPITAL: Canberra 399,000
LANGUAGE: English

Bangladesh
CONTINENT: Asia
AREA: 56,977 sq mi (147,570 sq km)
POPULATION: 156,595,000
CAPITAL: Dhaka 15,391,000
LANGUAGE: Bangla (Bengali), English

Benin
CONTINENT: Africa
AREA: 43,484 sq mi (112,622 sq km)
POPULATION: 9,645,000
CAPITAL: Porto-Novo (constitutional) 314,000; Cotonou (seat of government) 924,000
LANGUAGE: French, Fon, Yoruba

Albania
CONTINENT: Europe
AREA: 11,100 sq mi (28,748 sq km)
POPULATION: 2,774,000
CAPITAL: Tirana 419,000
LANGUAGE: Albanian, Greek, Vlach, Romani, Slavic dialects

Angola
CONTINENT: Africa
AREA: 481,354 sq mi (1,246,700 sq km)
POPULATION: 21,635,000
CAPITAL: Luanda 5,068,000
LANGUAGE: Portuguese, Bantu, other African languages

Austria
CONTINENT: Europe
AREA: 32,378 sq mi (83,858 sq km)
POPULATION: 8,511,000
CAPITAL: Vienna 1,720,000
LANGUAGE: German, Slovene, Croatian, Hungarian

Barbados
CONTINENT: North America
AREA: 166 sq mi (430 sq km)
POPULATION: 253,000
CAPITAL: Bridgetown 122,000
LANGUAGE: English

Bhutan
CONTINENT: Asia
AREA: 17,954 sq mi (46,500 sq km)
POPULATION: 733,000
CAPITAL: Thimphu 99,000
LANGUAGE: Dzongkha, Tibetan dialects, Nepali dialects

Algeria
CONTINENT: Africa
AREA: 919,595 sq mi (2,381,741 sq km)
POPULATION: 38,290,000
CAPITAL: Algiers 2,916,000
LANGUAGE: Arabic, French, Berber dialects

Antigua and Barbuda
CONTINENT: North America
AREA: 171 sq mi (442 sq km)
POPULATION: 88,000
CAPITAL: St. John's 27,000
LANGUAGE: English, local dialects

Azerbaijan
CONTINENT: Asia/Europe
AREA: 33,436 sq mi (86,600 sq km)
POPULATION: 9,418,000
CAPITAL: Baku 2,123,000
LANGUAGE: Azerbaijani (Azeri)

Belarus
CONTINENT: Europe
AREA: 80,153 sq mi (207,595 sq km)
POPULATION: 9,463,000
CAPITAL: Minsk 1,861,000
LANGUAGE: Belarusian, Russian

Bolivia
CONTINENT: South America
AREA: 424,164 sq mi (1,098,581 sq km)
POPULATION: 11,020,000
CAPITAL: La Paz (administrative) 1,715,000; Sucre (legal) 307,000
LANGUAGE: Spanish, Quechua, Aymara

*Country population figures are provided by the U.S. Population Reference Bureau (mid-2013); captial city figures are from the United Nations Population Division (metropolitan areas, 2011).

Bosnia and Herzegovina
CONTINENT: Europe
AREA: 19,741 sq mi
(51,129 sq km)
POPULATION: 3,834,000
CAPITAL: Sarajevo 389,000
LANGUAGE: Bosnian, Croatian, Serbian

Botswana
CONTINENT: Africa
AREA: 224,607 sq mi
(581,730 sq km)
POPULATION: 1,866,000
CAPITAL: Gaborone 202,000
LANGUAGE: English, Setswana, Kalanga, Sekgalgadi

Brazil
CONTINENT: South America
AREA: 3,300,169 sq mi
(8,547,403 sq km)
POPULATION: 195,527,000
CAPITAL: Brasília 3,813,000
LANGUAGE: Portuguese

Brunei
CONTINENT: Asia
AREA: 2,226 sq mi
(5,765 sq km)
POPULATION: 407,000
CAPITAL: Bandar Seri Begawan 16,000
LANGUAGE: Malay, English, Chinese

Bulgaria
CONTINENT: Europe
AREA: 42,855 sq mi
(110,994 sq km)
POPULATION: 7,260,000
CAPITAL: Sofia 1,174,000
LANGUAGE: Bulgarian, Turkish, Roma

Burkina Faso
CONTINENT: Africa
AREA: 105,869 sq mi
(274,200 sq km)
POPULATION: 18,015,000
CAPITAL: Ouagadougou 2,053,000
LANGUAGE: French, indigenous languages

Burundi
CONTINENT: Africa
AREA: 10,747 sq mi
(27,834 sq km)
POPULATION: 10,892,000
CAPITAL: Bujumbura 605,000
LANGUAGE: Kirundi, French, Swahili

Cabo Verde (Cape Verde)
CONTINENT: Africa
AREA: 1,558 sq mi
(4,036 sq km)
POPULATION: 515,000
CAPITAL: Praia 132,000
LANGUAGE: Portuguese, Crioulo

Cambodia
CONTINENT: Asia
AREA: 69,898 sq mi
(181,035 sq km)
POPULATION: 14,406,000
CAPITAL: Phnom Penh 1,550,000
LANGUAGE: Khmer

Cameroon
CONTINENT: Africa
AREA: 183,569 sq mi
(475,442 sq km)
POPULATION: 21,491,000
CAPITAL: Yaoundé 2,432,000
LANGUAGE: French, English, indigenous languages

Canada
CONTINENT: North America
AREA: 3,855,101 sq mi
(9,984,670 sq km)
POPULATION: 35,250,000
CAPITAL: Ottawa 1,208,000
LANGUAGE: English, French

Central African Republic
CONTINENT: Africa
AREA: 240,535 sq mi
(622,984 sq km)
POPULATION: 4,676,000
CAPITAL: Bangui 740,000
LANGUAGE: French, Sangho, other indigenous languages

Chad
CONTINENT: Africa
AREA: 495,755 sq mi
(1,284,000 sq km)
POPULATION: 12,209,000
CAPITAL: N'Djamena 1,079,000
LANGUAGE: French, Arabic, Sara, other indigenous languages

Chile
CONTINENT: South America
AREA: 291,930 sq mi
(756,096 sq km)
POPULATION: 17,557,000
CAPITAL: Santiago 6,034,000
LANGUAGE: Spanish

China
CONTINENT: Asia
AREA: 3,705,405 sq mi
(9,596,960 sq km)
POPULATION: 1,357,372,000
CAPITAL: Beijing 15,594,000
LANGUAGE: Standard Chinese (Mandarin), Yue, Wu, Minbei, other dialects and minority languages

Colombia
CONTINENT: South America
AREA: 440,831 sq mi
(1,141,748 sq km)
POPULATION: 48,028,000
CAPITAL: Bogotá 8,743,000
LANGUAGE: Spanish

Comoros
CONTINENT: Africa
AREA: 719 sq mi
(1,862 sq km)
POPULATION: 792,000
CAPITAL: Moroni 54,000
LANGUAGE: Arabic, French, Shikomoro

Congo
CONTINENT: Africa
AREA: 132,047 sq mi
(342,000 sq km)
POPULATION: 4,355,000
CAPITAL: Brazzaville 1,611,000
LANGUAGE: French, Lingala, Monokutuba, other indigenous languages

Costa Rica
CONTINENT: North America
AREA: 19,730 sq mi
(51,100 sq km)
POPULATION: 4,713,000
CAPITAL: San José 1,515,000
LANGUAGE: Spanish, English

Côte d'Ivoire (Ivory Coast)
CONTINENT: Africa
AREA: 124,503 sq mi
(322,462 sq km)
POPULATION: 21,142,000
CAPITAL: Yamoussoukro (official) 966,000; Abidjan 4,288,000
LANGUAGE: French, Dioula, indigenous languages

Croatia
CONTINENT: Europe
AREA: 21,831 sq mi
(56,542 sq km)
POPULATION: 4,253,000
CAPITAL: Zagreb 686,000
LANGUAGE: Croatian

Cuba
CONTINENT: North America
AREA: 42,803 sq mi
(110,860 sq km)
POPULATION: 11,258,000
CAPITAL: Havana 2,116,000
LANGUAGE: Spanish

Cyprus
CONTINENT: Europe
AREA: 3,572 sq mi
(9,251 sq km)
POPULATION: 1,135,000
CAPITAL: Nicosia 253,000
LANGUAGE: Greek, Turkish, English

Czech Republic (Czechia)
CONTINENT: Europe
AREA: 30,450 sq mi
(78,866 sq km)
POPULATION: 10,521,000
CAPITAL: Prague 1,276,000
LANGUAGE: Czech

Democratic Republic of the Congo
CONTINENT: Africa
AREA: 905,365 sq mi
(2,344,885 sq km)
POPULATION: 71,128,000
CAPITAL: Kinshasa 8,798,000
LANGUAGE: French, Lingala, Kingwana, Kikongo, Tshiluba

Denmark
CONTINENT: Europe
AREA: 16,640 sq mi
(43,098 sq km)
POPULATION: 5,613,000
CAPITAL: Copenhagen 1,206,000
LANGUAGE: Danish, Faroese,
Greenlandic, German, English

Egypt
CONTINENT: Africa
AREA: 386,874 sq mi
(1,002,000 sq km)
POPULATION: 84,667,000
CAPITAL: Cairo 11,169,000
LANGUAGE: Arabic, English,
French

Ethiopia
CONTINENT: Africa
AREA: 437,600 sq mi
(1,133,380 sq km)
POPULATION: 89,209,000
CAPITAL: Addis Ababa 2,979,000
LANGUAGE: Oromo, Amharic,
Tigrinya, English, Arabic, Somali

Gambia
CONTINENT: Africa
AREA: 4,361 sq mi
(11,295 sq km)
POPULATION: 1,884,000
CAPITAL: Banjul 506,000
LANGUAGE: English, Mandinka,
Fula, Wolof, other indigenous
languages

Grenada
CONTINENT: North America
AREA: 133 sq mi (344 sq km)
POPULATION: 112,000
CAPITAL: St. George's 41,000
LANGUAGE: English, French
patois

Djibouti
CONTINENT: Africa
AREA: 8,958 sq mi
(23,200 sq km)
POPULATION: 939,000
CAPITAL: Djibouti 496,000
LANGUAGE: French, Arabic,
Somali, Afar

El Salvador
CONTINENT: North America
AREA: 8,124 sq mi
(21,041 sq km)
POPULATION: 6,307,000
CAPITAL: San Salvador 1,605,000
LANGUAGE: Spanish, Nahua

Fiji Islands
REGION: Australia/Oceania
AREA: 7,095 sq mi
(18,376 sq km)
POPULATION: 860,000
CAPITAL: Suva 177,000
LANGUAGE: English, Fijian,
Hindustani

Georgia
CONTINENT: Asia/Europe
AREA: 26,911 sq mi
(69,700 sq km)
POPULATION: 4,541,000
CAPITAL: T'bilisi 1,121,000
LANGUAGE: Georgian, Russian,
Armenian, Azeri, Abkhaz

Guatemala
CONTINENT: North America
AREA: 42,042 sq mi
(108,889 sq km)
POPULATION: 15,428,000
CAPITAL: Guatemala City
1,168,000
LANGUAGE: Spanish,
indigenous languages

Dominica
CONTINENT: North America
AREA: 290 sq mi (751 sq km)
POPULATION: 71,000
CAPITAL: Roseau 14,000
LANGUAGE: English, French
patois

Equatorial Guinea
CONTINENT: Africa
AREA: 10,831 sq mi
(28,051 sq km)
POPULATION: 761,000
CAPITAL: Malabo 137,000
LANGUAGE: Spanish, French,
Fang, Bubi

Finland
CONTINENT: Europe
AREA: 130,558 sq mi
(338,145 sq km)
POPULATION: 5,440,000
CAPITAL: Helsinki 1,134,000
LANGUAGE: Finnish, Swedish

Germany
CONTINENT: Europe
AREA: 137,847 sq mi
(357,022 sq km)
POPULATION: 80,572,000
CAPITAL: Berlin 3,462,000
LANGUAGE: German

Guinea
CONTINENT: Africa
AREA: 94,926 sq mi
(245,857 sq km)
POPULATION: 11,793,000
CAPITAL: Conakry 1,786,000
LANGUAGE: French,
indigenous languages

Dominican
Republic
CONTINENT: North America
AREA: 18,704 sq mi
(48,442 sq km)
POPULATION: 10,260,000
CAPITAL: Santo Domingo
2,191,000
LANGUAGE: Spanish

Eritrea
CONTINENT: Africa
AREA: 46,774 sq mi
(121,144 sq km)
POPULATION: 5,765,000
CAPITAL: Asmara 712,000
LANGUAGE: Afar, Arabic, Tigre,
Kunama, Tigrinya, other Cushitic
languages

France
CONTINENT: Europe
AREA: 210,026 sq mi
(543,965 sq km)
POPULATION: 63,851,000
CAPITAL: Paris 10,620,000
LANGUAGE: French

Ghana
CONTINENT: Africa
AREA: 92,100 sq mi
(238,537 sq km)
POPULATION: 26,088,000
CAPITAL: Accra 2,573,000
LANGUAGE: English, Asante,
Ewe, Fante, Boron, Dagomba,
Dangme, other native languages

Guinea-Bissau
CONTINENT: Africa
AREA: 13,948 sq mi
(36,125 sq km)
POPULATION: 1,667,000
CAPITAL: Bissau 423,000
LANGUAGE: Portuguese,
Crioulo, indigenous languages

Ecuador
CONTINENT: South America
AREA: 109,483 sq mi
(283,560 sq km)
POPULATION: 15,789,000
CAPITAL: Quito 1,622,000
LANGUAGE: Spanish, Quechua,
other indigenous languages

Estonia
CONTINENT: Europe
AREA: 17,462 sq mi
(45,227 sq km)
POPULATION: 1,283,000
CAPITAL: Tallinn 400,000
LANGUAGE: Estonian, Russian

Gabon
CONTINENT: Africa
AREA: 103,347 sq mi
(267,667 sq km)
POPULATION: 1,601,000
CAPITAL: Libreville 686,000
LANGUAGE: French, Fang,
Myene, Nzebi, Bapounou/
Eschira, Bandjabi

Greece
CONTINENT: Europe
AREA: 50,949 sq mi
(131,957 sq km)
POPULATION: 11,081,000
CAPITAL: Athens 3,414,000
LANGUAGE: Greek

Guyana
CONTINENT: South America
AREA: 83,000 sq mi
(214,969 sq km)
POPULATION: 800,000
CAPITAL: Georgetown 127,000
LANGUAGE: English,
indigenous languages, Creole,
Caribbean Hindustani, Urdu

Haiti
CONTINENT: North America
AREA: 10,714 sq mi
(27,750 sq km)
POPULATION: 10,421,000
CAPITAL: Port-au-Prince
2,207,000
LANGUAGE: French, Creole

Indonesia
CONTINENT: Asia
AREA: 742,308 sq mi
(1,922,570 sq km)
POPULATION: 248,527,000
CAPITAL: Jakarta 9,769,000
LANGUAGE: Bahasa Indonesia,
English, Dutch, Javanese, other
indigenous languages

Italy
CONTINENT: Europe
AREA: 116,345 sq mi
(301,333 sq km)
POPULATION: 59,831,000
CAPITAL: Rome 3,298,000
LANGUAGE: Italian, German,
French, Slovene

Kenya
CONTINENT: Africa
AREA: 224,081 sq mi
(580,367 sq km)
POPULATION: 44,184,000
CAPITAL: Nairobi 3,363,000
LANGUAGE: English, Kiswahili,
indigenous languages

Laos
CONTINENT: Asia
AREA: 91,429 sq mi
(236,800 sq km)
POPULATION: 6,736,000
CAPITAL: Vientiane 810,000
LANGUAGE: Lao, French,
English, ethnic languages

Honduras
CONTINENT: North America
AREA: 43,433 sq mi
(112,492 sq km)
POPULATION: 8,555,000
CAPITAL: Tegucigalpa 1,088,000
LANGUAGE: Spanish,
indigenous languages

Iran
CONTINENT: Asia
AREA: 636,296 sq mi
(1,648,000 sq km)
POPULATION: 76,521,000
CAPITAL: Tehran 7,304,000
LANGUAGE: Persian (Farsi),
Turkic dialects, Kurdish, Luri,
Gilaki, Mazandarani

Jamaica
CONTINENT: North America
AREA: 4,244 sq mi
(10,991 sq km)
POPULATION: 2,712,000
CAPITAL: Kingston 571,000
LANGUAGE: English, English
patois

Kiribati
REGION: Australia/Oceania
AREA: 313 sq mi (811 sq km)
POPULATION: 106,000
CAPITAL: Tarawa 44,000
LANGUAGE: I-Kiribati, English

Latvia
CONTINENT: Europe
AREA: 24,938 sq mi
(64,589 sq km)
POPULATION: 2,018,000
CAPITAL: Riga 701,000
LANGUAGE: Latvian, Russian,
Lithuanian

Hungary
CONTINENT: Europe
AREA: 35,919 sq mi
(93,030 sq km)
POPULATION: 9,892,000
CAPITAL: Budapest 1,737,000
LANGUAGE: Hungarian

Iraq
CONTINENT: Asia
AREA: 168,754 sq mi
(437,072 sq km)
POPULATION: 35,095,000
CAPITAL: Baghdad 6,036,000
LANGUAGE: Arabic, Kurdish,
Assyrian, Armenian

Japan
CONTINENT: Asia
AREA: 145,902 sq mi
(377,887 sq km)
POPULATION: 127,301,000
CAPITAL: Tokyo 37,217,000
LANGUAGE: Japanese

Kosovo
CONTINENT: Europe
AREA: 4,203 sq mi
(10,887 sq km)
POPULATION: 1,824,000
CAPITAL: Prishtina 145,000
LANGUAGE: Albanian, Serbian,
Bosnian, Turkish, Roma

Lebanon
CONTINENT: Asia
AREA: 4,036 sq mi
(10,452 sq km)
POPULATION: 4,822,000
CAPITAL: Beirut 2,022,000
LANGUAGE: Arabic, French,
English, Armenian

Iceland
CONTINENT: Europe
AREA: 39,769 sq mi
(103,000 sq km)
POPULATION: 323,000
CAPITAL: Reykjavík 206,000
LANGUAGE: Icelandic, English,
Nordic languages, German

Ireland
CONTINENT: Europe
AREA: 27,133 sq mi
(70,273 sq km)
POPULATION: 4,598,000
CAPITAL: Dublin 1,121,000
LANGUAGE: Irish (Gaelic),
English

Jordan
CONTINENT: Asia
AREA: 34,495 sq mi
(89,342 sq km)
POPULATION: 7,309,000
CAPITAL: Amman 1,179,000
LANGUAGE: Arabic, English

Kuwait
CONTINENT: Asia
AREA: 6,880 sq mi
(17,818 sq km)
POPULATION: 3,459,000
CAPITAL: Kuwait 2,406,000
LANGUAGE: Arabic, English

Lesotho
CONTINENT: Africa
AREA: 11,720 sq mi
(30,355 sq km)
POPULATION: 2,242,000
CAPITAL: Maseru 239,000
LANGUAGE: Sesotho, English,
Zulu, Xhosa

India
CONTINENT: Asia
AREA: 1,269,221 sq mi
(3,287,270 sq km)
POPULATION: 1,276,508,000
CAPITAL: New Delhi 22,654,000
(part of Delhi metropolitan area)
LANGUAGE: Hindi, 21 other
official languages, English

Israel
CONTINENT: Asia
AREA: 8,550 sq mi
(22,145 sq km)
POPULATION: 8,054,000
CAPITAL: Jerusalem 791,000
LANGUAGE: Hebrew, Arabic,
English

Kazakhstan
CONTINENT: Asia/Europe
AREA: 1,049,155 sq mi
(2,717,300 sq km)
POPULATION: 17,031,000
CAPITAL: Astana 664,000
LANGUAGE: Kazakh (Qazaq),
Russian

Kyrgyzstan
CONTINENT: Asia
AREA: 77,182 sq mi
(199,900 sq km)
POPULATION: 5,665,000
CAPITAL: Bishkek 837,000
LANGUAGE: Kyrgyz, Uzbek,
Russian

Liberia
CONTINENT: Africa
AREA: 43,000 sq mi
(111,370 sq km)
POPULATION: 4,357,000
CAPITAL: Monrovia 750,000
LANGUAGE: English, indigenous
languages

Libya
CONTINENT: Africa
AREA: 679,362 sq mi
(1,759,540 sq km)
POPULATION: 6,518,000
CAPITAL: Tripoli 1,127,000
LANGUAGE: Arabic, Italian,
English

Madagascar
CONTINENT: Africa
AREA: 226,658 sq mi
(587,041 sq km)
POPULATION: 22,550,000
CAPITAL: Antananarivo 1,987,000
LANGUAGE: French, Malagasy,
English

Malta
CONTINENT: Europe
AREA: 122 sq mi (316 sq km)
POPULATION: 448,000
CAPITAL: Valletta 198,000
LANGUAGE: Maltese, English

Micronesia
REGION: Australia/Oceania
AREA: 271 sq mi (702 sq km)
POPULATION: 107,000
CAPITAL: Palikir 7,000
LANGUAGE: English, Chuukese,
Kosrean, Pohnpeian, Yapese,
other indigenous languages

Morocco
CONTINENT: Africa
AREA: 274,461 sq mi
(710,850 sq km)
POPULATION: 32,950,000
CAPITAL: Rabat 1,843,000
LANGUAGE: Arabic, Berber
dialects, French

Liechtenstein
CONTINENT: Europe
AREA: 62 sq mi (160 sq km)
POPULATION: 37,000
CAPITAL: Vaduz 5,000
LANGUAGE: German,
Alemannic dialect

Malawi
CONTINENT: Africa
AREA: 45,747 sq mi
(118,484 sq km)
POPULATION: 16,338,000
CAPITAL: Lilongwe 772,000
LANGUAGE: English, Chichewa,
Chinyanja, Chiyao, Chitumbuka

Marshall Islands
REGION: Australia/Oceania
AREA: 70 sq mi (181 sq km)
POPULATION: 56,000
CAPITAL: Majuro 31,000
LANGUAGE: Marshallese,
English

Moldova
CONTINENT: Europe
AREA: 13,050 sq mi
(33,800 sq km)
POPULATION: 4,114,000
CAPITAL: Chisinau 677,000
LANGUAGE: Moldovan, Russian,
Gagauz

Mozambique
CONTINENT: Africa
AREA: 308,642 sq mi
(799,380 sq km)
POPULATION: 24,336,000
CAPITAL: Maputo 1,150,000
LANGUAGE: Portuguese, Emak-
huwa, Xichangana, Elomwe,
Cisena, Echuwabo

Lithuania
CONTINENT: Europe
AREA: 25,212 sq mi
(65,300 sq km)
POPULATION: 2,956,000
CAPITAL: Vilnius 546,000
LANGUAGE: Lithuanian,
Russian, Polish

Malaysia
CONTINENT: Asia
AREA: 127,355 sq mi
(329,847 sq km)
POPULATION: 29,794,000
CAPITAL: Kuala Lumpur
1,556,000
LANGUAGE: Bahasa Malaysia,
English, Chinese, Tamil, Telugu,
Malayalam, Punjabi, Thai

Mauritania
CONTINENT: Africa
AREA: 397,955 sq mi
(1,030,700 sq km)
POPULATION: 3,712,000
CAPITAL: Nouakchott 786,000
LANGUAGE: Arabic, Pulaar,
Soninke, Wolof, French,
Hassaniya

Monaco
CONTINENT: Europe
AREA: 0.8 sq mi (2.0 sq km)
POPULATION: 37,000
CAPITAL: Monaco 35,000
LANGUAGE: French, English,
Italian, Monegasque

Myanmar (Burma)
CONTINENT: Asia
AREA: 261,218 sq mi
(676,552 sq km)
POPULATION: 53,259,000
CAPITAL: Nay Pyi Taw (admin-
istrative) 1,060,000; Yangon
(Rangoon; legislative) 4,457,000
LANGUAGE: Burmese, ethnic
languages

Luxembourg
CONTINENT: Europe
AREA: 998 sq mi (2,586 sq km)
POPULATION: 543,000
CAPITAL: Luxembourg 94,000
LANGUAGE: Luxembourgish,
German, French

Maldives
CONTINENT: Asia
AREA: 115 sq mi (298 sq km)
POPULATION: 360,000
CAPITAL: Male 132,000
LANGUAGE: Maldivian Dhivehi,
English

Mauritius
CONTINENT: Africa
AREA: 788 sq mi (2,040 sq km)
POPULATION: 1,297,000
CAPITAL: Port Louis 151,000
LANGUAGE: Creole, Bhojpuri,
French

Mongolia
CONTINENT: Asia
AREA: 603,909 sq mi
(1,564,116 sq km)
POPULATION: 2,792,000
CAPITAL: Ulaanbaatar 1,184,000
LANGUAGE: Khalkha Mongol,
Turkic, Russian

Namibia
CONTINENT: Africa
AREA: 318,261 sq mi
(824,292 sq km)
POPULATION: 2,410,000
CAPITAL: Windhoek 380,000
LANGUAGE: English, Afrikaans,
German, indigenous languages

Macedonia
CONTINENT: Europe
AREA: 9,928 sq mi
(25,713 sq km)
POPULATION: 2,066,000
CAPITAL: Skopje 499,000
LANGUAGE: Macedonian,
Albanian, Turkish

Mali
CONTINENT: Africa
AREA: 478,841 sq mi
(1,240,192 sq km)
POPULATION: 15,461,000
CAPITAL: Bamako 2,037,000
LANGUAGE: French, Bambara,
other indigenous languages

Mexico
CONTINENT: North America
AREA: 758,449 sq mi
(1,964,375 sq km)
POPULATION: 117,574,000
CAPITAL: Mexico City 20,446,000
LANGUAGE: Spanish, Maya,
Nahuatl, other indigenous
languages

Montenegro
CONTINENT: Europe
AREA: 5,415 sq mi
(14,026 sq km)
POPULATION: 623,000
CAPITAL: Podgorica 156,000
LANGUAGE: Serbian, Monte-
negrin, Bosnian, Albanian,
Croatian

Nauru
REGION: Australia/Oceania
AREA: 8 sq mi (21 sq km)
POPULATION: 11,000
CAPITAL: Yaren 10,000
LANGUAGE: Nauruan, English

Nepal

CONTINENT: Asia
AREA: 56,827 sq mi
(147,181 sq km)
POPULATION: 26,810,000
CAPITAL: Kathmandu 1,015,000
LANGUAGE: Nepali, Maithali,
Bhojpuri, Tharu, Tamang,
Newar, Magar, Awadhi

Nigeria

CONTINENT: Africa
AREA: 356,669 sq mi
(923,768 sq km)
POPULATION: 173,615,000
CAPITAL: Abuja 2,153,000
LANGUAGE: English, Hausa,
Yoruba, Igbo (Ibo), Fulani

Palau

REGION: Australia/Oceania
AREA: 189 sq mi (489 sq km)
POPULATION: 21,000
CAPITAL: Melekeok, 400
LANGUAGE: Palauan, Filipino,
English, Chinese

Philippines

CONTINENT: Asia
AREA: 115,831 sq mi
(300,000 sq km)
POPULATION: 96,209,000
CAPITAL: Manila 11,862,000
LANGUAGE: Filipino (based
on Tagalog), English

Russia

CONTINENT: Europe/Asia
AREA: 6,592,850 sq mi
(17,075,400 sq km)
POPULATION: 143,493,000
CAPITAL: Moscow 11,621,000
LANGUAGE: Russian, many
languages

Netherlands

CONTINENT: Europe
AREA: 16,034 sq mi
(41,528 sq km)
POPULATION: 16,798,000
CAPITAL: Amsterdam 1,056,000
LANGUAGE: Dutch, Frisian

North Korea

CONTINENT: Asia
AREA: 46,540 sq mi
(120,538 sq km)
POPULATION: 24,720,000
CAPITAL: Pyongyang 2,843,000
LANGUAGE: Korean

Panama

CONTINENT: North America
AREA: 29,157 sq mi
(75,517 sq km)
POPULATION: 3,850,000
CAPITAL: Panama City 1,426,000
LANGUAGE: Spanish, English

Poland

CONTINENT: Europe
AREA: 120,728 sq mi
(312,685 sq km)
POPULATION: 38,517,000
CAPITAL: Warsaw 1,723,000
LANGUAGE: Polish

Rwanda

CONTINENT: Africa
AREA: 10,169 sq mi
(26,338 sq km)
POPULATION: 11,116,000
CAPITAL: Kigali 1,004,000
LANGUAGE: Kinyarwanda,
French, English, Kiswahili

New Zealand

REGION: Australia/Oceania
AREA: 104,454 sq mi
(270,534 sq km)
POPULATION: 4,450,000
CAPITAL: Wellington 410,000
LANGUAGE: English, Maori

Norway

CONTINENT: Europe
AREA: 125,004 sq mi
(323,758 sq km)
POPULATION: 5,084,000
CAPITAL: Oslo 915,000
LANGUAGE: Bokmal Norwegian,
Nynorsk Norwegian, Sami

Papua New Guinea

REGION: Australia/Oceania
AREA: 178,703 sq mi
(462,345 sq km)
POPULATION: 7,179,000
CAPITAL: Port Moresby 343,000
LANGUAGE: Melanesian pidgin,
indigenous languages

Portugal

CONTINENT: Europe
AREA: 35,655 sq mi
(92,345 sq km)
POPULATION: 10,460,000
CAPITAL: Lisbon 2,843,000
LANGUAGE: Portuguese,
Mirandese

Samoa

REGION: Australia/Oceania
AREA: 1,093 sq mi
(2,831 sq km)
POPULATION: 190,000
CAPITAL: Apia 37,000
LANGUAGE: Samoan, English

Nicaragua

CONTINENT: North America
AREA: 50,193 sq mi
(130,000 sq km)
POPULATION: 6,043,000
CAPITAL: Managua 970,000
LANGUAGE: Spanish, English,
Miskito, other indigenous
languages

Oman

CONTINENT: Asia
AREA: 119,500 sq mi
(309,500 sq km)
POPULATION: 3,983,000
CAPITAL: Muscat 743,000
LANGUAGE: Arabic, English,
Baluchi, Urdu, Indian dialects

Paraguay

CONTINENT: South America
AREA: 157,048 sq mi
(406,752 sq km)
POPULATION: 6,798,000
CAPITAL: Asunción 2,139,000
LANGUAGE: Spanish, Guarani

Qatar

CONTINENT: Asia
AREA: 4,448 sq mi
(11,521 sq km)
POPULATION: 2,169,000
CAPITAL: Doha 567,000
LANGUAGE: Arabic, English

San Marino

CONTINENT: Europe
AREA: 24 sq mi (61 sq km)
POPULATION: 33,000
CAPITAL: San Marino 4,000
LANGUAGE: Italian

Niger

CONTINENT: Africa
AREA: 489,191 sq mi
(1,267,000 sq km)
POPULATION: 16,916,000
CAPITAL: Niamey 1,297,000
LANGUAGE: French, Hausa,
Djerma

Pakistan

CONTINENT: Asia
AREA: 307,374 sq mi
(796,095 sq km)
POPULATION: 190,709,000
CAPITAL: Islamabad 919,000
LANGUAGE: Urdu, English,
Punjabi, Sindhi, Siraiki, Pashto,
Balochi, Hindko

Peru

CONTINENT: South America
AREA: 496,224 sq mi
(1,285,216 sq km)
POPULATION: 30,475,000
CAPITAL: Lima 9,130,000
LANGUAGE: Spanish, Quechua,
Aymara, other indigenous
languages

Romania

CONTINENT: Europe
AREA: 92,043 sq mi
(238,391 sq km)
POPULATION: 21,269,000
CAPITAL: Bucharest 1,937,000
LANGUAGE: Romanian,
Hungarian

Sao Tome
and Principe

CONTINENT: Africa
AREA: 386 sq mi (1,001 sq km)
POPULATION: 188,000
CAPITAL: São Tomé 64,000
LANGUAGE: Portuguese

Saudi Arabia
CONTINENT: Asia
AREA: 756,985 sq mi
(1,960,582 sq km)
POPULATION: 30,054,000
CAPITAL: Riyadh 5,451,000
LANGUAGE: Arabic

Singapore
CONTINENT: Asia
AREA: 255 sq mi (660 sq km)
POPULATION: 5,444,000
CAPITAL: Singapore 5,188,000
LANGUAGE: Mandarin, English,
Tamil, Malay, Hokkien, Canton-
ese, Teochew

South Africa
CONTINENT: Africa
AREA: 470,693 sq mi
(1,219,090 sq km)
POPULATION: 52,982,000
CAPITAL: Pretoria (administra-
tive) 1,501,000; Bloemfontein
(judicial) 468,000; Cape Town
(legislative) 3,562,000
LANGUAGE: IsiZulu, IsiXhosa

St. Kitts and Nevis
CONTINENT: North America
AREA: 104 sq mi (269 km)
POPULATION: 55,000
CAPITAL: Basseterre 12,000
LANGUAGE: English

Swaziland
CONTINENT: Africa
AREA: 6,704 sq mi
(17,363 sq km)
POPULATION: 1,238,000
CAPITAL: Mbabane (admini-
strative) 66,000; Lobamba
(legislative and royal) —
LANGUAGE: English, siSwati

Senegal
CONTINENT: Africa
AREA: 75,955 sq mi
(196,722 sq km)
POPULATION: 13,497,000
CAPITAL: Dakar 3,035,000
LANGUAGE: French, Wolof,
Pulaar, Jola, Mandinka

Slovakia
CONTINENT: Europe
AREA: 18,932 sq mi
(49,035 sq km)
POPULATION: 5,414,000
CAPITAL: Bratislava 434,000
LANGUAGE: Slovak, Hungarian

South Korea
CONTINENT: Asia
AREA: 38,321 sq mi
(99,250 sq km)
POPULATION: 50,220,000
CAPITAL: Seoul 9,736,000
LANGUAGE: Korean, English

St. Lucia
CONTINENT: North America
AREA: 238 sq mi (616 sq km)
POPULATION: 170,000
CAPITAL: Castries 21,000
LANGUAGE: English, French
patois

Sweden
CONTINENT: Europe
AREA: 173,732 sq mi
(449,964 sq km)
POPULATION: 9,592,000
CAPITAL: Stockholm 1,385,000
LANGUAGE: Swedish, Sami,
Finnish

Serbia
CONTINENT: Europe
AREA: 29,913 sq mi
(77,474 sq km)
POPULATION: 7,136,000
CAPITAL: Belgrade 1,135,000
LANGUAGE: Serbian, Hungarian,
Slovak, Romanian, Croatian,
Rusyn

Slovenia
CONTINENT: Europe
AREA: 7,827 sq mi
(20,273 sq km)
POPULATION: 2,060,000
CAPITAL: Ljubljana 273,000
LANGUAGE: Slovene,
Serbo-Croatian

South Sudan
CONTINENT: Africa
AREA: 248,795 sq mi
(644,329 sq km)
POPULATION: 9,782,000
CAPITAL: Juba 269,000
LANGUAGE: English, Arabic,
indigenous languages

St. Vincent
and the Grenadines
CONTINENT: North America
AREA: 150 sq mi (389 sq km)
POPULATION: 108,000
CAPITAL: Kingstown 31,000
LANGUAGE: English, French
patois

Switzerland
CONTINENT: Europe
AREA: 15,940 sq mi
(41,284 sq km)
POPULATION: 8,078,000
CAPITAL: Bern 353,000
LANGUAGE: German, French,
Italian, Romansch

Seychelles
CONTINENT: Africa
AREA: 176 sq mi (455 sq km)
POPULATION: 93,000
CAPITAL: Victoria 27,000
LANGUAGE: English, Creole

Solomon Islands
REGION: Australia/Oceania
AREA: 10,954 sq mi
(28,370 sq km)
POPULATION: 581,000
CAPITAL: Honiara 68,000
LANGUAGE: English, Melane-
sian pidgin, other indigenous
languages

Spain
CONTINENT: Europe
AREA: 195,363 sq mi
(505,988 sq km)
POPULATION: 46,647,000
CAPITAL: Madrid 6,574,000
LANGUAGE: Castilian Spanish,
Catalan, Galician, Basque

Sudan
CONTINENT: Africa
AREA: 718,775 sq mi
(1,861,484 sq km)
POPULATION: 34,186,000
CAPITAL: Khartoum 4,632,000
LANGUAGE: Arabic, English,
Nubian, Ta Bedawie, Fur

Syria
CONTINENT: Asia
AREA: 71,498 sq mi
(185,180 sq km)
POPULATION: 21,898,000
CAPITAL: Damascus 2,650,000
LANGUAGE: Arabic, Kurdish,
Armenian, Aramaic, Circassian

Sierra Leone
CONTINENT: Africa
AREA: 27,699 sq mi
(71,740 sq km)
POPULATION: 6,242,000
CAPITAL: Freetown 941,000
LANGUAGE: English, Mende,
Temne, Krio

Somalia
CONTINENT: Africa
AREA: 246,201 sq mi
(637,657 sq km)
POPULATION: 10,383,000
CAPITAL: Mogadishu 1,554,000
LANGUAGE: Somali, Arabic,
Italian, English

Sri Lanka
CONTINENT: Asia
AREA: 25,299 sq mi
(65,525 sq km)
POPULATION: 20,501,000
CAPITAL: Colombo (adminstra-
tive) 693,000; Sri Jayewardene-
pura Kotte (legislative) 126,000
LANGUAGE: Sinhala, Tamil

Suriname
CONTINENT: South America
AREA: 63,037 sq mi
(163,265 sq km)
POPULATION: 558,000
CAPITAL: Paramaribo 278,000
LANGUAGE: Dutch, English,
Sranang Tongo (Taki-Taki), Carib-
bean Hindustani, Javanese

Tajikistan
CONTINENT: Asia
AREA: 55,251 sq mi
(143,100 sq km)
POPULATION: 8,085,000
CAPITAL: Dushanbe 739,000
LANGUAGE: Tajik, Russian

Tanzania
CONTINENT: Africa
AREA: 364,900 sq mi
(945,087 sq km)
POPULATION: 49,122,000
CAPITAL: Dar es Salaam
2,930,000; Dodoma (legislative)
83,000
LANGUAGE: Swahili, English,
Arabic, indigenous languages

Thailand
CONTINENT: Asia
AREA: 198,115 sq mi
(513,115 sq km)
POPULATION: 66,185,000
CAPITAL: Bangkok 8,426,000
LANGUAGE: Thai, English, ethnic
and regional dialects

Timor-Leste
(East Timor)
CONTINENT: Asia
AREA: 5,640 sq mi
(14,609 sq km)
POPULATION: 1,108,000
CAPITAL: Dili 180,000
LANGUAGE: Tetum, Portuguese,
Indonesian, English

Togo
CONTINENT: Africa
AREA: 21,925 sq mi
(56,785 sq km)
POPULATION: 6,168,000
CAPITAL: Lomé 1,524,000
LANGUAGE: French, Ewe, Mina,
Kabye, Dagomba

Tonga
REGION: Australia/Oceania
AREA: 289 sq mi (748 sq km)
POPULATION: 103,000
CAPITAL: Nuku'alofa 25,000
LANGUAGE: Tongan, English

Trinidad and Tobago
CONTINENT: North America
AREA: 1,980 sq mi (5,128 sq km)
POPULATION: 1,341,000
CAPITAL: Port-of-Spain 66,000
LANGUAGE: English, Caribbean
Hindustani, French, Spanish,
Chinese

Tunisia
CONTINENT: Africa
AREA: 63,170 sq mi
(163,610 sq km)
POPULATION: 10,882,000
CAPITAL: Tunis 790,000
LANGUAGE: Arabic, French

Turkey
CONTINENT: Asia/Europe
AREA: 300,948 sq mi
(779,452 sq km)
POPULATION: 76,083,000
CAPITAL: Ankara 4,194,000
LANGUAGE: Turkish, Kurdish

Turkmenistan
CONTINENT: Asia
AREA: 188,456 sq mi
(488,100 sq km)
POPULATION: 5,240,000
CAPITAL: Ashgabat 683,000
LANGUAGE: Turkmen, Russian,
Uzbek

Tuvalu
REGION: Australia/Oceania
AREA: 10 sq mi (26 sq km)
POPULATION: 11,000
CAPITAL: Funafuti 5,000
LANGUAGE: Tuvaluan, English,
Samoan, Kiribati

Uganda
CONTINENT: Africa
AREA: 93,104 sq mi
(241,139 sq km)
POPULATION: 36,890,000
CAPITAL: Kampala 1,659,000
LANGUAGE: English, Ganda
(Luganda), other indigenous
languages, Swahili, Arabic

Ukraine
CONTINENT: Europe
AREA: 233,090 sq mi
(603,700 sq km)
POPULATION: 45,513,000
CAPITAL: Kiev 2,829,000
LANGUAGE: Ukrainian, Russian

United Arab
Emirates
CONTINENT: Asia
AREA: 30,000 sq mi
(77,700 sq km)
POPULATION: 9,346,000
CAPITAL: Abu Dhabi 942,000
LANGUAGE: Arabic, Persian
(Farsi), English, Hindi, Urdu

United Kingdom
CONTINENT: Europe
AREA: 93,788 sq mi
(242,910 sq km)
POPULATION: 64,092,000
CAPITAL: London 9,005,000
LANGUAGE: English, Welsh,
Scots, Scottish Gaelic, Irish
Gaelic, Cornish

United States
CONTINENT: North America
AREA: 3,794,083 sq mi
(9,826,630 sq km)
POPULATION: 316,158,000
CAPITAL: Washington, D.C.
4,705,000
LANGUAGE: English, Spanish

Uruguay
CONTINENT: South America
AREA: 68,037 sq mi
(176,215 sq km)
POPULATION: 3,392,000
CAPITAL: Montevideo 1,672,000
LANGUAGE: Spanish, Portunol,
Brazilero

Uzbekistan
CONTINENT: Asia
AREA: 172,742 sq mi
(447,400 sq km)
POPULATION: 30,215,000
CAPITAL: Tashkent 2,227,000
LANGUAGE: Uzbek, Russian,
Tajik, Kazakh, Karakalpak

Vanuatu
REGION: Australia/Oceania
AREA: 4,707 sq mi
(12,190 sq km)
POPULATION: 265,000
CAPITAL: Port-Vila 47,000
LANGUAGE: pidgin (known
as Bislama or Bichelama),
indigenous languages

Vatican City
CONTINENT: Europe
AREA: 0.2 sq mi (0.4 sq km)
POPULATION: 798
CAPITAL: Vatican City 798
LANGUAGE: Italian, Latin,
French

Venezuela
CONTINENT: South America
AREA: 352,144 sq mi
(912,050 sq km)
POPULATION: 29,679,000
CAPITAL: Caracas 3,242,000
LANGUAGE: Spanish, indigenous
languages

Vietnam
CONTINENT: Asia
AREA: 127,844 sq mi
(331,114 sq km)
POPULATION: 89,721,000
CAPITAL: Hanoi 2,955,000
LANGUAGE: Vietnamese,
English, French, Chinese, Khmer

Yemen
CONTINENT: Asia
AREA: 207,286 sq mi
(536,869 sq km)
POPULATION: 25,235,000
CAPITAL: Sanaa 2,419,000
LANGUAGE: Arabic

Zambia
CONTINENT: Africa
AREA: 290,586 sq mi
(752,614 sq km)
POPULATION: 14,187,000
CAPITAL: Lusaka 1,802,000
LANGUAGE: English, Bemba,
Nyanja, Tonga, Lozi, Lunda,
Kaonde, Luvale

Zimbabwe
CONTINENT: Africa
AREA: 150,872 sq mi
(390,757 sq km)
POPULATION: 13,038,000
CAPITAL: Harare 1,542,000
LANGUAGE: English, Shona,
Sindebele, other indigenous
languages

Glossary

Note: Terms defined within the main body of the atlas text are not listed below.

ANTARCTIC CONVERGENCE a climate and marine boundary (approximately 55° S–60° S) where cold, slightly less saline Antarctic waters meet the southern extremes of the Atlantic, Pacific, and Indian Oceans; waters south of the Antarctic Convergence are sometimes referred to as the Southern Ocean (p. **125**)

ARID CLIMATE type of dry climate in which annual precipitation is often less than 10 inches (25 cm); experiences great daily variations in day-night temperatures (pp. **20–21**)

ASYLUM a place where a person can go to find safety; to offer asylum means to offer protection in a safe country to people who fear being persecuted or who have been persecuted in their own country (pp. **34–35**)

BATHYMETRY measurement of depth at various places in the ocean or other body of water (p. **11**)

BIODIVERSITY biological diversity in an environment as indicated by numbers of different species of plants and animals (pp. **28**, **108**)

BOREAL FOREST *see* Northern coniferous forest

BOUNDARY line established by people to separate one political or mapped area from another; physical features, such as mountains and rivers, or latitude and longitude lines sometimes act as boundaries (p. **10**)

BREADBASKET a geographic region that is a principal source of grain (p. **64**)

CANADIAN SHIELD region containing the oldest rock in North America; areas are exposed in much of eastern Canada and some bordering U.S. regions (pp. **56**, **62**)

CLIMATE CHANGE any significant change in the measures of climate, such as temperature, precipitation, or wind patterns, resulting from natural variability or human activity and lasting for an extended period of time (p. **29**)

COASTAL PLAIN any comparatively level land of low elevation that borders the ocean (p. **64**)

CONTINENTAL CLIMATE midlatitude climate zone occurring on large landmasses in the Northern Hemisphere and characterized by great variations of temperature, both seasonally and between day and night; continental cool summer climates are influenced by nearby colder subarctic climates; continental warm summer climates are influenced by nearby mild or dry climates (pp. **20–21**)

COORDINATED UNIVERSAL TIME (UTC) the basis for the current worldwide system of civil (versus military) time determined by highly precise atomic clocks; also known as Universal Time; formerly known as Greenwich Mean Time (p. **13**)

CULTURE HEARTH center from which major cultural traditions spread and are adopted by people in a wide geographic area (p. **90**)

CYBERCAFÉ a café that has a collection of computers that customers can use to access the Internet (p. **52**)

DEGRADED FOREST a forested area severely damaged by overharvesting, repeated fires, overgrazing, poor management practices, or other abuse that delays or prevents forest regrowth (p. **28**)

DESERT AND DRY SHRUB vegetation region with either hot or cold temperatures that annually receives 10 inches (25 cm) or less of precipitation (pp. **24–25**)

DIFFUSE BOUNDARY an evolving boundary zone between two or more tectonic plates with edges that are not clearly defined (p. **17**)

ECOSYSTEM term for classifying Earth's natural communities according to how all things in an environment, such as a forest or a coral reef, interact with each other (pp. **10**, **15**, **68**, **79**, **118**)

FAULT break in Earth's crust along which movement up, down, or sideways occurs (pp. **16–17**)

FLOODED GRASSLAND wetland dominated by grasses and covered by water (pp. **24–25**)

FOSSIL FUEL a fuel, such as coal, petroleum, and natural gas, derived from the remains of ancient plants and animals (p. **48**)

GEOTHERMAL ENERGY heat energy generated within Earth (p. **47**)

GLACIER large, slow-moving mass of ice that forms over time from snow (p. **26**)

GLOBAL WARMING a theory about the increase of Earth's average global temperature due to a buildup of so-called greenhouse gases, such as carbon dioxide and methane, released by human activities (p. **78**)

GLOBALIZATION the purposeful spread of activities, technology, goods, and values throughout the world through the expansion of global links, such as trade, media, and the Internet (p. **50**)

GONDWANA name given to the southern part of the supercontinent Pangaea; made up of what we now call Africa, South America, Australia, Antarctica, and India (pp. **16**, **120**)

GREENWICH MEAN TIME *see* Coordinated Universal Time

GROSS DOMESTIC PRODUCT (GDP) the gross national product excluding the value of net income earned abroad (p. **44**)

GROSS NATIONAL INCOME PER CAPITA a country's annual earned income divided by its population (p. **36**)

GROSS NATIONAL PRODUCT (GNP) the total value of the goods and services produced by the residents of a country during a specified period (as a year) (p. **44**)

GROUNDWATER water, primarily from rain or melted snow, that collects beneath Earth's surface, in saturated soil or in underground reservoirs, or aquifers, and that supplies springs and wells (p. **27**)

HEMISPHERE one-half of the globe; the Equator divides Earth into Northern and Southern Hemispheres; the prime meridian and the 180 degree meridian divide it into Eastern and Western Hemispheres (p. **5**)

HIGHLAND/UPLAND climate region associated with mountains or plateaus that varies depending on elevation, latitude, continental location, and exposure to sun and wind; in general, temperature decreases and precipitation increases with elevation (pp. **20–21**)

HOST COUNTRY the country where a refugee first goes to find asylum (p. **34**)

HOT SPOT in geology, an extremely hot region beneath the lithosphere that tends to stay relatively stationary while plates of Earth's outer crust move over it; environmentally, an ecological trouble spot (p. **28**)

HUMAN DEVELOPMENT INDEX (HDI) a way of measuring development that combines both social and economic factors to rank the world's countries based on health, education, and living standards (pp. **36–37**)

HUMID SUBTROPICAL CLIMATE region characterized by hot summers, mild to cool winters, and year-round precipitation that is heaviest in summer; generally located on the southeastern margins of continents (pp. **20–21**)

ICE CAP CLIMATE one of two kinds of polar climate; summer temperatures rarely rise above freezing and what little precipitation occurs is mostly in the form of snow (pp. **20–21**)

INDIGENOUS native to or occurring naturally in a specific area or environment (p. **116**)

INFILTRATION process that occurs in the water, or hydrologic, cycle when gravity causes surface water to seep down through the soil (p. **26**)

INTERNALLY DISPLACED PERSON (IDP) a person who has fled his or her home to escape armed conflict, generalized violence, human rights abuses, or natural or man-made disasters; unlike a refugee, such a person has not crossed an international border but remains in his or her own country (p. **34**)

LANDFORM physical feature shaped by uplifting, weathering, and erosion; mountains, plateaus, hills, and plains are the four major types (p. **22**)

LANGUAGE FAMILY group of languages that share a common ancestry (pp. **40–41**)

LATIN AMERICA cultural region generally considered to include Mexico, Central America, South America, and the West Indies; Portuguese and Spanish are the principal languages (p. **38**)

LIFE EXPECTANCY the average number of years a person can expect to live, based on current mortality rates and health conditions (p. **36**)

LLANOS extensive, mostly treeless grasslands in the Orinoco River basin of northern South America (p. **72**)

LOWLANDS fairly level land at a lower elevation than surrounding areas (p. **14**)

MANGROVE VEGETATION tropical trees and shrubs with dense root systems that grow in tidal mudflats and extend coastlines by trapping soil (pp. **24–25**)

MARGINAL LAND land that has little value for growing crops or for commercial or residential development (p. **28**)

MARINE WEST COAST type of mild climate common on the west coasts of continents in midlatitude regions; characterized by small variations in annual temperature range and wet, foggy winters (pp. **20–21**)

MEDIAN AGE midpoint of a population's age; half the population is older than this age; half is younger (p. **33**)

MEDITERRANEAN CLIMATE a mild climate common on the west coasts of continents, named for the dominant climate along the Mediterranean coast; characterized by mild, rainy winters and hot, dry summers (pp. **20–21**)

MEDITERRANEAN SHRUB low-growing, mostly small-leaf evergreen vegetation, such as chaparral, that thrives in Mediterranean climate regions (pp. **24–25**)

MELANESIA one of three major island groups that make up Oceania; includes the Fiji Islands, New Guinea, Vanuatu, the Solomon Islands, and New Caledonia (pp. **112–113**)

MELANESIAN indigenous to Melanesia (p. **116**)

MICROCLIMATE climate of a very limited area that varies from the overall climate of the surrounding region (p. **22**)

MICRONESIA one of three major island groups that make up Oceania; made up of some 2,000 mostly coral islands, including Guam, Kiribati, the Mariana Islands, Palau, and the Federated States of Micronesia (pp. **112–113**)

MICRONESIAN indigenous to Micronesia (p. **116**)

MONSOON seasonal change in the direction of the prevailing winds, which causes wet and dry seasons in some tropical areas (p. **94**)

MOUNTAIN GRASSLAND vegetation region characterized by clumps of long grass that grow beyond the limit of forests at high elevations (pp. **24–25**)

NONRENEWABLE RESOURCES elements of the natural environment, such as metals, minerals, and fossil fuels, that form within Earth by geological processes over millions of years and thus cannot readily be replaced (pp. **48–49**)

NORTHERN CONIFEROUS FOREST vegetation region composed primarily of cone-bearing, needle- or scale-leaf evergreen trees that grow in regions with long winters and moderate to high annual precipitation; also called boreal forest or taiga (pp. **24–25**)

OCEANIA name for the widely scattered islands of Polynesia, Micronesia, and Melanesia; often includes Australia and New Zealand (pp. **110–121**)

PAMPAS temperate grassland primarily in Argentina between the Andes and the Atlantic Ocean; one of the world's richest agricultural regions (pp. **70, 72**)

PATAGONIA cool, windy, arid plateau region primarily in southern Argentina between the Andes and the Atlantic Ocean (p. **72**)

PER CAPITA INCOME the total national income divided by the number of people in the country (p. **37**)

PLAIN large area of relatively flat land; one of the four major kinds of landforms (p. **18**)

PLATEAU large, relatively flat area that rises above the surrounding landscape; one of the four major kinds of landforms (pp. **18–19**)

POLAR CLIMATES climates that occur at very high latitudes; generally too cold to support tree growth; include tundra and ice cap (pp. **20–21**)

POLYNESIA one of three major regions in Oceania made up mostly of volcanic and coral islands, including the Hawaiian and the Society Islands, Samoa, and French Polynesia (pp. **112–113**)

POLYNESIAN indigenous to Polynesia (p. **116**)

PREDOMINANT ECONOMY main type of work that most people do to meet their wants and needs in a particular country (pp. **44–45, 61, 77, 87, 97, 107, 117**)

PROVINCE land governed as a political or administrative unit of a country or empire; Canadian provinces, like U.S. states, have substantial powers of self-government (p. **63**)

RAIN FOREST see Tropical moist broadleaf forest

RENEWABLE FRESH WATER water that is replenished naturally, but the supply of which can be endangered by overuse and pollution (p. **26**)

RIVER BASIN area drained by a single river and its tributaries (p. **72**)

RURAL pertaining to the countryside, where most of the economic activity centers on agriculture-related work (pp. **38–39**)

SAHEL in Africa the semiarid region of short, tropical grassland that lies between the dry Sahara and the humid savanna and that is prone to frequent droughts (p. **104**)

SALINE/SALINITY measure of all salts contained in water; average ocean salinity is 35 parts per thousand (p. **125**)

SAMPAN a flat-bottomed boat used in eastern Asia and usually propelled by two short oars (p. **98**)

SAVANNA tropical tall grassland with scattered trees (pp. **24–25**)

SELF-SUSTAINABILITY the ability of a system or community to maintain itself without benefit of external support or input (p. **39**)

SELVA Portuguese word referring to tropical rain forests, especially in the Amazon Basin (p. **78**)

SEMIARID dry climate region with great daily variation in day-night temperatures; has enough rainfall to support grasslands (pp. **20–21**)

SILT mineral particles that are larger than grains of clay but smaller than grains of sand (p. **78**)

STATELESS PEOPLE those who have no recognized country (p. **35**)

STEPPE Slavic word referring to relatively flat, mostly treeless, temperate grasslands that stretch across much of central Europe and central Asia (p. **92**)

SUBARCTIC CLIMATE region characterized by short, cool, sometimes freezing summers and long, bitter-cold winters; most precipitation falls in summer (pp. **20–21**)

SUBTROPICAL CLIMATE region between tropical and continental climates characterized by distinct seasons but with milder temperatures than continental climates (pp. **20–21**)

SUBURB a residential area on the outskirts of a town or city (p. **38**)

SUNBELT area of rapid population and economic growth south of the 37th parallel in the United States; its mild climate is attractive to retirees, and a general absence of labor unions has drawn manufacturing to the region (p. **60**)

TAIGA see Northern coniferous forest

TEMPERATE BROAD-LEAF FOREST vegetation region with distinct seasons and dependable rainfall; predominant species include oak, maple, and beech, all of which lose their leaves in the cold season (pp. **24–25**)

TEMPERATE CONIFEROUS FOREST vegetation region that has mild winters with heavy precipitation; made up of mostly evergreen, needle-leaf trees that bear seeds in cones (pp. **24–25**)

TEMPERATE GRASS-LAND vegetation region where grasses are dominant and the climate is characterized by hot summers, cold winters, and moderate rainfall (pp. **24–25**)

TERRITORY land under the jurisdiction of a country but that is not a state or a province (p. **57**)

TROPICAL CONIFEROUS FOREST vegetation region that occurs in a cooler climate than tropical rain forests; has distinct wet and dry seasons; made up of mostly evergreen trees with seed-bearing cones (pp. **24–25**)

TROPICAL DRY CLIMATE region characterized by year-round high temperatures and sufficient precipitation to support savannas (pp. **20–21**)

TROPICAL DRY FOREST vegetation region that has distinct wet and dry seasons and a cooler climate than tropical moist broadleaf forests; has shorter trees than rain forests and many shed their leaves in the dry season (pp. **24–25**)

TROPICAL GRASSLAND AND SAVANNA vegetation region characterized by scattered individual trees; occurs in warm or hot climates with annual rainfall of 20 to 50 inches (50–130 cm) (pp. **24–25**)

TROPICAL MOIST BROADLEAF FOREST vegetation region occurring mostly in a belt between the Tropic of Cancer and the Tropic of Capricorn in areas that have at least 80 inches (200 cm) of rain annually and an average annual temperature of 80°F (27°C) (pp. **24–25**, **78–79**)

TROPICAL WET CLIMATE region characterized by year-round warm temperatures and rainfall ranging from 60 to 150 inches (150–400 cm) annually (pp. **20–21**)

TROPOSPHERE region of Earth's atmosphere closest to the surface; where weather occurs (p. **5**)

TUNDRA vegetation region at high latitudes and high elevations characterized by cold temperatures, low vegetation, and a short growing season (pp. **24–25**)

TUNDRA CLIMATE region with one or more months of temperatures slightly above freezing when the ground is free of snow (pp. **20–21**)

UNIVERSALIZING RELIGION one that attempts to appeal to all people rather than to just those in a particular region or place (p. **42**)

UPLAND CLIMATE see Highland/upland climate

URBAN pertaining to a town or city, where most of the economic activity is not based on agriculture (pp. **38–39**)

URBAN AGGLOMERATION a group of several cities and/or towns and their suburbs (p. **38**)

Web Sites

Activities and Lessons: http://education.nationalgeographic.com/education/?ar_a=1

Antarctica: http://www.coolantarctica.com

Cultural Diffusion: http://www2.geog.okstate.edu/users/lightfoot/lightfoot.html

Earth's Climates: http://www.worldclimate.com

Earth's Vegetation: http://earthobservatory.nasa.gov/Features/LandCover

Education Resource: education.nationalgeographic.com/education/standards/national-geography-standards/?ar_a=1

Environmental Hot Spots: Quiz for Students: http://www.myfootprint.org

Flags of the World: http://www.fotw.us/flags/index.html

Globalization: http://www.globalization101.org

Map Projections: http://www.colorado.edu/geography/gcraft/notes/mapproj/mapproj.bak2

National Geographic Kids Atlases Home Page: http://www.nationalgeographic.com/kids-atlases/index.html

Natural Hazards:
   Earthquakes: http://earthquake.usgs.gov
   Tsunamis: http://www.tsunami.noaa.gov
   Volcanoes: http://www.geo.mtu.edu/volcanoes

Political World: https://www.cia.gov/library/publications/the-world-factbook/index.html

Quality of Life: http://hdr.undp.org/en/content/human-development-report-2013

Reading Maps: http://education.usgs.gov/secondary.html#geography

Time Zones: http://tycho.usno.navy.mil/tzones.html

World Cities: http://esa.un.org/unup

World Conflicts: http://www.cnn.com/interactive/maps/world/fullpage.global.conflict/world.index.html

World Energy: http://www.bp.com/en/global/corporate/about-bp/energy-economics/statistical-review-of-world-energy-2013.html

World Food: http://www.cgiar.org/impact/research/index.html

World Languages: http://www.ethnologue.com/web.asp
   Interactive for Students: http://www.ipl.org/div/hello

World Population: http://www.census.gov/population/international/data/idb/informationGateway.php; http://www.prb.org/Publications/Datasheets/2013/2013-world-population-data-sheet.aspx

World Refugees: http://www.unhcr.org/cgi-bin/texis/vtx/home

World Religions: http://www.adherents.com

World Water: http://www.worldbank.org/en/topic/water

Note: All Web sites were viable as of publication date. In the event that a site has been discontinued, a reliable search engine can lead you to new sites with helpful information.

Thematic Index

Boldface indicates illustrations; *italics* indicates maps.

Place-Name Index

Boldface indicates
    illustrations; *italics*
    indicates maps.

Illustration Credits

FRONT COVER

(Earth), leonello calvetti/Shutterstock; (background), DTKUTOO/Shutterstock; (arch), Michal Bednarek/Shutterstock; (jaguar), Mustang_79/iStockphoto; (St. Basil's), Vladitto/Shutterstock; (Statue of Liberty), Nikada/iStockphoto; (Machu Picchu), Lori Epstein/National Geographic Creative; (koala), Joe Scherschel/National Geographic Creative

BACK COVER

(Florence, Italy), S. Borisov/Shutterstock; (Antarctic penguins), kkaplin/iStockphoto; (woman with cell phone), David Evans/National Geographic Creative

SPINE

(Earth): leonello calvetti/Shutterstock

Locator globes: Theophilius Britt Griswold
Artwork & graphs: Stuart Armstrong

FRONT OF THE BOOK

1, leonello calvetti/Shutterstock; 2 (le), Andrew Burton/Getty Images; 2 (rt), Mattias Klum/National Geographic Creative; 3 (uple), Lori Epstein/National Geographic Creative; 3 (lole), Paul Banton/iStockphoto.com; 3 (rt), kkaplin/iStockphoto; 4 (le), David Aguilar; 4–5, NASA; 10, Belinda Pretorius/Shutterstock; 12 (le), kai hecker/Shutterstock; 12 (rt), Corbis; 24 (far le), TTphoto/Shutterstock; 24 (le), Lane V. Erickson/Shutterstock; 24 (rt), Elena Elisseeva/Shutterstock; 24 (far rt), Sai Yeung Chan/Shutterstock; 25 (far le), Nic Watson/Shutterstock; 25 (le), EcoPrint/Shutterstock; 25 (rt), FloridaStock/Shutterstock; 25 (far rt), EcoPrint/Shutterstock; 26 (le), Steve Winter/National Geographic Creative; 26 (rt), Annie Griffiths Belt/National Geographic Creative; 27 (le), Hervé Collart/Sygma/Corbis; 27 (rt), Mark Thiessen, NGS; 28 (le), Steve McCurry/National Geographic Creative; 28 (rt), Scientific Visualization Studio/Goddard Space Flight Center/NASA; 29 (le), Joseph Sohm/Visions of America/Corbis; 29 (rt), © Rolex Awards/Thierry Grobet; 32, Yann Layma/The Image Bank/Getty Images; 34, Isaac Kasamani/AFP/Getty Images; 35, Patrick Barth/Getty Images; 37, Ulrich Baumgarten via Getty Images; 38, WH Chow/Shutterstock; 39 (le), Tony Karumba/AFP/Getty Images; 39 (rt), Rebecca Hale, NGS; 40, Les Stone/Sygma/Corbis; 41 (le), Jeremy Horner/Corbis; 41 (rt), Ric Ergenbright/Corbis; 42 (le), Lindsay Hebberd/Corbis; 42 (rt), Annie Griffiths Belt/Corbis; 43 (le), Adrees Latif/Reuters/Corbis; 43 (rt), Joseph Sohm/Visions of America/Corbis; 44 (le), Lynsey Addario/Corbis; 44 (ctr), Phil Schermeister/National Geographic Creative; 44 (rt), James P. Blair/National Geographic Creative; 45 (le), James L. Stanfield/National Geographic Creative; 45 (rt), Ariel Skelley/Blend Images/Getty Images; 46 (le), Mark Thiessen, NGS; 46 (rt), Merrill Dyck/Shutterstock; 47 (le), stoonn/Shutterstock; 47 (rt), Steve Raymer/National Geographic Creative; 49 (le), Sarah Leen/National Geographic Creative; 49 (ctr), Bob Krist/National Geographic Creative; 49 (rt), Ayan82/Photolibrary/Getty Images; 50, Joe Raedle/Newsmakers/Getty Images; 51, David Evans/National Geographic Creative; 52, Rich LaSalle/Stone/Getty Images; 53 (le), Jodi Cobb/National Geographic Creative; 53 (rt), Louise Gubb/Corbis SABA

NORTH AMERICA

54–55, Noppawat/Flickr/Getty Images; 68 (uple), Woodfin Camp & Associates; 68 (uprt), Ravi Miro Fry; 68 (lo), Andrew Burton/Getty Images

SOUTH AMERICA

70–71, JLR Photography/Shutterstock; 78 (up), Mattias Klum/National Geographic Creative; 78 (lole), Bill Curtsinger/National Geographic Creative; 78 (lort), Michael Nichols/National Geographic Creative; 79, Michael Nichols/National Geographic Creative

EUROPE

80–81, S.Borisov/Shutterstock; 88 (up), Sven Hoppe/iStockphoto; 88 (lole), schmidt-z/ iStockphoto; 88 (lort), Cristian Gusa/Shutterstock; 89, Mark III Photonics/Shutterstock

ASIA

90–91, Lori Epstein/National Geographic Creative; 98 (up), China Photos/Getty Images; 98 (lole), Byun Yeong-Wook/AFP/Getty Images; 98 (lort), Hoang Dinh Nam/AFP/Getty Images; 99, VOISHMEL/AFP/Getty Images

AFRICA

100–101, DLILLC/Corbis; 108 (up), Christine Eichin/iStockphoto.com; 108 (lo), Paul Banton/iStockphoto.com; 109, Eliza Snow/iStockphoto.com

AUSTRALIA & OCEANIA

110–111, Selfiy/Shutterstock; 118 (up), Tim Laman/National Geographic Creative; 118 (lo), Reuters/Corbis; 119 (up), David Doubilet; 119 (lo), Tim Laman/National Geographic Creative

ANTARCTICA

120–121, kkaplin/iStockphoto; 125 (up), Gentoo Multimedia Limited/Shutterstock; 125 (lole), Steve Oehlenschlager/Shutterstock; 125 (lort), George F. Mobley/National Geographic Creative

Published by the National Geographic Society

Gary E. Knell
President and Chief Executive Officer

John M. Fahey
Chairman of the Board

Declan Moore
Executive Vice President; President, Publishing and Travel

Melina Gerosa Bellows
Publisher; Chief Creative Officer, Books, Kids, and Family

Prepared by the Book Division

Hector Sierra
Senior Vice President and General Manager

Nancy Laties Feresten
Senior Vice President, Kids Publishing and Media

Jennifer Emmett
Vice President, Editorial Director, Kids Books

Eva Absher-Schantz
Design Director, Kids Publishing and Media

Jay Sumner
Director of Photography, Kids Publishing

R. Gary Colbert
Production Director

Jennifer A. Thornton
Director of Managing Editorial

Staff for This Book

Priyanka Sherman, *Project Editor*

Suzanne Patrick Fonda, *Project Manager*

Martha Sharma, *Writer, Researcher, and Chief Consultant*

David M. Seager, *Art Director*

Lori Epstein, *Senior Photo Editor*

Angela Terry, angela terry design, *Designer*

Stuart Armstrong, *Graphics Illustrator*

Ariane Szu-Tu, *Editorial Assistant*

Callie Broaddus, *Design Production Assistant*

Margaret Leist, *Photo Assistant*

Carl Mehler, *Director of Maps*

Matthew Chwastyk, *Map Production Manager*

Mapping Specialists, LTD. and XNR Productions, *Map Research and Production*

Catherine Farley, *Copy Editor*

Dianne Hosmer, *Indexer*

Grace Hill, *Associate Managing Editor*

Mike O'Connor, *Production Editor*

Lewis R. Bassford, *Production Manager*

Susan Borke, *Legal and Business Affairs*

Production Services

Phillip L. Schlosser, *Senior Vice President*

Chris Brown, *Vice President, NG Book Manufacturing*

George Bounelis, *Senior Production Manager*

Nicole Elliot, *Director of Production*

Rachel Faulise and Robert Barr, *Managers*

The National Geographic Society is one of the world's largest nonprofit scientific and educational organizations. Founded in 1888 to "increase and diffuse geographic knowledge," the Society's mission is to inspire people to care about the planet. It reaches more than 400 million people worldwide each month through its official journal, *National Geographic*, and other magazines; National Geographic Channel; television documentaries; music; radio; films; books; DVDs; maps; exhibitions; live events; school publishing programs; interactive media; and merchandise. National Geographic has funded more than 10,000 scientific research, conservation and exploration projects and supports an education program promoting geographic literacy.

For more information, please visit nationalgeographic.com, call 1-800-NGS LINE (647-5463), or write to the following address:

NATIONAL GEOGRAPHIC SOCIETY
1145 17th Street N.W., Washington, D.C. 20036-4688 U.S.A.

Visit us online at nationalgeographic.com/books

For librarians and teachers: ngchildrensbooks.org

National Geographic supports K–12 educators with ELA Common Core Resources. Visit www.natgeoed.org/commoncore for more information.

More for kids from National Geographic: kids.nationalgeographic.com

For information about special discounts for bulk purchases, please contact National Geographic Books Special Sales: ngspecsales@ngs.org

For rights or permissions inquiries, please contact National Geographic Books Subsidiary Rights: ngbookrights@ngs.org

The Library of Congress has cataloged the 2001 edition as follows:

National Geographic Society (U.S.)
National Geographic student atlas of the world.
p. cm.
Includes index and glossary.
ISBN 978-1-4263-0446-0 (pbk.)
ISBN 978-1-4263-0445-3 (hc.)
ISBN 978-1-4263-0458-3 (library)
ISBN 978-1-4263-1775-0 (2014 pbk.)
ISBN 978-1-4263-1777-4 (2014 hc.)
ISBN 978-1-4263-1776-7 (2014 library)
  1. Children's atlases. 2. Earth—remote-sensing images. 3. Physical geography—Maps for children. [1.Atlases.] I. Title: Student atlas of the world. II. Title.
G1021 .N42 2001
912–dc21   00-030006

14/CK-CML/1
Printed in the United States of America